MW00352795

ANCHORING INNOVATION DISTRICTS

ANCHORING INNOVATION DISTRICTS

The Entrepreneurial University and Urban Change

COSTAS SPIROU

JOHNS HOPKINS UNIVERSITY PRESS | Baltimore

This book has been brought to publication with the generous assistance of the Robert L. Warren Endowment.

9 8 7 6 5 4 3 2 1

Johns Hopkins University Press
2715 North Charles Street
Baltimore, Maryland 21218-4363
www.press.jhu.edu

Library of Congress Cataloging-in-Publication Data
Names: Spirou, Costas, author.
Title: Anchoring innovation districts : the entrepreneurial university
    and urban change / Costas Spirou.
Description: Baltimore : Johns Hopkins University Press, 2021. |
    Includes bibliographical references and index.
Identifiers: LCCN 2020025909 | ISBN 9781421440590 (hardcover) |
    ISBN 9781421440606 (ebook)
Subjects: LCSH: Urban universities and colleges—Economic aspects—United States. |
    Community and college—Economic aspects—United States. |
    Community development, Urban—United States. |
    Entrepreneurship—United States.
Classification: LCC LB2328.42.U6 S75 2021 | DDC 370.9173/2—dc23
LC record available at https://lccn.loc.gov/2020025909

A catalog record for this book is available from the British Library.

Special discounts are available for bulk purchases of this book. For more information, please contact Special Sales at specialsales@jh.edu.

Johns Hopkins University Press uses environmentally friendly book materials, including recycled text paper that is composed of at least 30 percent post-consumer waste, whenever possible.

To the memory of my father,
Plutarch-Stelios Spirou (1940–2019),
for his unwavering commitment to family, education,
and community

CONTENTS

THE GENESIS of this project goes back to the spring of 2017, when I had the opportunity to meet with Rafael Bras, who was provost and executive vice president for Academic Affairs at Georgia Institute of Technology from 2010 until 2020. A few months earlier, I was awarded an American Council on Education (ACE) Fellowship and was exploring the possibility of a placement at the Institute. During that preliminary conversation, Rafael shared with me information about the Technology (Tech) Square initiative, across the highway, on the other side of the Fifth Street bridge in Midtown Atlanta. Committed to its continued advancement, he described the setting as a vibrant environment where university activities and corporate research were intersecting, driving economic development. As an urban affairs scholar and someone interested in the broader issues facing higher education, I was intrigued by the enterprising venture and its impact and implications for the local community. Furthermore, this part of Midtown was rapidly changing, with construction sprouting everywhere.

This book examines a recent trend in higher education as universities are actively investing resources in the establishment of innovation districts. Embedded in the urban environment, the creation of these entities is fueled by the formation of structures to support and attract entrepreneurial activity, primarily emanating from the commercialization of technology. This direction has significant implications for both higher education and the city. Engaging universities with the surrounding communities in this manner departs from past practices which viewed university campuses as isolated entities. As a result, the lines of where the university ends and the community begins are blurred. At the same time, these initiatives are contributing to the continuous rebirth of the urban core and adjacent neighborhoods. By embracing an interdisciplinary perspective, this work expands the scholarship in entrepreneurial science, higher education, technological innovation, and the university as a driver of urban economic development.

The contextual framework for this analysis rests within the broader response to the continued decline of public trust in higher education which has intensified in recent years. Beyond questions about the rising costs of a college education and the relevance of a degree in a society that is undergoing rapid change, universities cannot continue to rely primarily on resources derived from tuition and fees, as well as federal and state appropriations. In the long run these mechanisms are simply unsustainable. The effects of the unprecedented economic crisis of 2008 powerfully brought these issues to the forefront, requiring institutions to reorient themselves by pursuing bolder strategic plans that incorporated unique mindsets and embraced risk to become impactful innovators.

A successful innovation ecosystem also has major economic ramifications. Close links to business interests, not only bring highly established Fortune 500 companies into these districts, but attract entrepreneurs trying to breathe life into start-ups. The 2008 financial circumstances resulted in a call to realign higher education practices. While the growth of university-driven innovation districts stalled, the economic rebound that ensued fueled a tremendous expansion. This book affords distinct insights into the operational aspects of the entrepreneurial university.

Most recently, the COVID-19 global pandemic will likely have similar implications. Already facing pressures from demographic transitions, the spread of the virus caused academic leaders to face monumental challenges. The spring of 2020 brought major upheaval as instruction shifted abruptly to remote delivery. Billions of dollars were returned to students and families because of interrupted services, and future operations became uncertain with budget cuts and enrollment declines. Outside of the hospitality industry, health care and education proved to be the second-hardest hit sectors of the economy.

Like previous downturns, higher education will recover following a few years of adjustments. However, innovation districts will fare much better and experience a more rapid ascent largely for two reasons. First, compared with the pre-2008 crisis, a more robust technology cluster infrastructure is currently in place. This will support long-term growth. Second, innovation districts have been formulated around technological innovation, a direction which will remain vital to future economic prosperity. Research activity in these settings is already contributing to the fight against the COVID-19 pandemic by aiding vaccine research and other health care needs. The post-coronavirus downturn will reveal growth opportunities as technology start-ups will once again become central to economic recovery.

Within this larger perspective, this study draws from six cases. The first four involve research-intensive universities that are located in major metropolitan regions and serve as anchors of innovation districts. The remaining two are regional comprehensives in medium-sized cities that are increasingly playing a critical role in the promotion of similar strategies. Regarding the research universities, the conceptualization and execution of these projects, as well as the potential implications for higher education and urban change, can be significant. The mission and scope of the two comprehensive universities are different from the previous four since their location presents distinct challenges. How do these two institutions, without the research clout and resources of the previous cases, participate with their communities to further innovation and urban growth? This type of analysis diversifies the list of cases and offers insights that can prove beneficial to universities and cities across the country that either are contemplating similar projects, are in the early planning stages, or have already entered the process of pursuing innovation districts in their cities.

In some of these anchor cases, the original intent was an expansion of services since increases in enrollment may necessitate higher demand for classrooms, laboratories, office space, student housing, and even recreational facilities. Hence, land acquisition and construction to launch a new campus location is a response to specific conditions facing the organization. A product of these circumstances, such projects would have enjoyed significant success and would have been declared entrepreneurial if their eventual spatial function, at full maturity, resulted in retail presence and other uses. Furthermore, in cases where an area's previous status was long abandoned or mostly blighted, this kind of transformation would have been highly regarded and broadly acclaimed.

However, following their formation and with institutional support, some of these settings mature into densely occupied collections of startups and corporate centers that focus on experimenting with new ideas to advance technology transfer. Subsequently, the unfolding connections between university research activities and these entities give birth to neighborhoods which power robust ecosystems of technological innovation. Because of all this, the university vision may slowly evolve with more initiatives to further this reconstituted direction. In other cases, the creation of an innovation district was the primary intent, and the universities crafted a carefully planned strategy to achieve their objectives.

A central aspect of university innovative districts is the role of private-public partnerships. These are evident throughout the various stages of development. For example, project finance can take various forms, depending on the specific circumstances. In some cases, the university plays a vital role, while in others the private and public sectors can be significant contributors. It is apparent that entrepreneurial institutions and leaders always consider strategic collaborations to support their efforts and maximize success. Innovation districts become the settings where government, higher education, and businesses intersect. The spatial restructuring that ensues drives economic growth, even the possibility for historic preservation and sustainability, while contributing to the upsurge of new mixed-use neighborhoods, infusing a unique character to the community and contributing to urban regeneration.

The economic contributions though come at a considerable cost given the socioeconomic implications. Because of their mission, operational goals, and composition, innovation districts have the capacity to produce significant restructuring in the form of gentrification and displacement. Although gentrification occurs at different levels and at various stages, the social characteristics of those engaged in these clusters are likely to foster social exclusion rather than social inclusion. For example, new-build developments are geared toward professional and technical residents and not for those in the working class. Social mixing is thus discouraged, eventually pushing out existing residents while weakening diversity and the potential benefits of long-term growth for current occupants. Beyond housing, the gentrification forces also yield a restructured cultural component. Consumer goods, fashion and advertising, desired services, and even unique architecture give rise to distinct capital accumulation, which, in turn, creates new commodities and conveys a differentiated cultural meaning. In the process, these forces come to revitalize localized, ailing geographies while also perpetuating social inequality.

A comparative analysis on the role and impact of university-anchored districts within a broader framework of technological and business growth reveals that these districts can be viewed as innovative learning types that focus on recasting traditional models through the pursuit of partnerships, research, education, and policy. This can inform the future of academia in light of entrepreneurial engagement trends in higher education and recent directions of the university as an urban agent of change. For innovation districts to succeed, it is essential that continuing attention to funding is present, the university works closely with private sector entities, relationships with the government are systematic and cooperative, and potential conflicts with the surrounding community are addressed immediately and are part of an ongoing, intentional collaboration.

The present volume is directed at university administrators (presidents, provosts, deans, VPs of finance and administration, VPs of university advancement, VPs for research) and others involved in the promotion of similar proposals at their institutions. The book can also benefit local and state government officials interested in better understanding how they can partner with universities to induce economic growth and revitalize urban neighborhoods. University board members and regents or other representatives at state systems of higher education will also find this book insightful. Finally, faculty and graduate students with related research agendas in education, sociology, urban studies, science and technology, public policy, economics, and others can benefit from this scholarship.

WRITING THIS book has been a rewarding experience, and there are many individuals who have contributed to its development and eventual completion. I am thankful to Rafael Bras, provost and executive vice president for Academic Affairs at Georgia Institute of Technology, for his guidance and support. Rafael encouraged me at various stages to pursue this project and I greatly value his time and ideas on this and many other topics during my time as an American Council on Education Fellow (2017–2018) in the Office of the Provost at Georgia Tech. I learned quite a bit from my conversations and interactions with Rafael, including the vital importance of innovation in higher education and the role of technology.

George P. "Bud" Peterson, president of Georgia Tech from 2009 to 2019, proved instrumental in helping me gain a deeper understanding of the entrepreneurial university. Over a 10-year period, President Peterson led the rapid ascent of Technology Square from a cluster of buildings to a national model of a university-driven innovation district. He shared with me key perspectives about Tech Square, was very responsive, and always willing to offer important observations that added to my knowledge base. His vision of advancing this ambitious undertaking by fostering and maintaining partnerships proved invaluable. I am indebted to Jennifer Herazy, chief administrative officer for Academics and Research at Georgia Tech, who made the fellowship appointment possible, and in the process created one of the most professionally rewarding experiences of my academic career. I am deeply appreciative of Jennifer's insights and assistance.

I am grateful to President Steve Dorman at Georgia College and to Chancellor Kelli Brown at Western Carolina University who promoted and ensured my participation in the American Council on Education Fellows Program. Furthermore, both of these individuals have been extraordinarily supportive of my professional development and have guided my administrative journey. I have learned much from them about leadership and management in higher education. They are committed to assisting those around them grow and succeed. As mentors and colleagues, they have been generous with their time. Because of my interactions with them, I have developed a broader and deeper understanding of navigating various operational aspects critical to the role and function of colleges and universities. President Dorman also read a portion of the manuscript and offered helpful feedback. I am also thankful to Larry Bennett, professor emeritus of political science at DePaul University, and Dennis R. Judd, professor emeritus of political science at the University of Illinois at Chicago, for their many years of supporting my scholarship.

Gregory Britton, editorial director at Johns Hopkins University Press, provided extensive assistance and direction. When I initially approached him with a manuscript proposal that focused exclusively on Tech Square, he did what great editors do and challenged me to think more broadly, thus expanding my perspective. It is because of my conversations with Greg that the scope of the book includes more cases and a comparative analysis. I believe the book has improved significantly from its initial conceptualization because of his recommendations and encouragement. I am also appreciative of the staff at Johns Hopkins University Press, including production editor Hilary Jacqmin and assistant acquisitions editor Kyle Gipson, and of copyeditor Ashley Lachance as well as Brooks Hinton, Victoria Fowler, and Omar Odeh at Georgia College & State University for their assistance in bringing the book to completion.

This book is dedicated to my father, Plutarch-Stelios Spirou, who passed away in the summer of 2019. His value and commitment to education was unprecedented. As an educator for many decades on Samos

Island, Greece, he worked fervently, in multiple settings, to advance teaching and learning, and he led a life with integrity and a spirit of positivity. Over many decades he contributed greatly to civic affairs in an exemplary manner by assisting various local organizations dedicated to uplifting the intellectual life on the island. A teacher, author, and a strong believer in the importance of education, he left an indelible mark on all with whom he interacted, including myself.

My deep appreciation is also extended to my wife, Patrice, who has been with me tackling every book project going back to the 1990s. She has been a central part of my life in many ways, including as an intellectual partner. Her continued understanding and support of these academic endeavors has been invaluable.

ANCHORING INNOVATION DISTRICTS

The New Entrepreneurial University

ON JULY 1, 2017, Gary May arrived in Davis, California, as the new chancellor of the University of California, Davis. On September 25, he delivered his first major address to the university community titled "Future Forward." Chancellor May covered many topics during that speech including the importance of upholding and strengthening academic excellence, his commitment to diversity, and the value of furthering the common good. He outlined various institutional strengths and the many opportunities awaiting UC Davis. But May also took this moment to articulate his pursuit of a bold, new initiative called Aggie Square, an innovation district to be developed in nearby Sacramento.

A few months later, representatives from the City of Sacramento, the university, and the community held a press conference in the neighborhood of Oak Park to announce that Aggie Square would be constructed there on 25 acres of university-owned property. With more than one million square feet of space, the project would include room for research and teaching activities while incorporating parks and entertainment venues. Additionally, private sector housing could be built nearby. May argued at the event that the project would "create a hub of innovation and community-building here in Sacramento to advance both our academic and research missions and to bolster the economic vitality of the city." Mayor Darrell Steinberg echoed the chancellor's sentiment by noting, "The direction is clear and cannot be repeated enough: as we grow a dynamic economy and take advantage of all of our institutions and assets, that growth must be tied to our neighborhoods, our communities, especially our communities of color." Similarly, Joany Titherington, president of the Oak Park Neighborhood Association, declared that "the opportunity is meaningful for our community . . . [T]his is equity for not just our community, but it helps to level the playing field for everyone else in Sacramento in other neighborhoods . . . We are absolutely thrilled about having this opportunity to have Aggie Square right here in the Oak Park area."[1]

Soon thereafter, an opposing perspective on locating the Aggie Square project in Oak Park predicted a very different outcome. The working-class residents of the area expressed concerns that gentrification caused by the project would force them to move out of their historically African American neighborhood. Oak Park and Tahoe Park were already experiencing housing pressures, and Aggie Square would surely exacerbate these conditions and cause displacement. It was argued that the aggressive timeline of developing this urban research district would not allow for an inclusive and collaborative approach to addressing housing concerns. An editorial by the *Sacramento Bee* advised that "whether Aggie Square ends up being a blessing or a heartbreak to working-class residents will depend largely on whether the City Council and UC Davis are serious about building more housing and are proactive about enacting policies that protect existing residents from displacement as home prices inevitably rise with demand . . . The families in those modest houses off Stockton Boulevard have been there for a long time and must not be taken for granted. Aggie Square has to factor their needs in."[2] In April 2019, UC Davis unveiled a preliminary design for phase I of Aggie Square on approximately 8.25 acres. Science, technology, and engineering facilities, classrooms, co-working and community serving spaces, and housing units would make up the core of the first phase. Full completion is expected to take until 2029.[3]

For Chancellor May, the concept of an innovation campus is not solely about science and technology. It is also about prosperity and economic development, both locally and regionally. May has been attentive to and has consistently called for a collaborative approach, given that Aggie Square "will bring together a diverse array of startups, established companies, community organizations and UC Davis researchers, faculty and students. It will be a place to discover new partners, launch businesses, scale ideas and provide economic opportunity to residents across demographics, skill levels and industries. It will leverage our strengths and partnerships in health, agriculture, food technology, clean energy, clean transportation and more."[4] The new location in Sacramento would benefit the university in other ways. For example, it would house classrooms, labs, and offices that are currently at the main campus. Along with opportunities to expand enrollments, the university would also generate revenue from managing additional real estate holdings. These entrepreneurial pursuits will need to be balanced against the interest of the local community and the ability of its advocates to effectively articulate and advance that agenda.

Like UC Davis, many universities are continuously exploring growth opportunities, and partnerships among higher education, local government, and businesses are becoming increasingly more common. A few years ago, a story in the *Washington Post* titled "Under Pressure to Contain Tuition, Colleges Scramble for Other Revenue" focused on how leaders in higher education attempted to creatively address some of the challenges facing their organizations. In the article, one university president commented, "You can't function as a school, state or private, thinking there's an endless supply of money." Another cautioned, "When the market stops growing and costs keep going up, you can either cut your costs or try to raise more revenue."[5] In response to such concerns, Northeastern University in Boston founded the Office of New Ventures to identify creative ideas that the institution could cultivate in hopes of generating additional revenue. Likewise, Johns Hopkins University began an internally produced ratings software program that evaluates and ranks child care and education programs. The university invested not only in the technical aspect of the project but also in its marketing to customers around the country and abroad. These types of approaches are evident across both public and private universities, those operating in urban, suburban, or rural areas, as well as among institutions undifferentiated by the size of their endowments or by the numbers of students that they serve. Because of rapidly evolving conditions, now more than ever, higher education has embraced highly complex agendas and has engaged in the types of activities that a few decades earlier would have been improbable.

In this work, I focus on one major response to these pressures: the shifting of the university into an entrepreneurial mode to more broadly serve as an agent of change. My study examines how science and innovation fuel technology transfer to industry, emerging as forces of economic development and urban revitalization. It also investigates how, in their pursuits of complicated growth agendas, universities can have a significant impact in reshaping the urban environment. For example, during the 1960s, institutions of higher education actively participated in urban renewal initiatives as a way to clear land and protect their campuses from surrounding blight, efforts that were not without controversy. However, more recently, we observe a different orientation that is giving rise to considerably more ambitious endeavors. These extend from a variety of urban beautification initiatives to projects that are aimed at expanding student services, providing retail, transportation, and housing amenities, with commercial real estate playing an increasingly substantive role. Strengthening the overall social well-being of adjoining neighborhoods is another strategy that universities are currently pursuing.

When considering these major changes, it is apparent that the traditional role of the university, which has historically emphasized educating students in the classroom and conducting basic research, is being revisited. Reconstituted student preparation activities outside the classroom such as studying abroad, internships, multifaceted economic development pursuits that involve the community, and emphasis on the commercialization of knowledge are now accepted as central university functions. Furthermore, the quest to create new and to solidify existing partnerships between industry and government that will allow access to national and regional innovation systems is equally important. This is especially noteworthy given that these entities play a critical role in supporting high technology, which has given birth to scientific advancements.

The Evolving Nature of the University

Historically, colleges and universities have been viewed as elite, as exclusive centers of thought, discovery, and information. The commonly utilized reference to the university as the "ivory tower" conveys the notion of an isolated entity, detached from modern reality. For centuries having a sequestered establishment guided the culture of European institutions and was eventually transmitted to the United States with the formation of the American system of higher education. The image of the lofty university disconnected from everyday life remains and is reflected in the media of both the United States and Europe. A newspaper reporter in San Diego recently reminded readers that "colleges and universities have traditionally set themselves apart in ivory tower enclaves of deep thinking—unsullied by the dirt, grime and daily hassles around them. Faculty typically look for research opportunities halfway around the world, not in their own backyard."[6] Nicholas Kristof, a writer for the New York Times, wrote in an opinion essay that "some of the smartest thinkers on problems at home and around the world are university professors, but most of them just don't matter in today's great debates." His commentary was pointing to the state of isolation present in higher education.[7] In the United Kingdom, an article in the Economist titled "Time to Leave the Ivory Tower" outlined a proposal to create a new framework of excellence that would rate universities for the quality of their teaching. As a response to rising costs, only universities with appropriate teaching results would be allowed to raise their tuition. The findings of this assessment were released for the first time in the summer of 2017.[8]

The contrasting ideas of university external engagement versus disengagement became points of conversation for the first time during the unfolding of the New Deal as the United States prepared to embark on World War II. At the 1939 Harvard University graduation, President James Bryant Conant identified the importance of "[b]alancing within a university the quiet privileges of the ivory tower against the outside world." In 1940, President Franklin D. Roosevelt, speaking at a University of Pennsylvania event noted, "This is no time for any man to withdraw into some ivory tower and proclaim the right to hold himself aloof from the problems, yes, and the agonies of his society." Then, in 1942, shortly after the United States entered the war, Robert M. Hutchins, president of the University of Chicago, called for a new institutional direction: "When war has been declared, long run activities must be sacrificed to the short run activity of winning the war. We have stood for liberal education and pure research. What the country needs now is vocational training and applied research."[9]

By the end of World War II, the nature of higher education in America had been altered. The GI Bill of 1944 poured sizable government subsidies into education. Upon entering the 1960s and 1970s, college-aged baby boomers embraced the value of the postsecondary degree as a fundamental determinant of success in life. In a mere 10 years, enrollments surged from 6 million in 1965 to 11 million in 1975. The number of new public colleges and universities grew dramatically to meet the rising demand. Once reserved for the few, a college degree was now available to anyone willing to pursue it. States rushed to provide financial support to an enterprise which, without competition, lacked any incentives to explore change. This period of expansion also gave rise to a diverse, complex set of postsecondary public institutions that included metropolitan universities, comprehensive regionals, and community colleges. Varying missions and changing admission requirements helped create a complicated, yet autonomous system of institutions across the nation.

The addition of a robust array of for-profit colleges and universities focusing almost exclusively on working adults brought another complexity to an already intricate structure. Such institutions of higher education have a long history in the United States, emphasizing career preparation and serving those who have been unable to access more traditional delivery formats. Less than one percent of degree-seeking students were served by these entities during the early 1970s. However, the founding of the University of Phoenix as a for-profit university in 1976, and its eventual success, led to an enrollment explosion. By the early 2000s, the University of Phoenix served 200,000 students with a 25 percent annual enrollment growth. As a result, many companies entered these rapidly unfolding, lucrative, and publicly traded corporations. By 2012, 12 percent of college students in the United States attended a for-profit institution. Critics pointed to how the high tuition costs relative to academic investments resulted in high profits, while proponents advocated for the importance of access, quick response, and expeditious innovation.

But this was not an entirely new controversy. Debates over the cost of higher education date back to the early part of the twentieth century. In 1927, at Brown University's 153rd commencement exercises, alumnus John D. Rockefeller argued that the cost of higher education was expected to increase to the point that endowments and gifts from wealthy benefactors alone would make it impossible to meet the rising demand. Rockefeller noted that there was a shift underway from when those who entered college were interested in ministry, teaching, and an overall desire to serve the public good to "today [when] the majority of the students go to college for a good time, for social considerations or to fit themselves to earn money. The idea of service to the community is no longer the chief consideration . . . [U]nder these changed conditions the student might properly be expected to pay for the benefits he receives." On the other hand, Dean Huger W. Jervey of Columbia University Law School warned against tuition increases since "educational advantages will be open to the rich, rather than to the worthy."[10]

Though the conversation regarding the cost of higher education is not contemporary, the scope and impact on students and families today is more significant than ever. A year at Vassar in 1931 that included room, board, and tuition cost about $20,241 (2020 dollars). In 2020, tuition alone at Vassar was $58,770. In 1960, tuition, room, board, and fees at Bates was $17,453 (2020 dollars). Covering these same costs at Bates for one year in 2020 required $73,530.[11] In the 20-year period from 1996 to 2016, private colleges and universities saw a 5.68 percent average, compounded, annual tuition increase, with their public counterparts experiencing a 5.98 percent increase. These increases are substantial when considering that the consumer price index during that period was compounded at an annual rate of 2.44 percent.[12]

While the actual cost of attending public institutions is lower when compared to private colleges and universities, the situation of the former is equally problematic. From 1980 to 2015, students at public universities experienced quadrupled tuition increases to $9,139 (2014 dollars). A major reason for this relates to declining state appropriations to higher education. For example, state support in 1960 was $11.1 billion (2014 dollars). In 1975, the entry of baby boomers necessitated an increase to $48.2 billion (2014 dollars). State appropriations continued to grow to $86.6 billion in 2009, and while they declined after the economic recession, they rebounded to $81 billion (2014 dollars) in 2015. However, tuition rates remained unchanged. The Pell Grant program also grew significantly from $10.3 billion in 2000 to $34.3 billion (2014 dollars) in 2015.[13]

As the rise in tuition was unfolding, public discontent was becoming apparent around the nation. Overwhelming criticism from government officials, legislators, student advocates, parent groups, the media, and think tanks forced higher education leaders to place some controls on the rates of annual tuition increases. However, as these changes were going into effect, another set of costs was speedily mounting for students and their families: student fees. A story in the *Atlantic* cautioned its readers, "Think tuition is high? Now add fees for student activities, fees for athletics, fees for building maintenance, fees for libraries— even fees for graduation, the bills for which often arrive just as students and their families thought they were finally done paying for their higher education. All are frustratingly piled on top of a long list of expenses beyond tuition that many people never plan for or expect, or that can't be covered by financial aid—sometimes forcing them to take out more and more loans, or quit college altogether."[14]

Family incomes continued to lag in light of increases to the price of college. In an effort to better understand various forces and relevant trends, the Delta Cost Project by the American Institutes for Research has focused on key questions associated with spending in higher education, including "where does the money come from?" and "why do prices continue to increase?" Economists, accounting and law professors, sociologists, and education researchers as well as other higher education experts have pursued a variety of inquiries in an effort to better understand the dynamics impacting higher education. There is general agreement that a combination of factors has proved critical in shaping the current situation. For example, one factor is the rapid growth of campus amenities, as colleges and universities vie to provide services outside the classroom to expand or shape their enrollments. Additionally, curricular and cocurricular programming aimed at improving and differentiating the student experience have translated into a burgeoning of the administrative ranks. Undergraduate research, study abroad, community engagement, and sustainability initiatives are just a few examples from a large number of activities which are now playing a greater role across campuses. Furthermore, compliance with government regulations has grown rapidly, requiring considerable investment. The resulting decline of state support for higher education meant that costs would consequently get passed down to the consumers. Finally, increases in unsubsidized loans and other federally associated student aid programs directed colleges and universities to recalibrate their tuition rates.

The need to pay attention to labor market demands, employment patterns, and skills necessary to succeed in a rapidly developing economy surfaced as a routine topic of conversation and became frequently reported on by national media outlets. For example, stories on the declining role and applicability of the liberal arts, especially the humanities, became a common staple in newspapers, magazines, white papers, and reports, even among legislators and government officials. In 2011, Governor Rick Scott of Florida famously commented, "If I'm going to take money from a citizen to put into education then I'm going to take that money to create jobs. So, I want that money to go to degrees where people can get jobs in this state. Is it a vital interest of the state to have more anthropologists? I don't think so."[15] The importance of choosing the right field of study gained the favor of those covering higher education. A story in the US News and World Report aptly captures this sentiment, noting that computer science and business and accounting students are in demand since those pursuing these majors will experience high levels of professional success. Evaluating the employability of those holding college degrees is a relatively simple task, which in turn makes choosing a major a simple consumer choice. Accordingly, prospective students should review and evaluate projected labor outcomes, analyze employment data of recent graduates, and compare the return on investment for the degree. The reporter concludes by cautioning that anthropology and archeology, film, video and photographic arts, fine arts, philosophy, and religious studies should be avoided since these lead the list of the top least marketable college majors.[16]

It is thus evident that American higher education is undergoing significant changes, ushered in by external economic pressures and growing concerns about the capacity of the system to effectively meet employer requirements. Fluctuating workplace trends and shifting needs in high-demand professions mean that higher education has no other choice but to embrace and connect to the occupational conditions of society. As public institutions have seen sharp declines in state funds, private institutions have relied on endowments to support their operations and have discounted tuition to battle for enrollments. The only way for colleges and universities to move forward is to embrace innovation and an entrepreneurial mindset. Innovation should be applied to multiple facets of the enterprise, such as rethinking the curriculum and its delivery, cultivating new cutting-edge programs, reinventing career development centers, and by creating and implementing stronger and more meaningful assessment efforts. A reorientation of current align-ments with the private sector should be aggressively pursued through robust partnerships aimed at supporting experiential learning and at pioneering rewarding student opportunities. Peter McPherson, president of the Association of Public and Land-grant Universities, the nation's oldest higher education association, conveyed this urgency for innovation by noting, "Most of us feel that historical change is happening right now. Most believe our universities will look different, maybe very different, in 10 years. To most it is a question of whether we will work to shape that future or the future will shape us."[17]

The Push for Rethinking Higher Education after the 2008 Recession

Most would agree that the aftermath of the 2008 recession proved to have a significant impact on many economic sectors. There were massive bailouts of financial institutions aimed at addressing the crisis, the likes of which had not been seen for decades. The intervention was principally intended to bring stability and instill confidence in a troubled global financial system. It was expected that this injection of funds would allow for the time needed to address some of the leading causes behind the abrupt declines that ravaged the stock markets. After all, these had unsettled numerous industries including banking, housing, and various commodities. The crisis was so deeply felt, and its effect so widespread, that in early 2009 total global production was projected to be down for the first time since the World War II.

During the height of these unprecedented circumstances, as the first decade of the twenty-first century was coming to an end, a public conversation quickly unfolded. Debates ensued regarding the broader norms driving both the national and global economies. Questions surfaced in the media about existing assumptions related to the stock market, the dynamics of business, and the pursuit of profit as well as the inner workings of industries. For example, are there corporations whose extremely intimate and intricate connections to the economy have made them too big to fail? Was the massive intervention about ensuring financial stability, or was it, in effect, creating an uneven playing field and sustaining unfair practices? Furthermore, in light of these developments, should all industries and economic sectors pursue a self-evaluation to determine if their current practices are in line with future trends and directions?

The economic slowdown forced many within and outside higher education to caution that significant internal changes were on the horizon. The industry could not remain insular and indifferent to greater social, economic, cultural, and political shifts. In 2009, Molly Corbett Broad, who, at the time, was the recently appointed president of the American Council on Education, exhorted college and university leaders: "This is a time when the game is changing. Hunkering down is not a smart option."[18] A variety of voices contended that accountability, student-centeredness, responsiveness, inclusivity, and collaborative approaches to delivering educational services to students should take center stage. Accordingly, the focus should be placed on reform. The search for more efficient and effective practices was on since the current system of higher education had been labeled broken and simply unsustainable in its current form. One critic declared, "The 'glory days' of higher education are over."[19]

Although traditionally a highly resilient enterprise, higher education's growing interconnection with the consumer economy brought enrollment declines, the need for deeper tuition discounting, and an unexpected, severe reduction of financial contributions from government sources. In an open letter to President Barack Obama, the then-president of the University of Michigan, Mary Sue Coleman, sounded the alarm by noting that "American higher education—particularly public higher education—is one of the monumental achievements of our country. No other nation can rival the innovation, creativity, and intellectual fervor of our universities. Our institutions are responsible for America's knowledge security—an intellectual well-being that advances health and medicine, business, social science, the arts, public policy and national defense." She further argued, "It is essential that states reinvest in their public colleges and universities. Not doing so is shortsighted and threatens to cripple remarkable institutions of learning."[20]

But how can an enterprise as durable as higher education find itself in this position and affected in this manner? After all, colleges and universities hold a special place in American society, one which for decades came to be widely accepted as separate from the solely financially driven corporate entities at the center of this unparalleled crisis. Furthermore, significant tension and a clear demarcation of academic prestige exist among research, comprehensive, teaching, nonprofit, and for-profit organizations. While each of these institutional sectors was distinctly different, the recession affected every one of them.

The sharp criticism leveled against the US system of higher education contained a plethora of concerns beyond successive annual increases in tuition, overreliance on fees, and mounting student debt, trends that made it difficult for many to gain access to this pillar of upward mobility. Concerns arose in areas such as low student retention and graduation rates, and the delivery of highly specialized, esoteric course subjects, whose relevance was now questioned. Even the purpose and value of faculty tenure was scrutinized. An impression of the university as a place where athletics and student life were overtaking its primary purpose of preparing Americans to engage in an increasingly competitive, global arena was hotly debated. One higher education writer summarized, "The Great Recession has had a devastating effect on higher education, forcing many students across the country to pay more for colleges that offer less."[21]

Now under serious scrutiny, the academic community recognized that these broader economic conditions urgently required them to revisit their current practices and explore new ways of approaching the significant issues confronting the more than 4,000 four-year and two-year colleges and universities. The January 2010 Higher Education Policy Brief by the American Association of State Colleges and Universities (AASCU) captured this urgency by noting, "The current economic downturn has increased the focus on the value of postsecondary education for individuals, as well as for communities, states and the nation as a whole. The public's and lawmakers' attention to issues such as college access, affordability, accountability and cost containment will further spur state higher education leaders to redouble their efforts to innovate and collaborate and in so doing help fulfill American aspirations in the wake of the greatest recession since the Great Depression."[22] The New York Times observed that "colleges and universities across the country are responding (albeit sometimes slowly) to challenges threatening their traditional role in society if not their survival."[23] Following the recovery and improved financial climate across the country, public funding for higher education in 2017 was still $9 billion behind the outlays prior to the crisis, when adjusted for inflation.[24] This was the new normal.

So, what should the response be? Is it time for higher education to be regarded as a business and, like other industries, be subjected to the same forces facing each and every enterprise? What role, if any, can disruptive innovation play in higher education? Should higher education aggressively pursue the development of new or different practices? Are there ways for universities to develop a culture of innovation that is sustainable? What about entrepreneurship? Finally, should universities embrace reforms and become entrepreneurial in their practices, be publicly engaged, more relevant, and showcase how the ideas that they generate internally directly relate and add value to our society?

Public universities today must operate differently. Given the substantial disruptions brought forth by an assortment of economic forces they must explore alternative approaches to meeting various objectives. For example, economic development has been added to teaching and research as another key aspect of the institutional mission, making an entrepreneurial orientation essential. However, when investigating how universities engage through infrastructural development with their physical surroundings and social environment, this outlook unfolds in varying forms and degrees of engagement.

The New Entrepreneurial University

The entrepreneurial university is fast becoming the leading, iconic image of the modern institution of higher education. Observers have even argued that, for today's aspiring universities, there is no option other than the pursuit of this entrepreneurial mindset. Specifically, Holden Thorp and Buck Goldstein argue, "Ours is an era of entrepreneurship. Global forces have converged to enable individuals and small groups to undertake projects and enterprises of the kind that were once reserved only for large institutions. Large institutions are called upon to incorporate that same approach and way of thinking as a means of dramatically increasing the impact and efficiency of all that they do."[25] Such universities exhibit a set of common features and endeavor to cultivate a culture that not only recognizes the value of innovation, but also actively embraces strategies to further its institutionalization.

There are four general characteristics that can describe these organizational types. First, entrepreneurial universities are ambitiously willing to focus on the big issues. They often search for and even thrive on challenges. They tackle questions which are complex and issues that require considerable investments, necessitating multiple approaches. They are willing to recognize and embrace the notion that the successful pursuit of confronting big problems may require the establishment of interdisciplinary approaches. Second, entrepreneurial universities continuously attend to implementation processes and procedures, possessing an unwavering commitment to outcomes. Entrepreneurial universities do not lose sight of the goals that they have set out to achieve and are always assessing their progress in meeting those goals. They have the ability to be self-reflective, with unique familiarity with their strengths and weaknesses. From the beginning, they often recognize if their goals are placed far outside the limits of current institutional capacity. However, while knowing their limitations, they are also willing and not afraid to push, and if necessary, redraw operational boundaries. Third, entrepreneurial universities support the formation of robust partnerships. In developing these partnerships, they are willing to engage outside their institution and even outside academics. They search for entrepreneurs and other similarly calibrated organizations and are always prepared to contest preconceived notions or structural limitations. If and when it is needed, they are open to embracing alternative arrangements. Fourth, entrepreneurial universities are able to connect their actions to their missions. They are focused and can easily articulate how an initiative closely aligns with or furthers institutional priorities. In fact, a powerful connection is typically evident between the university and a given project.

Interestingly, the intentional drive toward innovation and entrepreneurialism is often embedded throughout the whole college experience. One example of such a comprehensive approach is at the University of Utah's Lassonde Studios, where residential floors are divided into themes. These themes include global impact and sustainability, digital media, design and the arts, and adventure and gear. The ground floor features 3D printers and an extensive array of tools that can be used to produce prototypes. Oriented as an environment that values and supports interdisciplinary learning, Lassonde Studios is branded as an innovation building with programming provided by the university's Lassonde Entrepreneurship Institute. During the grand opening, over 1,000 students applied to reside in this living-learning community that can house 400 residents. Similarly, Northwestern University introduced the 11,000-square-foot Garage in 2015, which is literally designed as a building for motor vehicles. Concrete floors, cinder block walls, and exposed ceiling beams make up the physical space. However, as the university's student accelerator, the Garage provides programming and resources to assist students in developing their professional skills, while also endeavoring to aid the creation of start-up companies.[26]

Innovation can occur at variable levels and degrees of intensity. For example, some universities focus on the delivery of their curriculum by injecting innovation in teaching and learning. Others embrace innovative practices in their internal operations to improve efficiency. A smaller number are innovative in executing their strategic directives, often formed around growth initiatives. To better recognize the complexities embedded in these institutional efforts, I identify below a typology which includes low, middle, and high levels of urban entrepreneurial activity in higher education. This typology takes into consideration the built environment since universities have the capacity to shape and reshape their surrounding physical locales. The first category includes institutional engagement resulting in the lowest form of urban entrepreneurialism. This entails colleges and universities that pursue the most common aim of real estate expansion centering on the acquisition or development of facilities for the purpose of providing fundamental services to students. While in support of this mission, the strategy is mostly limited to expansion of the existing footprint to house faculty and staff. There are plenty of examples of such cases across the nation.

In 2017, Oregon State University announced that it would occupy the second floor of the historic Meier & Frank building in downtown Portland, Oregon. This 15-story building once housed retail giant Macy's, which relocated a few years ago. In their efforts to redevelop the facility, the owners searched for new tenants. Subsequently, Oregon State signed a 10-year lease agreement for about $1.4 million. In a highly visible location, the building will serve as the center of activity in Portland for the Corvalis, Oregon–based institution.[27] Champlain College, a private institution in Burlington, Vermont, is another example. Their project proved a bit more complex than the Oregon State University case noted above, however, it still falls within the lowest form of entrepreneurial engagement. In 2017, the college broke ground to construct a new, six-story building to house 300 students in the city's downtown. At a cost of $36 million, Eagles Landing would provide housing to all college students with some retail space on the dormitory's first floor. The city has been supportive of the venture since it will aid the revitalization of downtown Burlington and is expected to also contribute 66 additional parking spaces open to the public.[28]

The second category of university urban entrepreneurial engagement includes institutions that pursue a far more complicated agenda. These institutions embrace real estate expansion to primarily meet two needs. The first focuses on achieving improved student services, along with housing for faculty and staff. The second incorporates aggressive commercial undertakings which have the capacity to yield additional revenue. The income may derive from retail, hotels, restaurants, and related activities. For example, in the summer of 2017, the University of California, San Diego, announced the creation of the Innovative Cultural and Education Hub in San Diego's downtown East Village, near Petco Park, home of the MLB's San Diego Padres. When fully realized, this new mixed-use project is expected to cost about $275 million and will include a 34-story tower with 426 residential units, retail, restaurant, office, and parking space. The UC San Diego Extension will be located at the site offering courses and workshops geared toward downtown workers who desire to achieve professional advancement. Chancellor Pradeep K. Khosla noted, "This new hub will support economic development downtown while delivering new educational opportunities for our students, faculty and staff and provide a greater connection to the communities throughout San Diego."[29]

Finally, the third category is inclusive of institutions that participate at the highest level of entrepreneurial engagement in the urban environment. These universities are capable of not only pursuing endeavors which further their ability to meet student, faculty, and staff needs by expanding their physical boundaries, but, like those in the second category, may also actively manage to diversify their outreach efforts with the goal of accomplishing various revenue generating objectives. However, what distinguishes these institutions from those noted earlier is that they intentionally embrace functions which aim to elevate their core mission. The real estate expansion of land holdings within this urban space allows them to strategically position themselves to develop strong partnerships with industry and advance science, technology, knowledge, and innovation with the aim of becoming catalysts for major urban revitalization and future economic growth. These university activities attract both residential development and industry to the area. Concerned with contributing to the community, and mindful of those interactions, they actively cultivate civic relationships. Their functions ooze into their surrounding areas, making it difficult to discern where the university ends and the rest of the city begins. This is in sharp opposition to past strategies which have historically resulted in intentionally separating, and even protecting, the university from the adjoining urban setting. The degree of community engagement and the complexity of external partnerships are key aspects which differentiate institutions in the third category, the "new entrepreneurial university."

Georgia Tech and Tech Square in Atlanta, MIT and Kendall Square in Cambridge, and Drexel University and University City in Philadelphia are examples of institutions that endeavor to manage a connection between the university and real estate expansion to meet multiple, complex goals which embrace the creation of major innovation spaces within the urban environment. This "new entrepreneurial university" is involved in substantive infrastructural strategies to generate a technological ecosystem that brings scientific research and business together to benefit students and expand economic development opportunities. Its efforts and operational activities are not separated, physically or otherwise. Rather they are conceptually attached to the campus and remain linked to the institutional mission. As a result, this type of institution finds itself trying to connect to the city, an engagement that is inherently multifaceted, especially at a time when cities themselves are undergoing considerable socioeconomic changes with population shifts, neighborhood revitalization initiatives, gentrification, and displacement.

In the City but Not of It: The Case of Cornell Tech

In 2009, as New York Mayor Michael R. Bloomberg was contemplating the forging of a state-of-the-art technological university in his city, the US economy was on the brink of collapse. His economic development initiative focused on bringing cutting-edge, high-tech research and industry together under the guidance of a major institution of higher education not even yet identified. The Bloomberg Administration felt that cultivating innovation and entrepreneurial thinking within the rapid forces of global change had the potential to fuel job creation and to safeguard New York City's position as an economic powerhouse for generations to come.

Luring an enterprising institution of higher education focused on science, technology, and engineering that was also capable of creating an ecosystem would not only attract and retain a high-tech workforce but could also attract businesses at varying stages of development. Marrying technology to entrepreneurialism was the primary consideration with the end goal of producing for New York, what Stanford University had done for Silicon Valley, San José, and San Francisco, and what MIT brought to Boston and Cambridge. The new campus would be constructed on city-owned land and an additional $100 million would be available to ensure all infrastructural improvements would be in place for the facilities. An advisory committee of university presidents, venture capitalists, business leaders, and others would be involved in the review process, ultimately making recommendations to the mayor. City Hall's October 28, 2011, deadline for the submission of bids brought in seven proposals from seventeen institutions representing a number of countries including the United States, Canada, England, India, and Israel. Most prominent among those were the proposed partnerships of Stanford University with the City College of New York, and Cornell University with Technion–Israel Institute of Technology. These two submissions were considered the frontrunners and both outlined the construction of a physical campus on Roosevelt Island.[30]

However, just before the announcement of the winning bid, Stanford withdrew from the competition, and Cornell informed the review committee that a $350 million gift from an alumnus was now available to support their project. At a press conference naming the Cornell-Technion partnership as the winning proposal, Bloomberg declared, "Today will be remembered as a defining moment . . . In a word, this project is going to be transformative, [the Cornell-Technion bid was] far and away the boldest and most ambitious [with an] incredibly aggressive schedule."[31] Following the announcement, the new university operated from Google's New York offices as it amassed $850 million for construction. In September of 2017, Cornell Tech, as it became known, opened the first phase of its campus on Roosevelt Island featuring three iconic buildings, the Bloomberg Center (the first academic building), the Bridge (a collaborative space), and the House (a residential building occupied by students and faculty). The Verizon Executive Education Center and a campus hotel will finalize the first of three consecutive building segments. Completion of the $2 billion, 12-acre campus is not expected until 2043.

The development site for Cornell Tech is on a two-mile-long island in New York's East River, located between Midtown Manhattan to the west and Queens to the east. With only 14,000 residents, Roosevelt Island narrowly stretches north and south and occupies 147 acres of land. In recent years, the area experienced significant growth with the addition of high rises. When the university opened, the average sale price of a housing unit was $1.1 million, significantly higher than the previous average price of $800,000 in 2014 and $660,000 in 2012. Rent started at about $2,500 per month for studios.[32] Due to its proximity to Manhattan and easy transportation access, values are expected to continue to rise.

While centrally located, Cornell Tech is isolated from the city, and that has been one of the primary criticisms leveled against this massive higher education investment. A writer for the *New Yorker* questioned

Roosevelt Island, home of Cornell Tech in New York City. Courtesy of user Emma Griffiths, Shutterstock Images.

the limited impact this institution would have on the built environment by asking, "Will this new campus be part of the city, an island destination, a model green neighborhood? Or, will this be Silicon Valley East, where commercial and educational buildings that appear transparent retreat behind an invisible security curtain? You can look, but you can't touch—not without a badge."[33] Other publications referred to the project as "fairly isolated and difficult to access . . . cars are only allowed on certain parts of the island"[34] and "the tech world in New York is developing . . . a massive tech 'campus' in one of the most isolated parts of the city: Roosevelt Island."[35] Finally, the New York Times commented, "Its isolation makes for . . . an unusually quiet atmosphere . . . the island's remove now offers Cornell Tech something unusual. It is in the city, but not of it."[36]

The New York initiative reveals the critical value that technologically focused academic institutions are expected to have on furthering growth. It is argued that accelerated technological progress is capable of improving productivity and forming financial opportunities. Consequently, aligning these projects with business endeavors holds special promise, placing research universities at the core of transformative change. However, there is an additional component that should be considered when assessing these investments. What about the built environment? How can these strategic directions and associated commitments contribute to strengthening local economic and community development? What about urban change? Cornell Tech will likely succeed in realizing many of its goals, but given its location, exceptional opportunities to meet some of these broader objectives will be missed. Connecting higher education driven by technological entrepreneurship and associated ecosystems to the fabric of the city can prove groundbreaking, under the right circumstances.

Anchoring Innovation and Higher Education

The Cornell Tech case above provides insights into an institution of higher education that engages in an entrepreneurial manner to create a technological powerhouse in teaching, learning, and research. However, the physical environment from which it is expected to operate fuels isolation. A recent higher education trend includes universities actively investing resources in the creation of innovation spaces and, in the process, operating as anchors for their establishment. Embedded in the urban environment, the development of these geographic districts is powered by the formation of structures to support and attract entrepreneurial activity, primarily emanating from the commercialization of technology. A 2014 study by the Brookings Institution concluded that "innovation districts constitute the ultimate mash up of entrepreneurs and educational institutions, start-ups and schools, mixed-use development and medical innovations, bike-sharing and bankable investments—all connected by transit, powered by clean energy, wired for digital technology, and fueled by caffeine."[37] This direction has significant implications for both higher education and the city. Such action positions the university away from past practices as an isolated entity; it must now engage in the urban environment and its surrounding communities. At the same time, these initiatives are expected to contribute to the continuous rebirth of the urban core and adjacent neighborhoods.

Consider a recent initiative at the University of Georgia. In the fall of 2019, the University System of Georgia approved the renovation of a building in downtown Athens to serve as a center of innovation and entrepreneurship. The goal is to bring together faculty, students, and professionals as well as community organizations to collaborate and provide solutions for various industry needs. The renovated facility will also support start-ups and further existing efforts in technology transfer and intellectual property development, including the commercialization of technology. What may be the most important part of this development is the fact that the new building will complement Studio 225, which opened in March 2019. Studio 225 focuses on supporting the student entrepreneurship program at the University of Georgia. The long-term goal is to create a dense infrastructure of integrated facilities that would produce an innovation district to support an ecosystem to promote local revitalization and economic development across the state of Georgia.[38] This type of development taking place at the University of Georgia is now becoming increasingly common.

Following World War II, innovation campuses sprouted in suburbs as research parks or corridors, typically alongside major highways. These sprawling settings, like Silicon Valley in California and Route 128 in Massachusetts, evolved to become destination hubs, ushering in a global technological revolution. Isolated from their surrounding environments, their emergence complemented the social and economic forces that gave rise to decentralization, including the formation of a dominant postwar metropolitan geography. However, the successful revitalization of urban areas in recent years, especially evident in older industrial centers, brought young people and empty nesters back to cities. It is within this framework that universities emerge as an anchor in the advancement of knowledge sectors, encompassing business incubators and accelerators, research institutes, and start-ups. Operating in dense quarters, with easy access to transportation, upgraded co-locating facilities, converted housing, and numerous new services and amenities, these rebranded places became magnets for those looking for opportunities in a fast-paced, rapidly unfolding, technology-based economy.

This unique interplay between universities and the city also furthers another function of higher education that extends beyond teaching and research. Innovation districts are helping redefine and reorient research activities from intellectual, often isolated exercises, to the pursuit of basic research that is informed by applied relevance. Embedding appropriate support services within these entrepreneurial centers in key areas such as strategic management and legal and human resources, along with connections to venture capital prospects, can fuel broader growth. In fact, because of their composition and highly concentrated level of activity, innovation districts and their associated institutions are emerging as key economic and technological drivers for their cities.

Unexpected economic downturns can have a significant impact on the continued growth of innovation districts. For example, the 2008 Great Recession slowed down various initiatives underway at the time.

The case of the Cortex Innovation Community in St. Louis is instructive. Founded in 2002, the Cortex is a 200-acre center located in historic neighborhoods west of downtown that connects biological science and university research at Washington University in St. Louis and St. Louis University to technological innovation and businesses commercialization. The district experienced considerable challenges during the recessionary period in the latter part of the 2000s since its ongoing strategy of encouraging major tenants to join the quickly unfolding, highly ambitious project did not prove viable or sustainable. Instead, the Cortex leaders had to adjust, focusing on the pursuit of different development strategies. The reconstituted plans included expanding the entrepreneurial outreach of the Cortex operations while emphasizing the creation of new amenities.[39] As the economy started to rebound, the Cortex announced in 2012 a $200 million expansion.[40] A few years later, in 2016, another $170 million expansion would add a hotel, apartments, and a parking garage to the area.[41] Similarly, following the 2008 recession, New York City emerged as one of the most robust technology ecosystems in the world. The financial crisis helped fuel investments in fintech and other areas. By 2015, more than $6 billion in venture capital poured in to support the launch of 14,500 start-ups. This, in turn, has helped transform the urban landscape and revived the local economy.[42] Thus, economic cycles can be disruptive yet generative.

The rise of innovation districts is particularly noteworthy since it offers a new, entrepreneurially guided, higher education orientation. It is the result of a more nuanced and intricate process, one born out of a dialectical relationship. This new entrepreneurial university is one that goes beyond development for development's sake. This is not merely for commonly prescribed purposes of solely generating revenue from various activities, accommodating needs for space, or simply providing student services. Its approach calls for establishing, cultivating, and growing a symbiotic relationship among higher education, commerce, and the community. It aims to intentionally marry institutional strengths with industry interests and needs, and in the process, give birth to an entity with its own unique and distinctive characteristics.

As the private sector invades the university campus, a reframed institutional entrepreneurialism is molded. This comes to involve the university in a more expansive role, one that fundamentally modifies key elements of the higher education enterprise.

However, this external engagement of bringing the university into the community has its challenges. As local economic growth unfolds, questions remain about three key areas. First, who benefits? Second, what are the social implications of the ensuing spatial restructuring? Finally, what does that mean for higher education? Colleges and universities are expected to have a liberating orientation and play a critical role in strengthening human and social development. Are the benefits produced inclusive? What may be the resulting distributional consequences?

The Book to Come

The book captures and merges two major areas of research to construct its analytic framework—the university as an entrepreneurial force of innovation and the university as an agent of urban economic and spatial growth. Chapter 2 offers a contextual perspective of the university as an urban innovator and an agent of change. Universities across the country find themselves in the precarious position of engaging in various physical regeneration initiatives in order to realize their mission. As a result, institutions will pursue ambitious but complicated agendas that necessitate the involvement of numerous external stakeholders. A number of initiatives are examined that connect physical (re)development to institutional advancement. The chapter discusses the role of these endeavors by highlighting potential implications in economic change, business expansion, new knowledge and discovery, and community transformation. Additionally, the university as an urban developer is considered since higher education has struggled to achieve positive relationships with its communities. The chapter concludes by pointing to contributions in organizational branding, city imaging, and regional distinction, as well as the rise of innovation districts as a recently promoted strategy of urban revitalization.

This discussion is followed by the first of five chapters that collectively present cases of university-driven innovation districts. The first four draw from research institutions in Atlanta, Boston, Philadelphia, and Phoenix. The fifth chapter presents two examples of regional comprehensives in Pensacola and Chattanooga. A concluding chapter identifies insights by employing a comparative perspective to consider best practices.

Specifically, chapter 3 examines Georgia Institute of Technology and its efforts leading to the 2003 opening of Tech Square in Midtown. A reconstructed bridge stretched the university across a massive highway into what once was one of the most blighted parts of the city. The district has since evolved into a robust array of start-ups and corporate innovation centers, thus transitioning Midtown into one of the most notable neighborhoods in the United States. The next chapter examines Kendall Square in Boston which, like Tech Square in the 1970s, was in a state of severe decline with streets lined by abandoned buildings and vacant lots. Today, driven by the Massachusetts Institute of Technology, this location is considered a global innovation center where technology entrepreneurs are engaged in a thriving environment to commercialize new ideas.

Chapter 5 captures the story of University City–City Center in Philadelphia, an area with a very long history of university-community interactions that includes the University of Pennsylvania (UPenn). In recent years, the location has undergone a new evolution with the launch of the massive Schuylkill Yards project, which is driven by Drexel University. This will not only reshape the west side of the city, but it will also position Philadelphia as a regional and national hub of entrepreneurial activity. The following chapter focuses on the role of Arizona State University in advancing initiatives spanning over 15 years in downtown Phoenix. These have led to the creation of an urban environment that is now conducive to revitalization. The launch of PHX Core, an innovation district in the Warehouse District, positions Arizona State University to play a critical role. The last chapter of the case studies portion of the book examines Pensacola and Chattanooga and involves both the University of West Florida (UWF) and the University of Tennessee at Chattanooga (UTC). These two institutions are different from the previous four in terms of their mission and history. They are also located in smaller cities with more limited resources. The chapter focuses on the role that UWF and UTC play in supporting innovation in these two mid-sized cities.

The concluding chapter discusses the implications for higher education and learning, university entrepreneurship, technological discovery, and community and economic development. Additionally, it analyzes how these initiatives can become major catalysts for new knowledge. The chapter views these districts as innovative learning types that focus on recasting traditional models through the pursuit of collaborations, informing research, education, and policy. Some of the comparison categories employed include (1) primary funding mechanism, (2) role of university leadership, (3) extent of private-public partnerships, (4) role of government, (5) level of functional connectedness to campus activities, (6) unique district features, (7) role of the community in the decision-making process including potential impact, and (8) level of university-district integration. Emphasis is placed on the significant economic contributions as well as the broader spatial and socioeconomic composition implications. For example, do these projects encourage gentrification and displacement? The chapter concludes with a discussion about how these cases inform the future of academia in light of entrepreneurial engagement trends in higher education and recent directions of the university as an urban agent of change. By drawing from these case studies, chapter 8 also includes insights into planning considerations that should be taken into account when pursuing comparable projects.

Conclusion

At a time when economic disruption has affected higher education, universities must now reengage in a quite different manner from that of the past. Specifically, they must reorient themselves and embrace a unique view to become impactful innovators. Because of the effects of the unprecedented economic crisis of 2008, institutions are more open to pursuing bolder strategic plans that incorporate unique mindsets and operate in an entrepreneurial manner. However, an innovation ecosystem that draws from technology and entrepreneurialism has major economic development ramifications. These pursuits, closely linked to business interests, range from bringing to these areas highly established Fortune 500 companies to attracting entrepreneurs trying to breathe life into start-ups.

Anchoring an innovation district necessitates appropriately executed university-community relations that provide favorable results to all stakeholders. Public-private partnerships are essential in producing desirable and sustainable outcomes. These are evident throughout the various stages of progress. For example, project finance can take multiple forms depending on the specific circumstances. In some cases, the university plays a central role, while in others, the private or public sector is a significant contributor. Access to a transportation network is also a key contributor for the effective evolution of a university anchored innovation district. But clustering talent, bringing investment, and supporting start-ups can produce significant complications. The spatial restructuring that ensues can support historic preservation but also contributes to the upsurge of new neighborhoods, infusing the community with a unique but often diverse character. These projects are capable of remaking entire neighborhoods, enticing newcomers and pushing out existing residents.

The next chapter focuses on the emerging and shifting nature of the university as an innovator, and its broader contributions as an agent of change to meet various needs. It provides a unique analytical lens and insights when examining the relationship between higher education, technological innovation, and urban development. Emphasis is placed on cases of institutions across the country that have focused on various physical redevelopment efforts. Cases that have struggled to develop positive relationships with their communities are also presented.

The University as Innovator and Urban Leader

A T THE 650-YEAR anniversary of the University of Pavia in Lombardi, Italy, Patricia McDougall-Covin, the William L. Haeberle Professor of Entrepreneurship at the Kelly School of Business of Indiana University, gave a lecture on entrepreneurship. Indiana University offered its first entrepreneurship course in 1959 and has since significantly expanded the curriculum to deliver highly distinguished undergraduate and graduate programs in the field. Today it is recognized as a leading institution in the subject, ranked consistently in the top-five best entrepreneurship programs in the nation. At that lecture, Professor McDougall-Covin exposed some of the myths of entrepreneurship, concluding that it is a mindset which includes a vision to recognize opportunities, a willingness to change, and a passion to embrace and pursue creative solutions. Extending this mindset across the entire university, she argued, would prove transformational since such action would offer insight into professional and personal development for students, faculty, and staff alike. Subsequently, this approach, she claimed, could lead to economic expansion and translate to job growth.

McDougall-Covin proceeded to share information about some of the progress taking place in this area at Indiana University. The Johnson

Center for Entrepreneurship & Innovation leads many initiatives that span across campus, beyond the traditional academic degrees and certificate programs. For example, law and business students provide legal assistance to faculty who aim to commercialize innovations. On the medical science front, the Indiana University School of Medicine focuses on transitioning medical life science innovations into products available on the general market. Students across academic programs are provided with their own space to identify innovations with commercial possibilities. In the Jacobs School of Music, entrepreneurship is part of the music education curriculum because these students have to independently develop their careers following graduation. Finally, internships in social entrepreneurship are part of the program of study in the School of Public and Environmental Affairs. McDougall-Covin concluded that Indiana University wants to be recognized as "The Entrepreneurship Campus of the 21st Century."[1]

Innovation and the Second Academic Revolution

The case of Indiana University is not unique. In fact, this movement has grown so strong that some scholars have argued that universities are currently undergoing a second revolution. Christopher Jencks and David Riesman in their classic The American Revolution (1968) assert that the first revolution was the addition of research to the teaching mission, with the latter coming to define university culture. Universities, they posited, focused on disciplinary research that professionalized the ranks of incoming faculty. As a response to the needs of a rapidly developing, knowledge-based society, this shift not only established the characteristics of the research university, but also created a system that reproduced itself by graduating its future professors. The first academic revolution then is defined by a cutting-edge research framework which also determines what it means to be a scholar.[2]

There has been a second academic revolution, one that necessitates an outward institutional orientation. It adds economic and social development to the university purpose and, in the process, helps define the innovative university. At the core of this new direction is the aggressive pursuit of the commercialization of intellectual property, with a primary objective of improving the local and regional conditions and contributing to the national and global economy. This new direction also helps improve the financial fortunes of the university and its faculty, simultaneously expanding opportunities for student engagement.[3] While the innovative university is most visible in the undertakings of research universities, other types of institutions (i.e., regional comprehensive, urban, liberal arts, etc.) have pursued activities which also complement this orientation.

An example of this trend is professional education, which is increasingly becoming a common strategy. Regardless of their size and mission, urban colleges and universities are especially active in this area, since offering educational opportunities for professional growth has proved highly profitable. Another type of engagement in non-research institutions involves civic entrepreneurship.[4] Southern Oregon University, a public liberal arts college, is credited with the success of the Oregon Shakespeare Festival in Ashland, Oregon. Through the creation of a long-lasting, symbiotic relationship with the city, the university managed to create and maintain "cultural clusters" which produced significant and sustained social and economic development. Even though the primary focus was the theater festival, its advancement resulted in the establishment of other related cultural forms, with music, art, and history forming collections of venues.[5] The notion of the university as a regional development force was also exemplified by the efforts of four institutions in southwest Ohio to attract the second headquarters of Amazon. In September of 2017, Jeff Bezos, founder and CEO, announced that the internet giant intended to locate this new complex in North America. Currently the biggest corporate employer in Seattle, Amazon promised to create 50,000 new jobs at its second headquarters site. The leadership of the University of Dayton, Wright State University, Sinclair College, and Clark State Community College committed themselves to supporting the retailer if it chose to locate in the area. Amazon received 238 proposals from cities competing for an anticipated investment estimated at over $5 billion.[6]

Stanford Professor Henry Etzkowitz claims that this second academic revolution was ushered in by the emergence of entrepreneurial universities, which pursued the transformation of knowledge into intellectual property. In the process, science has evolved from an educational activity to a revenue-generating force. This orientation, it is argued, is the result of the "triple helix model" (an interactive model which includes the university, industry, and government spheres) which fuels technological innovation.[7] Specifically, "in a knowledge-based economy, the university becomes a key element of the innovation system both as human capital provider and seed-bed of new firms. Three institutional spheres (public, private, and academic), that formerly operated at arm's length in laissez faire societies, are increasingly interwoven with a spiral pattern of linkages emerging at various stages of the innovation and industrial policy-making processes."[8]

MIT is an example of an institution of higher education that most characteristically reflects the second revolution's shift and typifies the notion of entrepreneurial science. Long in the shadow of Harvard University, MIT, in the middle decades of the twentieth century, went from struggling for relevancy to ascending as a globally recognized and highly prestigious university. The success was the result of MIT leaving behind "its traditional role within the U.S. innovation system as a producer of research output in science and engineering to an active participant in the technology commercialization process."[9] Furthermore, MIT influenced many other universities which have also attempted to advance through the implementation of the triple helix model.

The MIT course correction in the 1930s served as the basis for establishing a continually unfolding shift in science and research, which most recently included economic development as a central tenant of its orientation. Across higher education, the scope of this second academic revolution proved to be so profound that, in addition to giving rise to entrepreneurial science, it also created a new set of institutional norms.

These new functions added to teaching and research and produced numerous complexities. For example, during the biotech revolution of the 1970s and early 1980s, faculty participation in commercial activities created conflicts of interest and revealed ethical challenges. Additionally, issues surrounding academic entrepreneurship in biomedicine meant that to protect intellectual property in science research, other approaches needed to be developed. These included new ways to process information in a high-paced, competitive environment.[10]

Beyond some of the broader impacts, there are also other issues associated with the changing nature of academic research and how faculty need to rethink their professional roles as they operate within this refashioned structure. For example, a new set of guidelines must be negotiated, shifting the existing mindset from basic research (answers fundamental questions that lead to new products, technologies, and processes) to applied research (creates new products, technologies, and processes that lead to new fundamental questions), and from advancing knowledge to considering its commercialization implications. As one observer noted, "The privatization of the research continues to generate conflicts of interest and commitment. Chasing profits has become a common sideline in the life sciences—the university has become a more congenial place for entrepreneurs. As this institutional transition unfolded, the university's rules regarding faculty conduct have scarcely changed."[11] Furthermore, there is a general need to rethink the relationship between theory and practice, as well as the management of a continuous, back-and-forth interaction between industry and the academy.

An entrepreneurial orientation also has cognitive effects on academic culture. Securing funds from external sources, such as government agencies or businesses, to support staff in laboratories and research activities is emerging as a new and accepted metric in the tenure and promotion process. It is within this reconstituted framework that intellectual advancement gains commercial potential. This higher education entrepreneurialism also helps reformat the institutional mission by incorporating a strong social and economic development component.[12] But this orientation is not without critics. For example, theologian Jaroslav Pelikan in the *The Idea of the University: A Reexamination* (1992) argued that this new direction is antithetical to the nature of the university in which knowledge is at the core of the higher education enterprise, not as a means but as an end. In his more traditional view, that would complement the ivory tower orientation: research and teaching are intimately and intricately connected and should not deviate from their original intent.[13] Others have argued that universities are struggling with "unrealistic expectations as to what they can do to make the economy more competitive. At the same time, the political basis for balancing academic autonomy with these expectations is eroding."[14] Accordingly, this tension, leading to the "capitalization of knowledge,"[15] should be countered.

There are numerous factors that have contributed to the rise of entrepreneurial science and the drive for innovation in the academy. Possibly one of the most influential elements was the 1945 publication of *Science, The Endless Frontier* by Vannevar Bush. Vannevar Bush, who at that time served as director of the federal government's Office of Scientific Research and Development, was invited in 1944 by President Franklin D. Roosevelt to submit recommendations under the premise that the "information, the techniques, and the research experience developed by the Office of Scientific Research and Development and by the thousands of scientists in the universities and in private industry, should be used in the days of peace ahead for the improvement of the national health, the creation of new enterprises bringing new jobs, and the betterment of the national standard of living."[16] In the 30-page report, Bush argued for the advancement of an understanding of the "fundamental laws of nature" through the use of the "techniques of scientific research" and knowledge which is "founded on new principles and new conceptions, which in turn are painstakingly developed by research in the purest realms of science."[17] His orientation of focusing on basic research helped ease any political tension that could have ensued. In fact, the word "practical" was included on 17 occasions throughout the document, an approach that circumvented potential opposition. Bush noted that "without scientific progress no amount of achievement in other directions can insure our health, prosperity, and security as a nation in the modern world."[18] He proceeded to offer a model that advocated for a centralized format in which government would play the main role in sponsoring and funding research. The proposed new agency was subsequently created in 1950 as the National Science Foundation.

The publication of the Bush report proved critical in a number of ways. First, it propelled significant government spending in science and technology, with universities and industry becoming the major recipients of these resources. Second, it altered the public perception of science. Science is not just for those directly involved in its pursuit for the creation of knowledge. Rather, it is now recognized as having significant value in terms of its capability to improve the well-being of every citizen. Third, the advancement of science entered the public policy realm and came to be viewed by government officials, politicians, scholars, and the public as a major driver of economic and social development. Finally, on the higher education front, the report had considerable impact on institutional change. The emergence of the innovation-driven university—strengthened by internal knowledge creation, which has led to its expanding commercialization and associated technology transfer—has come to alter many of the norms governing the university. While these changes unfolded in stages, first visible in high-intensity research universities, by the latter part of the twentieth century, many institutions of higher education embraced this strategy with varying degrees of success.

Technological Innovation and the University

Silicon Valley in California and Route 128 in Massachusetts are two examples of well-known places where high-powered technological activity is associated with institutions of higher education. The first has been intimately connected with Stanford University and the latter with MIT. As major technology hubs, both of those locations have extraordinary clusters of skilled workers and an astonishing variety of high-tech activity. These locales have produced a remarkable concentration of innovative talent. They are recognized globally as epicenters of high technology that sustain a robust environment to support discovery, the advancement of knowledge, and commercialization.

The relationship between Stanford University and the adjoining communities in Santa Clara, California (what we now know as Silicon Valley), dates back to World War II and can be described as an ongoing cycle of innovation fueled by entrepreneurship. In the 1940s, as part of the war effort, Frederick Emmons Terman of Stanford University was invited by Vannevar Bush to lead an effort to develop equipment that would deter the effectiveness of enemy radar devices. Terman agreed to organize and lead the Radio Research Laboratory at Harvard University. Following completion of the project, he returned to Stanford, recognizing the critical importance of military research and its connection to technological innovation. Terman employed his extensive connections with the government to attract considerable federal funding. In 1951, he developed the Stanford Industrial Park, later renamed Stanford Research Park. As the first university-owned industrial site focusing on technology, the park endeavored to attract scientists and university faculty, encouraged students to develop their own companies, created new jobs, and contributed to the regional economy. In 1948, Russell H. Varian and Sigurd F. Varian founded Varian Associates, and their invention of the klystron would become foundational in the development of microwave tube technology. In 1953, Varian Associates established their headquarters in the park, and by the late 1950s almost 2,000 employees worked to create and support numerous existing industries. Steve Jobs founded NeXT Computer there after leaving Apple, and Hewlett-Packard, Xerox, General Electric, Lockheed, Facebook, and Tesla are some of the many companies located on the grounds. Terman, who had also served as dean of the School of Engineering and provost at Stanford, played the crucial role in the rise of Silicon Valley.[19] His contributions were so extensive that he was "credited as the academic architect of Silicon Valley."[20] The headline in the *San Francisco Chronicle* referencing his death in 1982 claimed, "Stanford's Terman Dies—He Launched Silicon Valley."[21]

The structural factors behind the rise of Silicon Valley were a combination of technological advancements and an atmosphere fostering the idea that scientific breakthroughs can be brought to the market quickly through the creation of new businesses. Clustering together services in finance, human resources, legal, accounting, and marketing assisted the rise of new firms. Government support and a committed relationship between Stanford University and industry led to early success, which, in turn, rapidly facilitated the development of additional companies. One of the most unique elements in the ascent of Silicon Valley has been its ability to diversify the industry sectors present within its geographical area. Electronics, computers, software, biotechnology, and networking are some of the industries that, over the years, viewed the place as a hub. Sustaining innovation and entrepreneurship is primary. Some of the guiding principles and unique characteristics that governed this environment included the notion that, when successful, high levels of financial reward should follow; intense worker mobility is desirable; failure is a foundational element of the culture; and encouraging the pursuit of new ideas and discoveries while at the same time protecting intellectual property is necessary. Because of these principles, Silicon Valley is expected to maintain its edge and global importance for many years to come.[22]

On the other side of the country, in 1951, the first segment of Route 128 opened in Massachusetts, approximately 15 miles outside of Boston. As a circumferential highway, Route 128 was perceived as a divider between the city and the rapidly growing suburbs. In May 1955, *Business Week* published an article titled "New England Highway Upsets Old Way of Life" referring to Route 128 as the "Magic Semicircle," the force that eventually came to symbolize Boston's high-tech rise. Research labs and entrepreneurs from Harvard and MIT introduced technologies that were quickly commercialized. This technological explosion on Route 128 was at the center of what became termed the "Massachusetts Miracle," a period of sharp economic growth in the 1980s following the devastating effects of deindustrialization in the 1970s. The economic revival was unexpected and unprecedented.[23]

Up until the late 1980s and early 1990s, Route 128 and Silicon Valley were comparable in the volume and scope of their technological activity. Both locations maintained strong military funding, access to venture capital, and connections to world class universities. They also sustained a diverse mix of large corporations, small companies, and start-ups. But Massachusetts's innovation economy then experienced a slowdown. The rapid rise of the personal computer ushered in dramatic changes nationally and globally. Its development found a home firmly positioned on the West Coast. A diverse assortment of parts necessary to power the new technological revolution required the creation of a myriad of application software and hardware components. The commercialization of the internet that followed necessitated continuous innovations in browser software, operating systems, email, VoIP, and instant messaging. Finally, the rise of e-commerce demanded the further acceleration of technological innovations, which in the process not only strengthened existing companies but also created new firms. The directory of Silicon Valley corporations would now include Apple, AMD, Electronic Arts, Cisco, Google, Nvidia, Netflix, Facebook, and Intel among many others.

This shift from the East Coast to the West Coast, and the resulting success and dominance of Silicon Valley in the 1990s, can be attributed to how the cultural conditions in the two areas evolved, even though the two locations experienced similar histories as cores of far-reaching technological breakthroughs. Specifically, on the one hand, the competitive advantage of Silicon Valley can be attributed to the development of a decentralized industrial system that supported cooperative conditions. On the other hand, Route 128 had developed a structure comprised of large companies that drove industrial change, with the majority maintaining a strong sense of autonomy. This nimbleness in Silicon Valley produced a fertile environment that bred innovation and valued risk-taking. Start-ups and spin-offs from existing corporations were encouraged. Developing alliances, sharing information, and supporting collaboration among colleagues across companies to give birth to new entities was the norm.

The different entrepreneurial cultures that emerged between Silicon Valley and Route 128 led to two very different trajectories and advancement paths. Technological innovation on the West Coast moved rapidly as new ideas and products were quickly integrated in existing activities that helped propel the creation of new markets. Silicon Valley also encouraged broader participation in new undertakings within the technology community.[24] According to an entrepreneur, "In Boston, if I said I was starting a company, people would look at me and say: 'Are you sure you want to take the risk? You are so well established. Why would you give up a job as vice president at a big company?' In California, I became a folk hero when I decided to start a company. It wasn't just my colleagues. My insurance man, my water deliverer—everyone was excited. It's a different culture out here."[25] Innovation eventually deteriorated along Route 128 as the vertical model of organizational culture began to inhibit business opportunities. On the other hand, the horizontal collaboration model on the west coast gave rise to many thriving, specialized companies. This led to product development and differentiation that powered success in systems integration.

In the preface to *Regional Advantage: Culture and Competition in Silicon Valley and Route 128* (1996), AnnaLee Saxenian, social scientist and dean of the School of Information at the University of California, Berkeley, wrote that "as a native of the Boston area, I may wish that the Route 128 region turns itself around quickly; as a scholar, I know that it is likely to take decades to overcome the management practices, culture, and institutions that have hindered the region in the past."[26] Today, Route 128 struggles to regain its dominance as a global innovation district. Additionally, during the last 30 years, suburban areas have lost their appeal as the revitalization of the urban core has attracted younger residents who value the vibrancy, density, diversity, historical significance, and a plethora of amenities—from transportation services to restaurants and bars—that urban neighborhoods provide. Boston's innovation ecosystem is similarly experiencing a rebirth but back in the city. Cambridge and Kendall Square are currently undergoing changes as Facebook,

View of the Massachusetts Institute of Technology, Cambridge, Massachusetts, campus from the Charles River. The Kendall Square Innovation District is visible on the right of the photo. Courtesy of user Wangkun Jia, Shutterstock Images.

Apple, Google, Amazon, and Microsoft have opened offices there, and new start-ups are rapidly launched and funded.

While Silicon Valley and Route 128 are widely associated with technological innovation and the role that Stanford and MIT played in their development, other universities have joined the hunt for strategies to engage in the transfer of technology from the institution to industry. The Bayh-Dole Act, formally referenced as the Patent and Trademark Act Amendments of 1980, became instrumental in the growth of technological innovation and the participation of universities in the process. Sponsored by Senators Birch Bayh of Indiana and Bob Dole of Kansas, the act required the involvement of federal agencies in supporting research to implement a patent policy. Before the act, any patents resulting from government support belonged to the government. The Bayh-Dole Act shifted control of patents away from the funding source to those that actually produced the invention. This shift proved significant for universities involved in research since before that time they could not retain ownership of their work.

The impact of the Bayh-Dole Act has been enormous. A 1997 survey by the Association of University Technology Managers found that between 1993 and 1997, 8,000 patents were granted to academic institutions. From 1980 to 1997, more than 2,200 companies were formed. Technologies generated by university research activities expanded commercialization and created new industries, resulting in over $30 billion of economic activity each year and supporting 250,000 jobs. The Council on Governmental Relations (COGR), an association of research universities, affiliated medical centers, and independent research institutes concluded that "as Vannevar Bush foresaw, enormous benefits to the U.S. economy have occurred because of federal funding of research . . . encouraging technology transfer. The licensing of new technologies has led to the creation of new companies, thousands of jobs, cutting-edge educational opportunities and the development of entirely new industries. Accordingly, the Bayh-Dole Act continues to be a national success story, representing the foundation of a successful union among government, universities, and industry."[27] In 2002, an editorial by the Economist noted that "possibly the most inspired piece of legislation to be enacted in America over the past half-century was the Bayh-Dole act of 1980. [It] unlocked all the inventions and discoveries that had been made in laboratories throughout the United States with the help of taxpayers' money. More than anything, this single policy measure helped to reverse America's precipitous slide into industrial irrelevance."[28]

The commercialization of innovation led to a significant expansion of patents filed, especially by institutions of higher education. For the first time, a large number of universities looked to create new structures that would nurture technology ventures. One of the most common approaches proved to be the development of research centers with physical incubators aiming to facilitate an environment of growth and success. In addition to incubators, "accelerators" were configured to accomplish these goals. Unlike incubators that are typically unstructured, accelerators operate with a short timeframe, typically three to four months. In addition to guidance, they also provide capital funds in exchange for equity in the company. On the other hand, start-up incubators do not have a set timeframe and the participating companies often benefit from services which are funded by university-secured grants. The primary goal of incubators and accelerators is to help nurture the value of the participating companies through expertise, mentoring, and financial assistance so that they can raise funds to function independently.

The Austin Technology Incubator (ATI) is a vibrant organization that works through the University of Texas at Austin (UT). Founded in 1989 by George Kozmetsky, who had served as dean of what is now the McCombs School of Business at UT, ATI assists start-ups that have made some progress to move to the next level by providing strategic planning services, advice, and funding. Over the years, ATI has maintained a focused approach, primarily emphasizing energy, health and bioscience, wireless communications, enterprise software, water, and transportation technologies. As one of the oldest start-up incubators in the country, ATI supports both university and non-university start-ups and is part of the IC^2 Institute (innovation, creativity, capital), which was also founded by Kozmetsky in 1977. The IC^2 Institute concentrates on furthering technological innovation by involving the university, government, and private entities to generate sustainable, regional economic development. According to UT President Bill Powers, "ATI has been integral to tapping into Austin's entrepreneurial spirit and making our city a technological capital."[29]

In recent years, the University of Washington in Seattle has also emerged as a hub of innovation and entrepreneurialism. The region is home to numerous Fortune 500 technology companies that include Amazon, Microsoft, and Expedia. Starbucks and Costco are also located in the metropolitan area. CoMotion is the university's start-up incubator. It originally began as the Center for Commercialization and focused on commercializing ideas that had bubbled up at the university. As a collaboration innovation hub, the organization has since significantly expanded its outreach outside the university and has proved very successful in boosting companies to grow to maturity and eventual independence. The mission of CoMotion has evolved into the pursuit of a broader strategy in search of economic and social impact. With a number of labs, they host start-ups in IT, engineering, life sciences, medical devices, clean technology, virtual reality (VR), and augmented reality (AR).

Startup Hall is a CoMotion Lab that opened in 2014 and is a partnership between the University of Washington, Techstars (start-up accelerator), and UP Global (nonprofit that organizes events for entrepreneurs). Located at the University of Washington, it provides an environment wherein IT and software start-ups can develop their companies. For example, Techstars Seattle aims to cultivate technical talent. The small number of companies that join the incubator as a result of a competitive application process receive access to mentors, investors, and many of the program's successful alumni. UP Global is a Seattle nonprofit that specializes in entrepreneurship. In 2017, CoMotion Labs @ Spokane was launched, an outreach effort to the community of Spokane, Washington, that focuses on "manufacturing, healthcare, agriculture and robotics."[30] University of Washington President Michael K. Young recently commented, "University start-ups give the American public a valuable return on their investment in academic research. UW start-ups deliver impact to the public from our life-changing discoveries."[31] Developing partnerships to expand the regional innovation ecosystem is a key approach to generating growth.

In the Midwest, the Research Park at the University of Illinois at Urbana-Champaign is another example of a technology hub that assists start-up companies and supports corporate research and development. A recent partnership with the University of Chicago's Polsky Center for Entrepreneurship integrates faculty from the highly ranked University of Illinois's College of Engineering to create a nucleus in Chicago's south side community of Hyde Park.[32] Similarly, the University Research Park (URP) in Madison, Wisconsin, focuses on aiding businesses in the early stages of development in various areas including computational and life sciences. The URP was established in 1984 and is affiliated with the University of Wisconsin–Madison. Finally, The Engine at MIT is a leading, highly focused ecosystem organized to propel groundbreaking discoveries from initial conceptualization to commercialization. Its mission is to embrace disruptive technologies that have the capacity to bring about significant change. The organization recently raised $200 million to assist incubators as they progress in addressing pressing challenges in emerging technologies. These include aerospace, advanced materials, genetic engineering, biotech, and renewable energy. According to MIT President L. Rafael Reif, "From the beginning, our vision for The Engine has been to foster the success of 'tough-tech' startups with great potential for positive impact for humanity. By enabling crucial investments in The Engine's first portfolio of companies, the funds announced today will also strengthen the local innovation ecosystem and the regional economy."[33]

These ambitious initiatives by public and private research universities across the country are intended to further technological innovation and reinforce entrepreneurship and commercialization. The competition is intense, and many institutions look to industry resources, government support, philanthropy, and unique partnerships to strengthen their position. Some have an advantage due to their past history, location, and research portfolio. But not all of these entities operate in an urban environment, nor are they the outcome of real estate expansion that has contributed to urban revitalization. In recent years, this aspect of community change has emerged as a unique component of university entrepreneurialism. Its singular characteristics constitute a distinctive focus of this book.

The University as an Urban Developer

In January of 2010, the *Chronicle of Higher Education* ran a cover story titled "The College President as Urban Planner." The essay discussed the efforts of Franklin & Marshall College (F&M), a private institution in Lancaster, Pennsylvania, to address some of the physical and social issues facing its home community. Like other cities experiencing deindustrialization, Lancaster underwent economic decline and depopulation during the 1960s, 1970s, and into the 1980s. Armstrong Flooring Inc., operated a factory in Lancaster. However, its footprint shrank, leaving behind derelict buildings. The challenge for the college was immediate given that Armstrong's structures not only were rapidly deteriorating but also were adjacent to the campus. Under the leadership of then-President John A. Fry, F&M "acquired, tore down, and cleaned up most of the former Armstrong World Industries facility—some 200 buildings on 47 acres, razed to make way for sports fields, a nursing college for the hospital, and perhaps other new development."[34] President Fry focused on creating and cultivating key partnerships with a number of stakeholders to achieve his objectives, including Armstrong World Industries, Lancaster General Health, Norfolk Southern, and state and local government officials. According to the director of economic development and neighborhood revitalization for the City of Lancaster, this redevelopment was crucial since it allowed for the hospital to continue to grow given that the old plant "would have been mothballed for some time to come . . . it was a huge undertaking. The coalition that F&M was able to bring to the table certainly benefited the redevelopment of the site." In the end, in addition to demolishing a factory, the project included moving a railyard and excavating a landfill.[35]

The case of F&M is not unique. Colleges and universities across the country do not have the option to relocate when the surrounding physical or social conditions undergo changes and deteriorate. Unlike businesses that have the option to move to a different environment that better meets their strategic objectives, or residents that, due to various demographic or economic shifts, can move to communities that offer better amenities, institutions of higher education are unable to leave behind their historic roots and often substantial campus investments. What is unique about the case of F&M is the ability of the leadership to ably respond to the circumstances threatening the institution.

When assessing the role of colleges and universities in urban development, it is important to keep in mind that organizational engagement varies extensively depending on specific circumstances. For example, the historical context, the socioeconomic conditions of the surrounding community, and the circumstances of the broader physical landscape are critical factors. Furthermore, the extent and intensity of prior and current institutional involvement must be considered since this can lead to favorable or unfavorable outcomes. For example, managing political and financial risks, addressing the intricacies that arise from real estate investments, and engaging with community organizations are all complicated propositions that necessitate strategic planning, patience, persistence, and coordination. The success of Franklin & Marshall was largely due to the fact that the institution did not have to engage in a contested arrangement to achieve its redevelopment goals. The challenge in this case had more to do with mobilizing the necessary resources.

Cities, in turn, are increasingly realizing the potentially positive force that colleges and universities can play in urban change, but success necessitates collaboration since multiple entities must work together to achieve the desired results. Town-gown relationships have become complicated in recent years for a number of reasons. First, in order to remain competitive, universities pursue the expansion of student services. This demand requires the utilization of additional space, which fuels the need for geographic enlargement in adjacent areas. The second reason relates to the fact that many cities are, in effect, reurbanizing. For example, population density, especially in or around core areas, has grown. Residential development often produces contested environments as existing institutions, real estate entrepreneurs, and incoming residents come into conflict with more established, less affluent communities who express discontent with property tax increases and ensuing gentrification.

The quest by universities to further their mission often positions them as umpires in the middle of these complicated forces, especially if development necessitates the displacement of residents and businesses. Creating a shared vision and then balancing mutually beneficial agendas is difficult. Government officials recognize these complexities, as well as the important contributions colleges and universities can make to urban revitalization. Mark Funkhouser, former mayor of Kansas City, Missouri, has argued, "Perhaps the next big thing in local government ought to be a 'higher education relations officer' who leverages universities' assets to benefit the cities they're in."[36] The relationships between higher education institutions and the communities within which they operate has received extensive coverage by the national media. Given their importance, the *Chronicle of Higher Education* and *Inside Higher Ed*, along with many other major newspapers and magazines, regularly publish stories on these issues. Interestingly, the release of the annual *Princeton Review*'s ranking of colleges now includes a listing of the worst and best town-gown relationships.

Institutional concerns of this nature are not unique. For instance, during the 1960s and 1970s, the University of Chicago was similarly worried about its long-term ability to excel as a world-class institution given the urban problems in adjacent Hyde Park and Woodlawn. The Penn agenda of community engagement during President Judith Rodin's years necessitated the commitment of over $1 billion between 1996 and 2006. A considerable injection of resources, the funds contributed to the start of a new wave of demographic change, accompanied by rapid economic shifts as residents with greater means moved to the area. Referenced as "Penntrification," this type of higher education–led gentrification has come to typify poor university-community relations.[37] The case of Penn and its surrounding neighborhoods reveals how complex and unpredictable the university-community relationships can become. Penn's early engagement with the community was by scorch and burn. Later, a more enlightened approach involved neighborhood actors and tried to be more holistic. However, this more inclusive approach still led to unanticipated outcomes by initiating gentrification. In short, an ambiguous story.

Urban colleges and universities across the country are trying to build relationships, foster successful strategies for civic involvement, and address complex socioeconomic challenges facing their surrounding communities. Strategies such as expenditures on beautification and the upgrading of adjacent infrastructure, developing retail and office space nearby, operating afterschool programs, creating new elementary schools, and encouraging faculty and staff to reside close to campus are some examples of efforts aimed at regeneration. It should be noted that these projects have varying degrees of success in achieving economic development. Furthermore, these investments alone often prove limited in strengthening community ties. The following cases of Yale, Northwestern, Brown, Columbia, and the University of Pittsburgh show the difficulties these institutions have experienced when managing community relations.

Over the years, Yale University has been unable to maintain a consistently constructive relationship with the City of New Haven, Connecticut. From the 1970s to the 1990s, Yale did not invest in adjoining areas, allowing neighborhoods to decay. This led to tensions between the privileged Ivy League institution and the disadvantaged residents. Repeated efforts to rebuild trust proved challenging as clerical and cafeteria workers went on strike in 1984, 1996, and 2003. Additionally, retail redevelopment efforts by the institution were met with criticism for pushing local commercial owners out of business. In 2013, former Yale President Richard Levin championed the reestablishment of a strong relationship with the city by noting, "A stronger Yale is good for New Haven, and a stronger New Haven is good for Yale. It is very important that both the president of Yale and the mayor of New Haven understand this, believe it and act on it."[38]

The situation is similar at Northwestern University which, for decades, has been at odds with the City of Evanston, Illinois. Like Yale, Northwestern is the dominant economic force in the north Chicago suburb. That status is at the center of a continuous controversy. For many years, government officials and residents have complained that the university was not making appropriate contributions for the services received from the community which it calls home. City representatives argue that millions of dollars from taxpayers go to the institution in the form of public services. Yet, the university, due to its nonprofit status, does not pay property taxes and fails to voluntarily make substantive offerings to help maintain city parks, roads, and related infrastructure. This tension grew, leading the two parties to file lawsuits against the other. In recent years, there has been a concerted effort to improve the relationship between the university and town.[39]

Facing significant enrollment increases in the 1960s, the University of Pittsburgh proceeded to develop a master plan to address future institutional growth needs. Conflicts emerged with the adjacent community of Oakland which expressed dissatisfaction with the university's strategy and the fact that they were not included in the planning process. By employing political channels, neighborhood coalitions applied pressure to alter the university's initial direction. The institution revisited its stance, eventually pursuing a collaborative approach with the community organizations.[40] Inviting community stakeholders to participate in planning initiatives may prove to have a more powerful impact than expected and can greatly help improve relationships.

Similar challenges have confronted other leading universities such as Brown and Columbia. Like Northwestern, Brown University struggled in Providence, Rhode Island. Brown also came under pressure to contribute more to the city for the services it received at a time of municipal fiscal stress.[41] In New York City, in the spring of 1968, Columbia University was entangled in a series of confrontations in nearby Harlem which caused outrage and political activism, forcing the university to rethink its stance and community outlook.[42]

It is apparent that when considering economic development and revitalization, urban universities face much more complicated circumstances than those located in suburban or rural settings. That is primarily because these institutions are operating in environments which have experienced significant decline during the 1970s and 1980s. In the end, as the realities of municipal crisis intersect with the desire of university leaders to grow campuses to attract and better serve students, a clash ensues which threatens the town-gown relationship. A collaborative and inclusive approach, perseverance, and transparency are key ingredients for success when universities partake in the urban developer role. But when examining the relationship between the university and the city, it is important to consider how the increasingly critical function of science and technology, stemming from academic research and the pursuit of commercializing knowledge, may impact change. This interaction between technological innovation and urban development is an essential component of any forward-looking inquiry.

Technological Innovation as a Source of Urban Change

At his acceptance speech as the recipient of the 1971 Nobel Prize for Economic Science, Simon Kuznets commented that "a technological innovation, particularly one based on a recent major invention, represents a venture into the partly unknown, something not fully known until the mass spread of the innovation reveals the full range of direct and related effects."[43] During that December 11 ceremony, Kuznets focused his remarks on the complicated and unpredictable nature of economic growth. Even though his work was broad, discussing modern economic expansion as a distinct historical epoch, it is apparent that the underlying dynamics and impact of technological innovation are equally complex when considering the effect of innovation on urban change. Technological innovation, unless it reaches a state of maturity, does not automatically lead to business expansion. For example, when assessing the relationship between employment density and patent intensity, research shows that the latter is maximized when a competitive market is in place and when the population is under 1 million residents. Higher population does not necessarily produce more patents since appropriate conditions are a prerequisite to success. In fact, the intensity of patents is maximized at an employment density of about 2,200 jobs per square mile. Under these conditions, the presence of patents are 20 percent higher.[44]

Understanding the relationship between technological innovation and urban change requires an exploration of the undercurrents necessary to create an environment conducive to development. Specifically, how does innovation contribute to the rise of a culture in cities that furthers its advancement? What are the catalytic forces that can alter the urban environment? In *Cities in Civilization* (1998), urban planner and geographer Sir Peter Hall examines how cities achieve great moments of success. His interdisciplinary approach is noteworthy because it embraces the work of historians, economists, and geographers. Hall focuses on the importance of creativity as a critical ingredient. Specifically, he asks, "How and why do innovative technologies, innovative ways of industrial management, create new growth; and how do they come to develop in certain places at certain times?"[45]

Hall employs the concept of the "innovative milieu," which he argues is evident in many historical periods. City size and complexity are key ingredients in creating urban networks of innovators. These are guided by creative individuals who challenge the current cultural conditions, eventually altering the social structure. He notes the importance of a balanced disruption by indicating that "creative cities are almost certainly uncomfortable, unstable cities, cities in some kind of basic collective self-examination. . . . Conservative, stable societies will not prove creative; but neither will societies in which all order, all points of reference, have disappeared."[46] The changing nature of the innovative milieu is evident through three stages of evolution. These include an early industrial period of eighteenth-century and early nineteenth-century cities, followed by a corporate era during the latter decades of the nineteenth and early part of the twentieth centuries exemplified by the many research sites clustered in Detroit, Michigan. Finally, after World War II, technical innovation was driven by military research, which helped create a plethora of scientific applications. While Hall offers key insights on innovation, creativity, and urban change, he also recognizes the influence of inherent complexities and concludes that "time and chance happeneth to them all; it is a question of finding the moment and seizing the hour."[47]

Sociologist and urbanist Manuel Castells has investigated the relationship between information society and globalization. Like Hall, Castells also utilizes the "milieux of innovation" to describe unique regions in which the accelerating pace of innovation is an outcome of the information technology revolution. These geographical locales form clusters with distinct characteristics that can innovate and are part of the globalization process. Hence, "These milieux required (and still do in early twenty-first century, in spite of on-line networking) the spatial concentration of research centers, higher-education institutions, advanced-technology companies, a network of ancillary suppliers of goods and services, and business networks of venture capital to finance start-ups"[48] and the "cluster does not consist simply of people landing together, it is about people working together and companies networking with each other . . . These kinds of territorial networks have expanded through global networks between territories . . . This is important for city development."[49]

So, what are the implications of the network society on the informational city? First, the rise of virtual interactions within highly interconnected global networks challenges some of the foundational aspects of long fixed production processes. Castells notes that "at its core, capital is global. As a rule, labor is local."[50] The emergence of these reconstituted conditions means that the capital is relying less and less on the traditional nature of labor, since it is now dispersed and unable to pursue collective action. This causes complications since "who are the owners, who the producers, who the managers, and who the servants become increasingly blurred in a production system of variable geometry, of teamwork, of networking, outsourcing, and subcontracting."[51] It is through these conditions that business relations are advanced. But the pace of technological transformation is so rapid that the formulation of the dual city is a direct outcome. Castells argues that mega cities are the new urban form that follows with a "distinctive feature of being globally connected and locally disconnected, physically and socially."[52] The pursuit of regional development through high technology during the 1980s and early 1990s gave rise to "technopoles." These industrial complexes serve as centers for the manufacturing of core materials and also shape the conceptual design and production process.[53] In more recent years, because of rising levels of interdependency and accelerated flows of capital and labor, these types of cities are more likely to cooperate than to compete with each other.

But what about the ramifications of all this at the local level? What are the ways that cultural innovation and creativity, as well as technological transformations, affect urban growth and shape the urban environment? What are the consequences at the neighborhood level? A number of researchers have offered perspectives on such issues, attempting to provide answers to these questions. For example, urban affairs scholar Richard Florida, in his highly influential The Rise of the Creative Class (2002), posits that technology workers and those engaged in creative work are the type of residents that can play a significant role in the revival of urban centers in ways no other public investment can achieve. Attracting and retaining those involved in creative occupations is a much better economic development strategy than offering tax breaks and associated incentives to entice corporations. When considering the sizable municipal expenditures required, the mere presence of these businesses does not guarantee the return of economic benefits that can lead to regeneration.

According to Florida, the creative class is comprised of tech-savvy professionals and entrepreneurs, as well as musicians, independent-minded individuals, gays, and lesbians, who are attracted to environments which offer vibrant urban scenes, loft living, cafés and trendy restaurants, farmer's markets, and a bohemian culture. This lifestyle experience is enticing to those neighborhood newcomers who are highly entrepreneurial, tolerant, community-minded, and socially engaged.[54] Two key descriptive characteristics of the creative class are that they are talented and possess high levels of tolerance. They also possess high levels of human capital as measured by educational attainment at or above a college degree. Because of these qualities, they are also likely to maintain high levels of sympathy for others, are attracted to diversity, and value cultural and nightlife amenities. Florida concludes that there is a strong association between high technology industries and talent. The presence of talent attracts high tech firms which aids the establishment of a broad collection of high technology commercial enterprises. This, in turn, helps fuel income growth.[55]

The creative class approach to economic development is not without challenges. The rise of gentrification has been a key outcome of this trend as the influx of creative people helped quickly raise the market value of housing. This led to property tax increases, new construction, and displacement in various neighborhoods that, at one time, were home to middle-class and lower-income residents of various racial and ethnic groups. Gentrification is also closely linked to improved amenities, which strengthen the quality of life and emerge as a major drive for urban growth. It is no surprise that, in recent decades, municipal leaders and civic boosters aggressively turn their attention to policies which focus on an economy that centers on urban tourism, leisure, and entertainment.[56]

Although creative class–focused economic development policy is controversial, many cities have sought to seed innovation districts, which has emerged as a formidable financial growth strategy. Enterprising mayors across the country pursue innovation districts aggressively because of their positive benefits. During his two-term tenure, Seattle Mayor Greg Nickels (2001–2009) was a strong promoter of urban life, advocating dense living and environmental sustainability. Nickels was instrumental in the growth of South Lake Union, located north of downtown to the southern tip of Lake Union. By expanding transportation options in the area and adding a street car line, these infrastructural investments contributed to the creation of an economically vibrant environment focusing on biotechnology and the life sciences. As a result, the community has transitioned from a setting that was once full of derelict warehouses into a booming neighborhood, making South Lake Union an exciting place that combines residential living, work opportunities, and entertainment options. On the opposite side of the country, a similar story is evident in Mayor Thomas Menino's (1993–2014) successful effort to revive Boston's downtown. Menino played a key role in the explosive development of office, retail, and housing projects in the South Boston Innovation District. Also known as the Seaport Innovation District, this initiative was introduced by Menino in 2010. The mayor envisioned and advocated for the transformation of more than 1,000 acres of abandoned waterfront land into a nucleus of information technology activities that encompassed the computer, digital, and media industries. Today, this innovation district continues to grow with live-and-work housing options and the presence of numerous cultural amenities. Both of these districts, in Seattle and Boston, have received extensive praise and accolades, nationally and internationally, as officials across the globe try to copy their success.

The cases of these government-spearheaded, highly successful Seattle and Boston locales typify the extraordinary potential of innovation centers for urban revitalization and scientific advancement. However, urban research universities are also essential, since their pursuit of commercialization of knowledge in science and technology can play a key role in regional economic development. A recent report by the Brookings Institution finds that research universities in downtowns have a significant impact due to their geographic advantages. The assemblage of innovation forces present in dense environments proves highly favorable due to inherent opportunities for growth. According to the report, "The knowledge economy is driven by the strategic interplay between universities, firms, entrepreneurs, research labs, and independent inventors who draw strength from each other in virtuous cycles of innovation. Innovation districts—employment hubs in the cores of cities that co-locate research, entrepreneurs, housing, and mixed-use amenities—are perhaps the most recent and tangible example of innovation clusters."[57] The analysis concludes by noting that research universities located in midtowns and downtowns produce more licensing deals, and receive more income from those deals, than do institutions in suburban or rural areas. Additionally, urban universities create a significantly higher number of start-ups, as well as unveil more inventions on a per student basis.

Conclusion

Technology and innovation are emerging as fundamental drivers of urban economic development. Institutions of higher education, along with governments and corporations, are playing a significant role in the creation of districts to support the commercialization of knowledge, develop an ecosystem of entrepreneurialism, and attract business investment. This direction complements the mission of universities as they search for financial growth opportunities and endeavor to improve their academic standing and provide experiential opportunities to students. Research-intensive universities are especially well-positioned to realize these goals because of their capacity to produce research and new knowledge. At the same time, due to their high level of complexity in both conceptualization and execution, the creation and maintenance of effective partnerships is required. Institutional leadership is also essential to ensuring success.

These newly formed geographic clusters also attract new residents who are highly educated, creative types, and high wage earners that are ambitious and entrepreneurial. As they occupy surrounding neighborhoods, they trigger new investment in housing and retail services, in the process aiding the regeneration of what were once ailing areas. At that point, it is the university and the community that find themselves connected, typically because institutional ventures may alter the built environment including the current residential composition. What further complicates these interactions is that university expansion is often tied to broader real estate strategies which may include the rental or sale of retail and office spaces. In fact, in some cases, even new condominium housing becomes part of the institutional strategy. While the approaches and results vary, there is observed consistency in producing reconstituted conditions that generally alter the socioeconomic conditions producing abrupt or long-term change, often resulting in gentrification and displacement.

The next chapter focuses on the rise of Technology (Tech) Square in Atlanta and the role of Georgia Institute of Technology (Georgia Tech) in its development. For years, the massive Interstate 75/85 kept the Georgia Tech campus separated from the community to its east until 2003 when Tech Square was unveiled in Midtown. The chapter discusses the historical circumstances leading to the construction of this multi-block neighborhood which has since evolved to become a nationally recognized technological ecosystem supporting commercialization and entrepreneurship. Additionally, corporate innovation centers attracted to the district in recent years include companies such as Panasonic, AT&T, Home Depot, Delta Airlines, Anthem, Chick-fil-A, Boeing, and Siemens. Currently, more than 30 corporations have opened innovation centers at Tech Square, making this a very unique project feature. The Tech Square case incorporates the role that business headquarters and offices, professional education, adjoining retail services, the Georgia Tech Foundation, and the Georgia Tech Hotel and Conference Center have played in the formation of the Tech Square environment. Recent changes to the physical layout of the area—including additional residential and commercial construction, mixed-use orientation, and other functions—are also addressed, as well as factors contributing to a culture of innovation and the implications for the neighborhood. The chapter considers structural forces in helping transition the vision of Tech Square from conceptualization to execution, including location, urban decline or revitalization, competition, and agency in the form of institutional leadership.

Anchoring a Redevelopment Renaissance

Tech Square in Atlanta

L OCATED JUST north of downtown Atlanta, Georgia Tech has historically operated in a densely urban, physically contained setting.
Over the years, the campus underwent various expansions and changes.
The university benefited from the 1996 Olympic Games as the recipient
of new facilities and global attention. North Avenue to the south and
Tenth Street to the north, together with the massive Interstate 75/85 to
the east and multiple railroad lines to the west, framed the campus
buildings and grounds until the early part of the 2000s. However, in
2003, the institute "jumped" the Downtown Connector (Interstate
75/85) to unveil an expansion to the east. Initially a complex of university and retail buildings, Technology Square (Tech Square), as it became
branded, has since evolved into a thriving district of corporate innovation centers, many of which are associated with Fortune 500 companies, incubators, accelerators, and start-ups. The district seamlessly
links the university to the adjoining Midtown neighborhood. What is
most remarkable about the case of the Tech Square development is
how rapidly it has unfolded. Just 15 years earlier, this was one of the
city's most socially and economically challenged communities. The
accelerated pace of the last five years has been especially noteworthy,

increasing demand and fueling additional development in the surrounding area.

In 2016, the American Planning Association (APA) recognized Midtown as one of just five *Great Places in America: Neighborhoods*. According to the APA, a key defining characteristic that propelled Midtown toward this distinction was the fact that "top-ranked anchor institutions bridging technology, healthcare, and the arts, foster innovation among corporations, start-ups, and entrepreneurs in Midtown Atlanta's Technology Square area."[1] The spring 2017 issue of *Innovation Leader* magazine published a list of leading innovation cities and hubs located within metropolitan areas. The publication ranked Atlanta as number six, identifying Georgia Tech as the "catalyst" that "in the late 1990s began buying up acreage and developing a blighted, underused zone between its campus and Midtown Atlanta. Atlanta has long been home to industry-defining global companies like Coca-Cola, United Parcel Service, Home Depot, and CNN, but this new neighborhood, dubbed Tech Square, became a petri dish for all sorts of new innovation activity. The result is one of the few places in the world where you can ride an elevator or walk a few steps to go between 15 innovation labs run by companies like AT&T, Anthem, Southern Co., ThyssenKrupp, Panasonic, and Delta Air Lines."[2]

Many other national publications have referenced the Tech Square development as an important agent of change. For example, *Harvard Business Review* pointed to the university and Tech Square by noting, "Because young technology firms often serve as test beds for future products, Georgia Tech has made Midtown Atlanta into an ideal environment for corporate research centers by supporting faculty and student startups and linking them to larger businesses. [Georgia Tech is] also taking great pains to improve the physical realm and animate public spaces to create an environment for creative thinking and collaboration." The publication concluded that these developments are a "leading indicator of where corporate research is headed."[3] Corporations, especially those focused on science and technology, have historically looked to universities. As mentioned previously, Stanford and

Silicon Valley along with MIT and Route 128 are two of the most obvious and notable examples. Currently, Tech Square is home to more than 30 corporate innovation centers, and that number is expected to grow. Panasonic was the first to establish an innovation center in 2012. Since then, the AT&T Foundry opened in 2013, followed by the Coca-Cola Development and Innovation Lab (2015), the Southern Company Energy Innovation Center (2015), Anthem Innovation Studio (2016), the Boeing Manufacturing Development Center (2017), and the Honeywell Software Development Center (2018), among many others.

The story of Tech Square in Atlanta is driven by the founding of a technological university in the southeast that ascended to become a top 5 public institution in the country. During that period, Georgia Tech housed the Olympic Village for the 1996 Olympic Games in Atlanta, hosting athletes from across the globe. The campus was also the site for some Olympic competitions. But the enrollment growth that followed and the need for upgraded facilities necessitated an initial expansion across a major interstate in the western part of Midtown, one of the city's most derelict areas. Furthermore, Georgia Tech wanted to create a more attractive and defined entrance to the school while also desiring to embrace a more business-minded orientation in its strategic outlook. In the last 10 years, the university's commitment to infusing technological innovation and entrepreneurship at the undergraduate and graduate levels fostered an environment that helped fuel the commercialization of knowledge, attracting corporate entities in search of talent and venture capital to a rapidly changing Technology Square. In the last few years, additional university development is enticing business headquarters and companies to construct office towers nearby. All this has quickly transformed Midtown into one of the most expensive neighborhoods in Atlanta, reshaping the socioeconomic standing of the community. Today, Tech Square is a vibrant ecosystem that is continuing its ascent, connecting entrepreneurs, student and faculty researchers, laboratories, and venture capitalists, blurring the lines between the university and the city in the process.

The Rise of a Technological University in the South

While noted for its research activities in science and technology, Georgia Tech has diversified its academic offerings in recent decades to provide academic programs in business, as well as the humanities and social sciences. The university was founded in 1885 as the American South was transitioning from an agrarian to an industrial economy. Atlanta emerged as the center of the "New South" movement, a term introduced in 1874 by Henry W. Grady, managing editor of the *Atlanta Constitution*. This shift eventually became closely associated with the staging of the International Cotton Exposition of 1881. The exposition was proposed by Edward Atkinson, who had called for a grand city event that would showcase the most advanced products, tools, and techniques in the cultivation of cotton. The latest crop planting and cotton seed cleaning methods would be displayed. Because of the event, many of the outdated practices of this rapidly flourishing industry would be reconsidered.

Born in Brookline, Massachusetts, Atkinson was president of the Boston Manufacturers Mutual Insurance Company. A leading entrepreneur in the management of textile mills in New England, he argued that education would be a key element in promoting economic investment and industrial growth by noting that the "south probably needed mechanical and industrial education more than his own region and warned that unless education preceded or accompanied capital, the latter would be almost worthless."[4] In a speech at the Exposition, Atkinson mentioned that his son, a student at Harvard at the time, was instructed in carpentry and blacksmithing. Atkinson also pointed to an exhibit for the Exposition by the School of Mechanic Arts at Boston Tech (later renamed MIT) as an example of the powerful connection between education and industrial progress.[5] Grady quickly supported the cause of creating a technological institution in Georgia. He, along with others, could see the value of such an investment. These included John F. Hanson, a Macon industrialist and owner of the *Macon Telegraph and Messenger*, and Nathaniel Harris, also from Macon, founder of the Bibb Manufacturing Company, a major textile and cotton enterprise that expanded into other parts of the state over the years to become one of the largest employers in Georgia.

Hanson prompted *Macon Telegraph and Messenger* editor Harry S. Edwards to publish an editorial calling for the establishment of a polytechnic with the goal of furthering agriculture, in a manner similar to how the state had earlier created the University of Georgia. This new institution, Edwards argued, would support the growing manufacturing industries just as legislatures had done in other parts of the country, especially in New York and Massachusetts. The article appeared in the newspaper on March 2, 1882. It eventually received the backing of the *Atlanta Constitution* and of legislators, who, in the spring of 1883, traveled to the northeast to visit Cooper Union, Stevens Institute of Technology, Boston Tech, and Worcester Free Institute of Industrial Sciences (later renamed Worcester Polytechnic Institute). Impressed by the two Massachusetts universities, Boston Tech and Worcester, the committee finally recommended that Worcester serve as a model for the new institution.[6] Founded as the Georgia School of Technology, the university was firmly part of the transition from the agricultural to the industrial economy. It was renamed the Georgia Institute of Technology in 1948 and in May 1961, under the leadership of President Edwin Harrison, the university voluntarily desegregated by admitting African American applicants. Since then, it has evolved from a regional technological institution to become globally noted as it focused on conducting groundbreaking scientific research through innovation.

Gerald Wayne Clough arrived at Georgia Tech in 1994 as the 10th president of the university and was the first alumnus to serve in that capacity. In collaboration with the Georgia Tech Foundation Inc., the university implemented in the mid-1990s a campus land acquisition program across the Fifth Street Bridge that was consistent with the campus master plan for the future use of the institute. Charlie Brown and Harry Hammond "Buck" Stith Jr. served as trustees and chairs of the Georgia Tech Foundation. Stith noted that in 1995, "At our annual meeting at The Cloister in Sea Island, after a long Executive meeting involving budgets, forecasts, fund-raising, all the problems associated with an institution faced with a growing student body, new disciplines, expanding physical needs on a campus that was essentially land-locked, our Chairman, Charlie Brown, said the four most feared words any executive, manager, leader or entrepreneur can hear—'Oh, by the way . . .' When you hear these words, look out! So, Charlie said, 'Oh, by the way, I've got an option on some old, worn-out buildings with some land growing up in weeds over across the interstate on 5th Street near The Biltmore.' Charlie persuaded us that this was 'thinking outside the box' and, after much discussion, we bought it—with absolutely no plan for its use."[7] By purchasing eight acres (later expanded to 13.3 acres of land to the south of Fifth Street for $11.9 million), the new asset could serve as a source of institutional enlargement. John Carter, who served as president and CEO of the Georgia Tech Foundation from 1999 to 2013, noted that "there was no specific purpose for the land. It was an option and the university could plan to do something with it or not. It could be 5 years or 25 years later. There was some activity in that area, a Cadillac dealership and some other stores, but everyone slowly moved away. The land was just sitting there, becoming a place of ill repute. All that was happening right next to the campus, not only at night, but also during the day. Following the purchase, we just maintained the parcels by keeping things clean."[8]

On numerous occasions Georgia Tech President G. Wayne Clough reminded the members of the foundation and various other university constituents of the importance of expansion for the future of the institute. He reiterated the rationale behind potential development by regularly reviewing facilities at other universities. At one speech to the Georgia Tech Foundation, Clough compared the facilities at the Darden School of the University of Virginia, the Anderson Management School at UCLA, and the Steinberg Conference Center of the University of Pennsylvania Wharton School with those housing the DuPree College of Management at Georgia Tech. The difference was stark. The College of Management was located on the west campus in an unassuming structure, one that was also in need of major upgrading. Additionally, the Georgia Center at the University of Georgia, and the Emory Conference Center and Hotel at Emory University, were not only highly functional but boosted programmatic opportunities at those institutions. Repeated reference was also made regarding how continuing education outreach at Georgia Tech had grown by 285 percent in the past 20 years. Between 1995 and 2000, the growth was 10 percent annually with 4,900 programs offered to 107,000 participants, generating 60,534 continuing education units from 605,000 hours of instruction.[9]

The university administration recognized that even though the institute had benefited from the Olympics, these were primarily athletic facilities and dormitories. The Olympics had expanded the southern and western edges of campus, but no options existed on the dense, northern residential edge. In a series of speeches, Clough began to reference the possibilities of a relationship between the institute and Midtown. At an administrative retreat in August of 1999, his comments focused on leadership and the future, noting that Midtown was a location which had the potential to be marketed as a high-tech hot spot given the synergy that already existed between the institute and the neighboring community across the Downtown Connector. He argued that start-ups had emerged in various parts of the area, and that the presence of numerous loft, condo, and apartment projects that were developing provided unique opportunities. Stimulating a Midtown renaissance through high-tech activities would be consistent with some of the economic development already taking place by the city and the state. Clough went on to specifically reference Fifth Street as a "spine" connecting the institute to Midtown.[10] Years later, he reflected, "We had other needs. I would drive across the Fifth Street Bridge and there were for sale signs everywhere. Many students, faculty and staff also entered the campus from that point, especially during the Olympic Games. That was the direction for the campus to grow."[11]

However, that area, the western part of Midtown, along with the rest of the community had been declining for years. This condition accelerated following decades of disinvestment as suburbanization propelled Atlanta's unprecedented growth. At another speech that same year, on the role of the university in urban revitalization at the Urban Land

Institute, Clough argued, "In creating Silicon Valley, Stanford University had the advantage of large tracts of undeveloped land nearby. In contrast, Atlanta's major universities are right in the city, where redevelopment requires collaboration. Atlanta is not really experiencing a revitalization or even a renaissance, but rather a reincarnation. Atlanta is not returning to its former glory; it is turning into something new."[12] Among Tech's leadership, a consensus emerged that any campus expansion would have to take place to the east, making crossing the Downtown Connector the only viable direction.

The University as a Collaborator: Georgia Tech Meets Midtown

At a carefully choreographed press conference on June 5, 2000, Georgia Tech presented its campus master plan to Atlanta, which included the institute's goal to undertake a multibuilding project on the property across Fifth Street. A number of dignitaries were present and invited to speak at that gathering, including Mayor Bill Campbell; Susan Mendheim, president and CEO of the Midtown Alliance, the most influential community organization in Midtown; and Sam Williams, president of the Metro Atlanta Chamber of Commerce. In his remarks, Clough commented on the history of the campus and the adjoining community boundaries, as well as the scope of the development, including its specific components. But he also gave attention to Midtown, emphasizing the collaborative university-community relationship which helped give rise to the project. He commented that Georgia Tech and the Midtown Alliance "began to consult and collaborate, and our respective development plans reflect that complementary, symbiotic relationship. The Midtown Alliance understands that Georgia Tech is the engine that will drive the development of a high-tech business community in Midtown. Georgia Tech understands the importance of quality housing, retail, restaurants, and cultural amenities to our effort to attract top-notch faculty, staff, and students. We both know that if we cooperate, we have the potential to make Midtown a dynamic live-learn-work-play community that will become a model for other cities. As the

Midtown Alliance and Georgia Tech developed a shared vision for this community, an exciting future for this particular part of the neighborhood began to emerge."[13] A year later, reflecting on that presentation, he noted that "we went to Susan Mendheim and the Midtown Alliance and more or less asked to be adopted. Over the past several years, we have been working closely with the Alliance in creating both the Midtown Blueprint and our own Campus Master Plan, so that these two documents complement each other. The goal of both of them is to create a model, urban, live-work-learn-play community. We want to put Midtown on the leading edge, not only in Atlanta but also in the United States, as an in-town neighborhood that offers all resources needed for a quality life."[14]

In the spring of 2004, a significant update was integrated into the 1997 Georgia Tech Campus Master Plan. The need for this revision, which still guides the university today, was the outcome of significant changes that took place in the previous few years. Chief among them was a rapidly expanding student enrollment, growing research activities, and the accompanying increases in faculty and staff. The plan also intended to respond to a number of unfolding strategic initiatives, including the formal depiction of the Technology Square expansion now found on the campus map. The update made it clear that its pursuit was firmly connected to the university's strategic, capital, and financial planning activities. Sustainability and accessibility—as well as attention to land use, parking, transportation, housing, athletics, and recreation—were elements that had always been part of previous planning efforts. But the 2004 plan update, for the first time, also included a focus on "collaborative planning with community constituents." It was an outward, rather than inward/defensive approach, which would subsequently inform the plan's future orientation.

The document presented a conceptual framework that offered a set of contrasting guiding principles. These called for shifting the university's alignment from a "traditional campus" to a "knowledge-based community." Additional characteristics included a transition from an "internally oriented" campus to one that is both "internally and externally"

View of Interstate 75/85 looking north cutting through Atlanta. To the left is the campus of Georgia Tech and to the right is Midtown. The second bridge is Fifth Street which connects the university campus to Tech Square. Courtesy of user ESB Professional, Shutterstock Images.

oriented, from a campus that is "Ivory Tower isolated and apart from the community" to one that is "engaged with the community in many different ways." Finally, the plan argued for a framework directed by "study/play/live/work community" principles.[15] As Clough noted, "Georgia Tech has had numerous folks in its history who wanted to make the campus safe by walling it off from its surrounding neighborhoods. Today we believe that a better approach is to work together with our surrounding neighborhoods to improve quality and safety. We want to reach out to the neighborhoods around us and blur the edges of our campus, so that those who live and work nearby can share the amenities we offer."[16] It is this concept of collaboration between the university and the community that characterized how the institute pursued the Fifth Street expansion and the eventual development of Technology Square.

Midtown was once home to a vibrant shopping district along Tenth and Peachtree Streets. But the construction of Lenox Square in 1959, an upscale shopping mall in Buckhead, and Ansley Mall in 1964, as well as the ensuing decentralization, resulted in significant population loss and the demolition of many area buildings during the 1960s and 1970s. The trend continued in the 1980s as empty lots and surface parking came to dominate much of the community. Any new commercial and residential development that took place occurred along the Peachtree and West Peachtree stretches of the Peachtree Corridor, cutting through Midtown between Buckhead and downtown. Underdeveloped and un-kept parking lots, vacant buildings, and adult-oriented businesses, along with some single occupancy residences in deteriorated struc-tures made this one of the most blighted parts of the city. Clough re-flected about the land across the Downtown Connector, "I thought to myself, we should buy this property."[17]

As a nonprofit organization, the Midtown Alliance has led Midtown's renaissance. Founded in 1978, the alliance has facilitated numerous community efforts toward urban revitalization over the years. Young urban professionals have been attracted to the various amenities, in-cluding the proximity to Atlanta's downtown to the south and Buck-head to the north. The primary goal of the Midtown Alliance has been to strengthen existing assets while supporting and guiding the creation of a commercial, retail, and residential hub to further Midtown as a dy-namic arts and cultural center. In order to meet these objectives, in 1997, the Midtown Alliance initiated *Blueprint Midtown*. It was a com-prehensive master plan that endeavored to ensure a sustainable future through the integration of sound planning principles and broad com-munity participation. The publication of *Blueprint Midtown* proved highly influential since it not only established a sound foundation for redevelopment in the area, it also informed the largest, single rezoning legislation in the history of the city of Atlanta. The document identified the area across the Fifth Street Bridge as a location to include mixed-use retail, entertainment, and low rise (five to six stories) office development. One of the key goals was to create an urban market center that could promote unique types of retail with parking decks nearby that would also offer ground level retail opportunities.[18] A follow-up version titled

Blueprint Midtown II was launched in 2003. Its focal points were placed on retail and restaurant additions, expanding residential growth, adding parks and plazas, and promoting effective mixed-use development practices.

Intimately connected with these efforts, the university engaged as one of many stakeholders and contributed to the conceptualization and execution of these plans. Shannon Powell, who served as executive vice president and chief operating officer at Midtown Alliance and was involved in formulating Blueprint Midtown, noted, "Georgia Tech was part of those conversations from the start and a contributor to our efforts. Representatives from the Institute participated in many meetings and collaborated on many occasions."[19] Robert Thompson, executive vice president for Administration and Finance at Georgia Tech, also played a central role and saw the expansion as an opportunity to connect the university with the community, stating, "It represents, to use a technology buzzword, a 'portal' to the Midtown technology corridor and community. More importantly, it represents a two-way connection between Georgia Tech and the community of which it is a part, allowing all who live, work, play and study in Midtown to make Georgia Tech and the Georgia Tech community a part of their everyday lives."[20] The City of Atlanta also contributed to these efforts, with then–Atlanta Planning Commissioner Michael Dobbins expressing strong support for the Midtown Alliance efforts. Dobbins openly recognized the critical importance of Blueprint Midtown and its long-term, positive implications for this community and across the city.[21]

Construction of Technology Square began in the fall of 2001, the result of a process that included developers, Midtown Alliance representatives, architects, and the university. The northern part of Fifth Street was privately developed and was scheduled to include the Advanced Technology Development Center (ATDC) and the Yamacraw Electronic Design Center. The ATDC was formed by the Georgia General Assembly following an effort by the state in the late 1970s and early 1980s to support partnerships between universities and businesses with the goal of launching new companies. Since its establishment, the ATDC has been headquartered in various parts of Midtown, though over the years the organization also created satellite operations in other parts of the state. The relocation to Technology Square would bring the ATDC even closer to the university. The Yamacraw Electronic Design Center was also planned to be placed at the north part of the street. As a statewide initiative introduced in 1999 by Governor Roy Barnes, the goal of the center was to help grow industries that focused on high technology. Identifying opportunities and supporting the commercialization of research activities was central to its mission. Even though the developers of the southern part of the street (Georgia Tech Foundation and Georgia Tech) were different from those involved in the northern part of the street (Kim King and Associates), it was critical that the final version of the design maintained a consistent architectural view, both functionally and visually. Thus, the guidelines were jointly developed by the foundation, the Midtown Alliance, and the architectural firm. This allowed for a plan that ensured the effective staging of the streetscape along the Fifth Street corridor.

Empowering Creativity and Entrepreneurship: Fueling Student and Faculty Engagement

G. P. "Bud" Peterson began his tenure at the Georgia Institute of Technology in 2009 as the 11th president of the university. Like most of the US economy, Atlanta was in the midst of an economic downturn not seen since the Great Depression. Just a year earlier, in the fall of 2008, Georgia Tech Interim President Gary B. Schuster instituted a moratorium on hiring and a freeze on position reclassifications. He placed limits on operations expenditures, travel, and equipment acquisitions, and even declared delays and deferments on already scheduled purchases. Schuster also announced permanent budget cuts of at least 6 percent in FY09 and possibly greater for FY10.[22]

Nevertheless, while facing these significant challenges, Peterson outlined from the start an ambitious direction for the university. In an opinion piece published in the *Atlanta Journal Constitution*, he argued that the future of the university should be firmly placed at the intersection of innovation, technology, and entrepreneurship. He wrote, "One of our goals is for Georgia Tech to be the 'Innovation Institute,' a place where technology, economics, business, public policy, law, commercialization and entrepreneurship co-mingle and thrive. This involves creating a culture that values not only the rewards of research, but also the economic and commercial impact of the results. Tech is already an economic engine for the state and known for its innovation. Our goal is to be known for innovation worldwide, preparing students to be innovative leaders whether in education, government, corporate, law or public policy environments."[23]

Like other public universities, Georgia Tech relied on support from state funds during declining economic conditions. At a welcoming event, prior to taking office, Peterson acknowledged that this "has to be one of most difficult times at Georgia Institute of Technology. These are challenging times, they are challenging times for Georgia Tech, they are challenging times for the state of Georgia, they are challenging times for the nation. We will have to continue to face challenges in the coming months but we will step up and address those challenges in a way that above all will ensure that we will not diminish the quality of the education and research programs at the Institute . . . first and foremost."[24] Georgia Tech indeed weathered the economic downturn as Peterson embarked on a 25-year strategic plan and surpassed the $1.5 billion goal for Campaign Georgia Tech by raising $1.8 billion. However, what may prove to be one of the most unique aspects of his presidency was a focus on recognizing and growing strong collaborative and strategic partnerships that centered on technological innovation and entrepreneurship. Thus, the development of an ecosystem where research and discovery, technology transfer, and business interests and needs comingled gave rise to a distinctive environment with the capacity to fuel economic growth and urban development. The Technology Square project would be the primary actor and central driver of this vision.

In 2010, the university launched a dynamic 25-year strategic plan, *Designing the Future: A Strategic Vision and Plan*. Innovation and entrepreneurship were prominently referenced. For example, the framework of the plan outlines that the institution should be "an economic driver for Atlanta, the state of Georgia" while encouraging faculty to be "both scholars and entrepreneurs."[25] In addition, the plan called for a continuous commitment to the adjacent community by noting that the university "will encourage and help create a revitalized Midtown development zone that will surround the campus and include quality housing, strong schools, world-class informal learning centers, cultural venues, and retail amenities." In addition, it promoted the importance of strengthening Midtown by forming an environment that supports economic opportunities through technological advancement. Thus, "As a test bed for research and innovation in the urban environment, the city of Atlanta will be populated with the industries that support innovation and new businesses. As such, it will become a laboratory for sustainable economic and social development that promotes technological change while celebrating the human spirit. Georgia Tech and Midtown Atlanta will attract alumni, global leaders, and venture capitalists to visit and contribute to the community—and it will be a place where faculty, students, and staff from around the world will choose to live, learn, work, and play."[26] Finally, the document identifies the value of collaborative partnerships by indicating, "Public-private partnerships with the community will be instrumental for economic development, research, educational innovations, and cultural venues."[27] The 2010 plan repositioned the university by identifying a framework for institutional advancement and offered a new conceptual direction that included a reconstituted purpose for the Technology Square expansion.

The university strategically embarked on a concerted effort to further hands-on student involvement, encouraging direct insights into laboratory settings. Expanding that engagement beyond the lab allowed for additional skills to develop, including collaboration and opportunities to tackle real-life challenges. By connecting science, engineering, and technology with an entrepreneurial orientation, students can build on their prior experiences and pursue solutions to more complex issues. This helps propel student research forward, crafting a more independent orientation beyond the isolation typically associated with the laboratory environment. Student competitions is one area that allows for this transition to unfold. For example, the VIP program stages the VIP Innovation Competition. Students taking a VIP course for credit can join a team tasked with generating a poster and an oral presentation that addresses a need, offers a solution, and identifies a customer who can benefit from their innovation. Beyond the VIP Innovation Competition, a number of other targeted initiatives help strengthen creativity and discovery. These include Ideas 2 Serve (I2S), the Global Social Venture Competition, Invention Studio, TI:GER, Capstone Design Expo, CREATE-X, and InVenture Prize.

I2S and the Global Social Venture Competition are both organized by the Institute for Leadership and Entrepreneurship, an interdisciplinary entity in the Scheller College of Business. They focus on encouraging values-based leadership and socially responsible entrepreneurship. I2S assists students in developing organizations that not only aspire to generate revenues, but are also deeply concerned about social and environmental issues. Improving the human experience and people's life chances are intimately linked to their strategic outlook. A competition of innovations that are either at an early stage or at a more mature phase is judged by investors and socially conscious business leaders. The more advanced Global Social Venture Competition shares some of the same core objectives of I2S. It provides mentoring and visibility to ambitious entrepreneurs, as well as $80,000 in prize money, that can help thrust their ideas forward in hopes of forming viable companies. These social venture initiatives can thus receive exposure, guidance, and support as part of an experiential learning process.

Open to all majors across the university, regardless of year of study or prior experience, the Invention Studio is a unique approach to encouraging innovation. As a student-run makerspace, the setting allows participants to explore and nurture original and unconventional concepts within a supportive environment that values responsibility, safety, and community ownership. The Convergence Innovation Competition urges the creation of innovative products and experiences.

These can be a part of class projects or fall outside the formal academic setting. As a biannual event, the categories for the fall competition are determined by the campus community. For the spring competition, they are established by industry partners that, for 2018, included four categories: health and wellness, smart cities and IoT (Internet of Things), arts and culture, and sports and fan experience.[28] The submissions are judged on the quality of prototypes which operate "on converged services, media, networks, services, and platforms."[29] The Georgia Tech Institute for People and Technology and the Research Network Operations Center are the organizers of the event.

However, what would probably be considered the highest profile programs in building the creative technology muscle are the InVenture Prize Competition and CREATE-X. The faculty-led InVenture Prize was launched in 2009. It provides undergraduate students the opportunity to showcase high-level technology projects with considerable business potential. The annual event draws significant interest beyond the university community. Finalists showcase their inventions before a panel of expert judges in a packed auditorium televised live by Georgia public television. The winner receives $20,000 from Google, a free US patent filing by Georgia Tech's Office of Technology Licensing (an approximate value of about $20,000), and acceptance into university start-up accelerator programs and mentoring services. The 2016 winning team included Zack Braun, who described the competition as an intense experience, commenting, "I felt a little star struck when I walked out on stage. The bright lights, 2,000 people cheering when you walk out, it's kind of crazy to have to talk right after that!"[30] Roger Pincombe, who tied for first place during the inaugural competition and after graduation pursued a career in San Francisco as a software engineer, admitted that the InVenture Prize competition "pushed me to go from just building things to thinking of startups."[31] The InVenture Prize is considered the nation's largest undergraduate invention competition.

CREATE-X started in 2014 as another faculty-led program. Undergraduate students gain knowledge and experience that will allow them to pursue entrepreneurial opportunities. Through various programmatic options that include coaching and legal assistance, participants are able to develop the skills necessary to launch their own start-ups. As a curricular-based program that offers academic credit, the goal is to support entities that are most likely to have a long-term impact and be sustained over time. In its relatively short lifespan, CREATE-X has evolved into a university signature program framed around three principles: (1) learn, (2) make, and (3) launch. Within it, a number of educational activities aid students' understanding of entrepreneurial orientation such as Startup Lab and Tech Ventures. These are yearlong credit hour courses that emphasize evidence-based entrepreneurship, creativity, and the theory and practice of start-ups. CREATE-X also supports the transition of concepts to products. "Idea to Prototype" provides legal advice and resources in the form of funding to create an archetype. Finally, students can intern as a way to launch their operations as they receive seed funding, legal services, space, mentorship, IP protection, and visibility to achieve their objectives.

All of these efforts at the university during the Peterson era played a central role in contributing to the development of a culture that connects technology and entrepreneurship, a multistage process. Initially, undergraduate research activities help form a fundamental core by encouraging students to engage in lab experiences. Those persisting students participate in programming which furthers creativity and discovery. Experiential opportunities at the next level allow students to combine entrepreneurial skills and pursue a more independent orientation toward technology development. Judged competitions at various levels, faculty mentoring, interactions with business leaders, exposure to relevant legal considerations, funding assistance, and a highly supportive institutional environment thrust promising ideas forward. This advanced stage includes an environment comprised of accelerators, incubators, and venture capital. Tech Square becomes the epicenter where this ecosystem unfolds.

Boosting the Technology Ecosystem: Supporting the Commercialization Process

An array of activities either directly sponsored by the university or the result of collaborations between the university and businesses contributes to the creation of a structure that fuels Tech Square's distinct vibe and identity. Additionally, attracted by the chance to interact and innovate in the district, unaffiliated private incubators and angel investors are part of the equation. For example, the Enterprise Innovation Institute (EI²) is the university's business organization aimed at providing assistance to industries, aiding technology commercialization, and strengthening economic development. One of the functions of EI² is to empower start-ups seeking to improve their competitiveness. EI² initiatives fall into three main categories: (1) commercialization, (2) entrepreneurship, and (3) business services. These include VentureLab, the Georgia Tech Integrated Program for Startups, the Advanced Technology Development Center (ATDC), Innovations Corps, and the Economic Development Lab. Outreach activities by the Procurement Assistance Center and the Contracting Education Academy help organizations improve business services. The long-term objective of EI² is to reorient the role of the technological university within a rapidly unfolding economy. Innovation Corps offers short courses to those entrepreneurs interested in commercializing research and building a start-up. The Economic Development Lab has a broad agenda that helps with the establishment of incubators, assists faculty in their commercialization program efforts, and contributes to assessing innovation in emerging technologies.

As a technology incubator, ATDC has played a central role in the development of Tech Square. Forbes named ATDC one of "12 business incubators changing the world."[32] The operation has graduated more than 200 companies by taking advantage of its access to university resources and through the delivery of a curriculum, coaching and mentoring from experts and business leaders, and support from various corporate partners and companies. The overwhelming majority of these companies continue to be active with many of them being acquired by major corporations. Some made it to the IPO stage. For example, founded in 2011, Clearleap is a software company that was acquired by IBM to help advance cloud video services. Partpic graduated from ATDC in 2017 after achieving at least one of three milestones set by the incubator and a few months later it was acquired by Amazon. Partpic developed search technologies that recognize objects. Tellabs acquired Future Networks, a maker of cable modems for $181 million. Future Networks was a 2001 ATDC graduate. S1 Corporation, a software company specializing in payment processing, went public and was later acquired by ACI Worldwide. ATDC is also well connected to local community organizations including the Technology Association of Georgia, the MIT Enterprise Forum in Atlanta, Invest Atlanta, and the Atlanta CEO Council. Finally, ATDC maintains strong relationships with venture capital firms.

VentureLab is an incubator and part of the university's EI^2 that supports students and faculty to create start-ups based on research conducted at Georgia Tech. Over the years, VentureLab aided the development of hundreds of start-ups which have been formed in aerospace, financials, materials, biomedical, clean technology, computing, pharmaceutical, security, and robotics, among other industries. The program works closely with the Georgia Tech Research Corporation (GTRC), which serves as the contracting agency for sponsored research at the university. GTRC also licenses all intellectual property. VentureLab ensures that the start-ups they work with are well positioned to pursue their business plans by managing the legal requirements which typically prove limiting for many teams during the early stages of development. Invention disclosures, intellectual property filings, and conflict of interest issues are some of the key areas for which VentureLab provides critical support. In 2014, UBI Index, an incubator consulting group, assessed 800 incubators from 66 countries and ranked Georgia Tech's VentureLab 2nd in the United States and 17th in the world.[33] A recent offshoot, the Georgia Tech Integrated Program for Startups, encourages entrepreneurship among university faculty, staff, and students. Emphasis is placed on licensing agreements and legal assistance for patents.

There are a number of other incubators and accelerators that are operating in Tech Square. For instance, the Advanced Manufacturing Program focuses on the creation of an environment for manufacturing start-ups by coordinating programs that include industry experts, corporations, and investors, along with university resources. In 2015, following a partnership with Wordpay U.S., the fintech program was launched to mentor financial technology start-ups and entrepreneurs. In the area of health care, Forge is an incubator that assists by bringing together investors, clinical professionals, and mentors to support new companies. Additionally, Cyberlaunch is a three-month-long accelerator program that engages start-ups in the area of information security. Finally, by embracing a data-driven orientation, NeuroLaunch is an accelerator for neuroscience start-ups.

However, two of the most notable accelerators in the Tech Square ecosystem are Engage and Flashpoint. Both of these accelerators are

Technology Square in Atlanta, south side of Fifth Street. Courtesy of Mary Eve Speach.

connected to university resources but also bring considerable funding portfolios. Flashpoint was founded in 2011 as part of the Center for Deliberate Innovation at Georgia Tech. More recently, its programs are offered through Flashpoint Management Company, a university spinoff. As a 10-week-long start-up accelerator, Flashpoint provides both for-profit and nonprofit start-ups with an opportunity to become part of a mentoring environment. The start-ups are exposed to a unique methodological approach through a curriculum that allows participants to learn and embrace tools to reduce risk and maximize success. This helps them to become intentional and more strategic in their orientation, thus allowing them to consider the potential for scalability. According to Merrick Furst, a faculty member who founded Flashpoint, "When the new administration at Tech decided to make accelerating entrepreneurship a central goal of the university, they pulled me in. We already had a first-rate incubator and other excellent programs, so we thought incremental improvements would just yield incremental results. I also knew that traditional approaches to starting companies, and to supporting founders, were unreliable. We needed a different approach. Flashpoint helps address the fundamental problem: how do you build scalable new companies that succeed?"[34] From 2012 to early 2018, Flashpoint collaborated with 150 start-ups with a collective market value of $1.2 billion.

Engage is a 90-day mentorship accelerator that started in 2017 and is managed by GATV, a Georgia Tech affiliate. Originally, 10 corporations cooperated to form this initiative. Among them were Fortune 500 companies such as AT&T, Delta Airlines, Invesco, Home Depot, and UPS. In spring 2015, Goldman Sachs Group Inc. joined the other corporations as the 11th member of Engage in Tech Square. The program works with early stage companies that are gearing up to enter the market. Leaders from these corporations join together to provide start-ups support to develop a competitive advantage. Once accepted, participating companies receive $75,000 in financial assistance. However, what is probably the most unique aspect of this initiative is Engage Ventures, a $15 million fund pooled by the corporate members and distributed to fledgling start-ups. The largest arrangement of its kind, Engage Ventures, which is managed by Tech Square Ventures, brings together major corporations in an independent firm. Former Mayor Kasim Reed advocated for the fund following a visit to Silicon Valley in 2013.

The Tech Square ecosystem includes a number of venture capital and seed fund investors. In addition to Flashpoint and Engage Ventures, Tech Square Ventures, Tech Square Labs, Mosley Ventures, Atlanta Seed Company, and Ninety10 Partners also operate in the area. Angel and venture capitalists are also part of a growing investment environment. Tech Square Ventures is a seed and early stage fund specializing in technology start-ups which support university spin-offs, as well as entrepreneurs that focus on the internet and the cloud. Some of the companies that have benefited from Tech Square Ventures include PreTel Health, a supplier of fetal monitoring systems; UserIQ, which assists companies with their customer retention efforts; and Cypress. io, which supports software developers by providing an all-in-one testing framework. Seed funding is also available through Tech Square Labs, an incubator in search of a range of companies, from very early stages of development to more established enterprises.

Collaborative working environments are also present in Tech Square and offer resources to aspiring entrepreneurs. Tech Square Labs operates a 15,000-square-foot co-working space. In 2016, The Garage was formed, a workspace and event venue that brings people together to interact and develop relationships. As part of the tech community of Atlanta, The Garage sponsors conferences, lectures, fireside chats, performances, parties, and celebrations. It also coordinates community outreach events that give back to various local organizations. One of the most successful recent happenings is the Atlanta Startup Crawl. Those curious about entrepreneurship and technology are invited to explore the facilities, interact with start-ups, and engage in the Sandbox ATL, a provider of shared experiences. An annual spring job fair is organized for hiring breakthrough companies, inviting prospective applicants by proclaiming "no suit, no resume, just you." All this aims at cultivating connections along the way that can lead to commerce.

Corporate Innovation Centers and Midtown's Future

In 2013, President Peterson spoke about the changing expectations in higher education at the (co)lab summit, a gathering of regional leaders sponsored by Leadership Atlanta designed to create collaborative strategies that would aid the growth of the metropolitan area. His remarks centered around three unfolding trends which were principally informed by the conditions born out of the recent economic crisis. These included attending to the employability of graduates and their adaptation to a continuously changing society; providing lifelong learning opportunities by utilizing advanced technology; and quickly transitioning research from the lab to the consumers.

The latter of these trends would prove critically important given its potential ramifications for economic development and job creation. This orientation also emerged as a major driver in the subsequent advancement of Technology Square since, as Peterson claimed, "All of these activities that are occurring there in Tech Square, in Midtown, Atlanta, are designed to . . . take ideas and research that we do at Georgia Tech and move that research into the business community."[35] He also identified the corporate innovation centers as a key step in giving Tech Square a concrete direction. Specifically, "The corporate innovation centers have been a great success. It was an organic process, one that involved many individuals. It was not clear right away. When our engagement with AT&T resulted in the opening of their Foundry in Atlanta in 2014, well that was a game changer. It brought legitimacy. We realized at that moment that we have a model. We had something special in place. We have worked really hard since that time to strengthen that effort."[36] Rafael L. Bras, who arrived as provost and executive vice president for Academic Affairs at Georgia Tech in 2010, echoed a similar sentiment, noting that "a real strategy started to take shape when some of the large corporations decided to move to Tech Square. Panasonic and AT&T entering the location was key since it allowed them to be innovative and agile. Following that, more corporations expressed interest in becoming part of that environment. That helped build confidence."[37]

The case of Anthem is notable because it exemplifies the long-term potential and implications of corporate innovation centers. Anthem, an $85 billion health care benefits company serving millions of customers, decided to create an innovation studio in Tech Square. In an interview with *Forbes*, Anthem CIO Tom Miller noted, "It was clear that breakthroughs were inevitable and that they would be largely enabled by technology—mobile care, the internet of things, digital. . . . Recognizing that there was so much going on that had the potential to disrupt our industry, we decided to launch the Anthem Innovation Studio. We also wanted it to be fast, however, I came to realize the criteria set that had to be in place for us to be productive in innovation. By May of 2016 we had built out our own studio. We now have a team of about twenty people that continuously innovate. They evaluate ideas, they shape those ideas, and they pilot them."[38] In October 2017, Anthem went a step further by announcing the construction of a 21-story office tower in Tech Square to house its IT center. The location will employ more than 3,000 information technology and software development professionals. CIO Tom Miller referenced Tech Square as a "hotbed for innovation."[39] In January 2018, NCR opened its global headquarters in Midtown, adjacent to Tech Square. The $450 million investment brought 5,000 jobs to the area. Bill Nuti, NCR chairman and CEO, noted during the opening, "Our move to Midtown is part of our vision for transforming Atlanta into the Silicon Valley of the East."[40] And there is more activity on the way. In 2019, Anthem began construction on another 20-story office tower after consolidating its operations in downtown Atlanta and nearby Buckhead. That same year, Norfolk Southern announced the construction of its $575 million headquarters in Midtown as part of its relocation from Virginia to Atlanta, mentioning the importance of nearby Georgia Tech and access to the city's technology workforce.[41]

The recent growth at Tech Square has been impressive, and its economic development implications are significant. In fact, when thinking about the technology scene in Atlanta, Tech Square is immediately referenced as the pacesetter. During its genesis, Tech Square did not have a direct impact on residential development, nor did the university engage in a contested arrangement with community organizations in Midtown. This portion of west Midtown was empty, abandoned land in need of a new purpose. Georgia Tech embraced and integrated community voices in the design of the area. However, in the last 10 years, Midtown has been in the midst of dizzying construction activity of dense residential and office buildings. From 2017 to 2021, it is expected that almost 7,000 new residential units and 5 million square feet of office and institutional space will be added, along with 300,000 square feet of retail and 1,100 hotel rooms. It's expected that, by 2021, an additional 3,097,500 square feet of office and institutional space and 1,774 residential units will come to the market, along with 684 hotel rooms and 81,700 square feet of retail. Developers are currently planning another 1 million square feet of office and institutional space, 2,686 residential units, 262,700 square feet of retail space, and 722 new hotel rooms. These figures do not include renovations of existing structures.[42]

Tech Square has contributed to reshaping Midtown into one of the most expensive neighborhoods in Atlanta. Millennials, Generation Xers, and even baby boomers who are empty nesters are attracted to the new Midtown because of the walkability, recreational opportunities, new and updated housing stock, and the robust employment opportunities in science and technology, law, and corporate settings. With more office construction slated to surround Tech Square, high-income workers will put more pressures on Midtown's real estate, escalating prices and making the area increasingly unaffordable. From this perspective, Tech Square will continue to impact the community beyond the western edge of Midtown. While it is unlikely that Georgia Tech will be able to access many more additional properties due to the rising cost of real estate in the area, its emergence and subsequent growth will have reshaped its neighborhoods for many years to come.

Conclusion

In Ann Breen and Dick Rigby's book *Intown Living: A Different American Dream*, they document the renaissance of American cities as increasingly younger people are deciding to reside in lively urban environments. Their chapter on Atlanta focused on Midtown, predicting that Tech Square would play a very important role in the future of the community as an exciting place to live and work. In 2005, just a couple of years after the unveiling of Tech Square, they write, "Next door is one of the engines of Midtown's prospective ascendancy as a great Atlanta urban neighborhood. One, being built by Georgia Tech, is a 600,000-square-foot, multiple-building undertaking. It is labelled Technology Square, and occupies eight acres across from the Biltmore [once a landmark hotel and now listed on The National Register of Historic Places] that had been vacant for years."[43]

Fifteen years later, Technology Square in Atlanta has emerged as the epicenter of innovation initiatives in business and technology in the southeast and a model for university-driven development, nationally and globally. Leadership has been essential to the district's rise. President Clough managed to engage the Georgia Tech Foundation in purchasing the land and expanding the university services across the interstate. That move proved to be a major step in establishing an early structure, creating a mix of activities, and bringing life to what was once an abandoned area of town. However, it would be the vision and decade-long dedication of President Peterson that followed which powered a culture of creativity and entrepreneurship, brought corporate innovation centers, and formulated sustained relationships with government and businesses. It was also during the Peterson era that additional growth came to Tech Square. In the spring of 2019, the university unveiled the 21-story, 750,000-square-foot Coda Building that brings together technology industry professionals with 700 Georgia Tech faculty, staff, and students. Just a few months later, in the fall of 2019, the university announced the third phase of Tech Square development. When completed, this stage will add more buildings at an estimated cost of $200 million, attracting more corporate entities to the area. Focusing on interdisciplinary research, commercialization, and sustainability, the expansion will also provide space to the nearby Scheller College of Business.

Since Tech Square is not developing in a state of isolation from the rest of the city, its long-term effects will be dramatic. In addition to driving the creation of a nationally recognized, robust ecosystem of technological innovation, cultivating partnerships, and fueling economic growth, the district also contributes to urban revitalization and community development. Historically, Georgia Tech has not pursued plans to "erect walls" to protect the institution. Rather it has endeavored to engage the surrounding communities and has jointly participated in various planning initiatives. The western section of Midtown was underdeveloped, with empty lots and surface parking areas. Abandoned and dilapidated, it was subjected to a long history of significant socioeconomic challenges. Thus, the Tech Square project did not entail the usual seizure of contested space, and the university did not overwhelm the community. In fact, there was no opposition. Rather, the university embraced the community of Midtown, which continues to be part of the conversation, thus ensuring an ongoing symbiotic relationship. The success of this project is also due to the fact that the university brought an established reputation as a leading technological and environmental institution. Therefore, it integrated sustainability concepts and attributes which resulted in a highly attractive, functional, mixed-use environment.

The next chapter focuses on the Kendall Square innovation district, which is anchored by the Massachusetts Institute of Technology (MIT). The area had been the recipient of federal funding support to house research activities for NASA after the Cambridge Redevelopment Authority cleared land for a sizable, multibuilding project. However, that would come to a halt as politics in Washington, DC, redirected these activities and the NASA headquarters to Houston, Texas. The rise of Route 128 outside downtown Boston also shifted potential investments to the suburbs, leaving Kendall Square in a state of isolation. In the 1990s, small start-ups moved into the area. Since its formation in 1999, the Cambridge Innovation Center has played a central role in the subsequent development of the co-working space model for entrepreneurs. Pharmaceutical companies and major technology firms such as

Facebook, Google, Amazon, Amgen, Novartis, Pfizer, Biogen, and Baxter subsequently established research centers in Kendall Square, producing a global hub comprised of some of the leading life sciences and biotech firms in the world. In recent years, it became apparent that, because of its dominant commercial nature, the area lacked amenities. In 2011, MIT pursued an aggressive plan that would not only attract more biotech and IT companies, but also rebalance the area away from its dominant orientation by introducing service features such as restaurants, retail, and vibrant clusters of activities. Following six years of discussion and debate about the future of Kendall Square, the City of Cambridge approved an MIT proposal to repurpose surface parking and eight of its properties to create a lively neighborhood. Since then, the ascent of Kendall Square's global dominance as a formidable district of innovation continues, while simultaneously exacerbating ongoing pressures on what was once a highly diverse residential community.

| 4 |

The Most Innovative Square Mile on the Planet

Kendall Square in Boston

ADJACENT TO THE Massachusetts Institute of Technology (MIT) in Cambridge, Massachusetts, rests Kendall Square. Today, it is considered a global hub for biotech and technology as firms cluster and occupy some of the most expensive real estate in the United States. Without a doubt this would be considered the most advanced form of a university-anchored innovation district in the world, since MIT has been the primary driving force behind what the Boston Consulting Group referenced in 2009 as "the most innovative square mile on the planet."[1] The city of Cambridge has also benefited from this development, becoming one of the most sought-after places to live and work. Technological innovation and entrepreneurship have become synonymous with Cambridge. In 2011, as a way of solidifying the district's status, the city and MIT established the Entrepreneur Walk of Fame on Main Street. The granite plaques embedded in the cement with a visible star in the upper corner of each one reminds one of the Hollywood Walk of Fame which showcases entertainers along Hollywood Boulevard and Vine Street in Hollywood, California. However, in this case, the celebrities are entrepreneurs whose technological innovations fueled worldwide economic growth. The inaugural class included some of the most iconic personalities: Bill Gates, Steve Jobs, Bill Hewlett, David Packard, Bob Swanson, Mitch Kapor, and Thomas Edison.[2] For Kendall Square and MIT, the goal is to be intimately identified with science and technology, as finance is associated with Wall Street in New York City and government with Washington, DC.

This has been a remarkable transformation since it was not that long ago that this part of the city was plagued by some of the most notable urban challenges typically associated with decline, including physical decay and social and economic isolation. In 1964, the Cambridge Redevelopment Authority (CRA), under the Housing Act of 1949, pursued an urban renewal plan for the Kendall Square area by demolishing buildings, clearing parcels of land, and relocating businesses. These efforts brought changes to the area, but it was not until the late 1970s and 1980s that MIT faculty research efforts fueled biological technology advancements, creating business endeavors and, ultimately, attracting pharmaceutical companies to the area. In the 1990s and 2000s, the Kendall Square ecosystem continued to mature. Dominated by office buildings, research centers, and laboratories, the area could not maintain essential services such as restaurants and retail. MIT recognized this issue and designed a plan which was submitted to the city for review in the spring of 2011. A revised document focused on affordable housing was introduced a few years later as a response to another significant demand expressed by residents.

This chapter focuses on the transformation of Kendall Square during the last three decades and the continuous role that MIT played in its ascent. The success of this innovation district has been intricately connected to the standing and upward trajectory of the university. However, this journey requires coordination and a balancing act of multiple stakeholders. Those include the university, the City of Cambridge, residents, real estate companies, corporations, nonprofits, and others. Furthermore, demands for additional growth in what is already a very dense physical setting places more pressures on key areas such as housing and transportation. The development of a culture that maintains a unique mix is now essential, a direction that is also critical to furthering innovation. This will be the major challenge facing Kendall Square in the coming years.

The Ascent of MIT and Industrial Decline

MIT was founded in 1861 by the Commonwealth of Massachusetts and William Barton Rogers, who served as the first president of the institution from 1862 to 1870. Previously a professor of natural philosophy at the University of Virginia, Rogers played a fundamental role even before the university received its official charter, advocating for many years that the formation of a university of its type in Boston was imperative. In a letter to his younger brother in 1846, Rogers argued that "ever since I have known something of the knowledge-seeking spirit, and the intellectual capabilities of the community in and around Boston, I have felt persuaded that of all places in the world it was the one most certain to derive the highest benefits from a Polytechnic Institution."[3] Rogers enclosed in that communication to his younger brother a "Plan for a Polytechnic School in Boston" outlining in great detail the structure of the institution and its day-to-day operational activities. Rogers also articulated that such an endeavor would not only be beneficial to those interested in intellectual pursuits because "the occupations and interests of the great mass of the people are immediately connected with the application for physical science, and their quick intelligence has already impressed them with just ideas of the value of scientific teaching in their daily pursuits."[4]

Two main forces can be identified behind the formation of MIT. The first was an embrace of a science-based model rooted in the technical and polytechnic schools evident in the educational structure of France, an approach distinctly different from the traditional liberal arts education. The second was a response to the powerful forces of industrialization led by technologists who, during the middle part of the nineteenth century, transformed social relations in the United States, including the economy. The addition of Boston boosters and government visionaries helped found the university first known as Boston

Tech. Initially located around Copley Square in Boston, in 1916, MIT moved its campus to Cambridge, just south of Kendall Square, a land infill along the Charles River. Over the years, the university significantly expanded its presence, with Main Street and Massachusetts Avenue serving as its boundaries.[5] The area benefited from Harvard Bridge and the construction of the Longfellow Bridge, a combination highway and railroad bridge. The Cambridge Tunnel, a subway tunnel, connected Boston to Harvard Square. In 1912, the project brought two stations to Cambridge at Central and Kendall Squares.[6]

During its early period, the university faced serious financial challenges, as it was dependent on tuition and attracted students from middle-class families. In fact, Harvard University President Charles William Eliot (1869–1909) unsuccessfully attempted, at least six times, to acquire MIT. During the 1930s, MIT President Karl Taylor Compton (1930–1948) and Vice President Vannevar Bush (1932–1938), who also served as dean of the MIT School of Engineering, focused on the importance of the pure sciences as a way to combat the vocational orientation that had typified the institute. According to a 1949 report to the faculty on education,

> During the thirties, the Compton administration undertook to enlarge the purpose and meaning of an M.I.T. education. The balance between science and technology was restored by an increasing support for work in the pure sciences. The curricula were revised to reduce the amount of required practical work in shops and drafting rooms. Subject matter was simplified and the significance of fundamentals as opposed to details was emphasized. These changes lifted the morale of the M.I.T. community and resulted in renewed confidence in the ability of the Institute to develop leadership in science as well as in engineering. The Institute was no longer dominated by the engineering point of view, and the engineering departments themselves became less narrowly vocational.[7]

The cooperation with the military and the defense research that followed, along with its connections to industry, helped propel MIT to its current international status.

However, unlike MIT, the area surrounding the university did not share the same continuous upward trajectory. When the university moved to Cambridge, the city was a robust industrial center that included a diverse array of factories that manufactured steam boilers, furniture, paper, glass, soap, bricks, and ladders. In 1920, the neighborhood of Cambridgeport to the west housed the "Simplex Wire & Cable Company, the National Biscuit Company [as well as] the Necco candy factory, the Riverside Press, and a Ford Motor Co. assembly plant."[8] In 1880, Edward Kendall founded the Kendall Boiler and Tank Company, originally under the name of Kendall & Davis. Kendall Square would be named after the steam boiler manufacturing founder. Candy was one of the most dominant industries along Main Street, which was affectionately called "Confectioner's Row." By the mid-1940s more than 60 confectionery manufacturers operated in the area.[9]

Unfortunately, like many other industrial centers of the Northeast and upper Midwest, the post-World War II era brought significant changes to Cambridge and Kendall Square. As the early stages of globalization began to set in, fueled by technological advancements and the rise of suburbanization and movement to the Sunbelt states, one after another, factories closed or relocated. Between 1950 and 1980, Cambridge lost a fifth of its population declining from 120,740 (1950) to 95,322 (1980). Empty lots, abandoned buildings, and urban blight defined the area. One observer described Kendall Square during the early 1960s as "a 43-acre district, once dense with factories that churned out soap, vulcanized rubber, and dozens of other products, had become a collection of forlorn, rickety structures that blighted the landscape."[10] Robert Simha, who served as director of planning for MIT from 1960 to 2000, was responsible for managing the expansion of the university campus from 4.5 million square feet to 9 million square feet. He described Kendall Square from the 1960s to the 1990s as a "moribund 19th-century district . . . Companies were sliding away. People were losing jobs. The city was losing income. The few plants that remained, like the vulcanized rubber plant, were smelly and polluted the air."[11] The rise of Route 128 outside downtown Boston shifted potential investments to the suburbs, leaving Kendall Square in a state of disrepair and isolation.

Out to the Suburbs: MIT and Route 128

As Cambridge and Kendall Square were struggling to manage urban decline, Boston's suburban communities were growing, undergoing a building boom, and rapidly becoming the preferred places to live. In 1951, Route 128 opened on the western edge of Boston, just 15 miles from downtown, at a cost of $18 million.[12] By 1965, the highway was completed, extending 65 miles from Gloucester to Braintree to eventually become Boston's inner beltway. In the 1950s and 1960s, as many nineteenth- and twentieth-century industries began to deteriorate, technology-based companies sprouted, either reclaiming empty spaces or building new facilities along the transportation stretch on the outskirts of the city. These firms prospered as they clustered together, helping to give birth to more companies. This dense concentration eventually produced a high technology corridor driven by innovation and change, significantly contributing to local economic growth. A number of forces converged to create what would eventually become known as "America's Technology Region."

First, the Route 128 location benefited from successful nearby companies that could fuel technological innovation. For example, Raytheon Corporation, already in Waltham, Massachusetts, was the third-largest defense contractor in the United States behind Boeing and Lockheed Martin. It was founded in Cambridge in 1922 as the American Appliance Company by Laurence Marshall, a civil engineer who graduated from Tufts University; Charles G. Smith, a Harvard University physicist; and Vannevar Bush, who would later have an illustrious career as an academic administrator at MIT and serve in leadership positions in the federal government. The company was first located near MIT but would later move to the suburbs. The most remarkable aspect of Raytheon was its ability to diversify its business ventures over the decades, including manufacturing tubes for radios, power equipment, electronic auto parts, industrial electronics, and microwave communications. In the 1940s, the defense industry shifted its focus to radar technologies. Through the Radiation Laboratory at MIT, Raytheon secured major contracts to produce the technology leading to advanced imaging capable of detecting enemy military weaponries. This rapid growth made Raytheon a global technology leader. During the war period, Raytheon sales increased from $3 million in 1940 to $168 million in 1945. After the war, the corporation continued to grow its business in various sectors including appliances, electronics, special aircrafts such as missiles, and cutting-edge radar systems.[13]

Second, the proximity to a robust array of institutions of higher education was another advantage that aided the growth of the region along Route 128. Research labs at MIT and Harvard fueled innovation by continuing to pioneer scientific advancements and technologies. The commercial transistor and the semiconductor served as the foundation for electronics and minicomputer research and helped to create a robust knowledge industry. A 1968 story in Mechanix Illustrated attempted to predict life 40 years in the future. At that time, the author posited that computers would manage traffic, prepare meals, create shopping lists, and even keep track of bank balances. Furthermore, he wrote, "[In 2008] computers also handle travel reservations, relay telephone messages, keep track of birthdays and anniversaries, compute taxes and even figure the monthly bills for electricity, water, telephone and other utilities. The single most important item in 2008 households is the computer."[14] The foundation for the realization of these predictions was the electronic and minicomputer revolution.

These developments combined with a strong environment of entrepreneurial activities that received support by venture capital brought together researchers, risk takers, and investors to conceive some of the most notable technology businesses in the world. Companies like Digital Equipment Corporation (founded in 1957), Lotus Software (founded in 1982), GTE (founded in 1955), Wang Laboratories (founded in 1951), Apollo Computer (founded in 1980), Prime Computer (founded in 1972), and many others were created or resided along Route 128. Their founders were connected to the prestigious Boston universities. Digital Equipment Corporation founder Ken Olsen, Apollo founder William Poduska, and Lotus Software founders Mitch Kapor and Jonathan Sachs were all MIT alumni. Wang founder An Wang attended Harvard University. Many of the Prime Computer founders were associated with building Multics, a computer operating system project at MIT.

An impressive ecosystem emerged that continued to attract companies, making the area ripe for growth. This also brought significant changes in real estate as developers realized the potential benefits of the technological revolution by introducing industrial parks with easy access to transportation routes. Between 1950 and 1957, more than $100 million in capital projects was invested in the area, with 53 businesses calling Route 128 home in 1955. By 1959 that number had grown to 223, and a decade later it exploded to an extraordinary figure of 729. Land value also rapidly changed from $450 per acre to $5,000 per acre in 1957 and continued to rise in the 1960s. By 1980, over 250,000 people were employed in an impressive array of technology-based companies with 75,000 workers added between 1975 and 1980.[15]

The triple helix model—an approach that drives innovation with the combined efforts of government, industry, and academic institutions—converged to create Route 128. First, on the government front, new federal agencies such as the National Science Foundation provided significant resources to further science and technology. Defense spending fueled by the Cold War proved substantial as Massachusetts emerged as a major beneficiary of government contracts. Second, an increase in global demand for computers in business and the commercialization of other technologies aided existing industries and forged new high-tech business opportunities. Finally, groundbreaking academic research at nearby universities and a strong entrepreneurial outlook was the last piece of the puzzle, bringing these forces together to produce the most remarkable geographic corridor of technological advancement.[16]

However, the recession of the 1980s and the declines in federal spending started to have a negative impact as these highly successful companies proved unable to continue their ascent. Due to their expansive size and increasing bureaucratic structures, they lacked agility, focusing on controlling the market rather than determining ways to innovate. Hence, the companies struggled to transition from the decline of the minicomputer, subsequently missing the advent of the personal computer. Instead, Silicon Valley in northern California rapidly and powerfully rose as the new center of technological discovery and business acumen, where spin-off companies gave birth to thriving new industries with global outreach.[17]

The Rebirth of Kendall Square

As urban decline was apparent in Kendall Square and across Cambridge, the need to pursue revitalization efforts was becoming increasingly essential. The federal government took the lead since this was a condition prevalent across many American cities. In the 1960s, Kendall Square was considered to serve as the location for the headquarters of NASA. There was an unsuccessful effort in 1961 by Massachusetts Governor John Volpe and Senator Benjamin Smith to make Cambridge the site for the Manned Spacecraft Center (MSC), for which NASA eventually selected Houston. Despite rumors to the contrary, John F. Kennedy wasn't involved in this effort: James Webb, who led the space agency from February 1961 until October 1968, commented that Kennedy had "intervened in no way to try to favor his own state of Massachusetts, or to rule it out of the game." The MSC, which in 1973 was renamed Johnson Space Center, opened in March 1962, almost two years before the November 1963 assassination of President Kennedy.[18] His successor, President Lyndon B. Johnson, ultimately identified Houston, Texas, as the space agency's command center.

Nevertheless, the failed effort opened the door for a different opportunity. In 1964, the federal government turned to the City of Cambridge and requested that land be provided to NASA for an Electronics Research Center (ERC). This entity would focus on the development of advanced electronics for spacecraft guidance to be employed by the space agency during the Apollo era. The Cambridge Redevelopment

Galaxy: Earth Sphere fountain is a sculpture in Kendall Square, erected at the intersection of Main Street and Broadway. The fountain is a gateway to Kendall Square and a centerpiece of Point Park, a highly visible plaza. Courtesy of user eskystudio, Shutterstock Images.

Authority (CRA) and the city adopted the Kendall Square Urban Renewal Plan for the project. From the start, the goal of clearing 42 acres, 15 of which were purchased by NASA, was met with local opposition since it included the removal of 94 businesses. The project also razed 50 buildings and required additional infrastructure development. Regardless of these concerns, in the fall of 1964, NASA opened the Electronics Research Center. Its location adjacent to MIT was expected to take advantage of the high-tech research activity at the university and the nearby electronics cluster of companies on Route 128. Additionally, graduate and postgraduate level opportunities for further professional development could be provided by MIT to NASA employees.

Scheduled to include more than 2,000 positions in professional, technical, and administrative capacities, at its peak in 1969, only 950 employees called the ERC their employment home. However, with very little notice, in June 1970 the center was closed. At that time, only six of the 14 planned buildings had been constructed.[19] John Volpe, who served as secretary of transportation (1969–1973) in the Nixon administration, helped to immediately repurpose the facility as the Transportation System Center, later renamed the Volpe Center.[20] The ERC and the Volpe Center brought some activity back to a rapidly deteriorating Kendall Square. The decline was abrupt and sustained. In the area between Broadway and Main Street once stood Lever Brothers, a soap factory that occupied 30 buildings. The structures stretched in an imposing way. Mike Bonislawski, a lifelong Cambridge resident reflected, "Lever Brothers was enormous . . . They had a little park there—in the middle of it was an ornamental fountain. I remember going there as a kid to run through the water. It was gigantic, block after block, and they had these big water towers. It was tall, too—it was an impressive site."[21] At its height, Lever Brothers employed 1,300 workers and the plant produced tens of thousands of tons of soap each year.[22]

Operating in Kendall Square since 1898, Lever Brothers decided to put the factory and the land up for sale and move out of state in 1959. Mayor Edward Crane reached out to James Killian, who at the time headed the MIT Corporation, to explore the possibility of converting the site into research space for the university. Killian had previously served as president of MIT and had a good understanding of the institute's mission, vision, as well as recent and future initiatives. He felt that gaining control of a large portion of the abandoned property would be beneficial for both the university and the city, something that would also strengthen the relationship between the institute and the immediate community.

In 1960, following a partnership with real estate development company Cabot, Cabot & Forbes, MIT announced a new 14-acre commercial center called Technology Square on land that also included part of the nearby Rogers Block. During that announcement, Killian made clear the intent of the initiative, noting, "We believe that enlarging the professional scientific and engineering community here would strengthen the universities and the industries in this area."[23] By 1967, four buildings were constructed on what was once the Lever Brothers parcel, attracting "IBM, Grumman Aircraft Engineering Corporation, Polaroid [headquarters], and several government agencies. Institute-related activities housed in the Square included a number of research groups such as Project MAC which grew into the Laboratory for Computer Science. The Square also housed MIT's Laboratory for Artificial Intelligence . . . [and] the adjacent construction of the Charles Stark Draper Laboratory."[24] An MIT official observed that "making a clean sweep of the area and starting afresh [fueled] the transition [of Kendall Square] from gradual change—one building at a time, one company at a time—to a more organized and more aggressive process of change."[25]

With the federal government and the university now actively engaged in Kendall Square, the revitalization possibilities were slowly becoming evident. The key sector that led the ensuing urban revival and remained a core activity surrounding the MIT campus would be biotechnology. Today, the number and close proximity of MIT-founded biotech companies, research institutes, and start-ups is astonishing and cannot be found anywhere else in the world. To understand how this happened, it is important to focus on the critical role that the MIT academic community played over the last few decades in discovery research. An insightful example of this would be the case of Phillip A. Sharp, an institute professor of biology at MIT and recipient of the 1993 Nobel Prize in Physiology or Medicine for his work on split genes. Credited with giving birth to biotech, Sharp spent time at Cal Tech and the Cold Spring Harbor Laboratory before joining MIT in 1974.[26] He was drawn to MIT because it was an environment that, in addition to providing the latest research tools, included a community of mentors and scholars conducting groundbreaking research. Sharp recognized that these colleagues shared a common passion for "strikingly important things we just don't know exist," adding that "discovering them through basic science changes the whole world."[27] Genetics research entered an exciting period during the 1960s when discoveries related to DNA properties informed our understanding of the inner workings of the cell. But this was also contentious given the potential ramifications of creating unexpected forms of microorganisms. Cell research was quite controversial during the early 1970s. But in 1976, the City of Cambridge passed an ordinance that created guidelines for genetic studies, a decision that fueled research in biotechnology.[28]

Though presented with a number of opportunities to leave the university, Sharp chose to stay and managed to combine research with the pursuit of business ventures that he felt could make a difference. According to Sharp, his recombinant DNA research "was a technology we knew was going to impact the world, but it was all located inside universities. There was no practical application for molecular biology."[29] In 1978, he cofounded Biogen (Biogen Idec) with a colleague from Harvard University. Now listed as a Fortune 500 corporation worth $90 billion (2015), this biotechnology company develops treatments for hepatitis, multiple sclerosis, and cancer, among other diseases. In 2002, Sharp cofounded Alnylam Pharmaceuticals, a biopharmaceutical company focusing on therapeutics. *Forbes* considered Alnylam one of the most innovative growth companies in the United States. Both Biogen and Alnylam are located around MIT.

These types of entrepreneurial initiatives—connecting science, technology, and commerce—helped drive the Kendall Square innovation ecosystem in life sciences. In addition to the companies and start-ups, the presence of research institutes proved critical. The Broad Institute of MIT and Harvard has raised more than $2 billion in funds for genetic research. The Koch Institute for Integrative Cancer Research connects biologists and engineers to collaborate on efforts to combat the disease. Eric Lander, director of the Broad Institute, noted that "in the entire known universe [there is no place] that has this concentration of people interested in the biological and biomedical sciences. If you draw a circle about two miles around this street corner, you probably capture something like 10 or 15 percent of all biomedical research in the United States."[30]

In 2003, Novartis, a Swiss-based pharmaceutical company that is one of the largest in the world today, moved to Kendall Square. Pfizer, Amgen, and Baxter followed with major research centers. Eighteen of the 20 major pharmaceutical companies now have a presence in Kendall

Square. Susan Hockfield, a professor of neuroscience at the David H. Koch Institute for Integrative Cancer Research, who also served as president of MIT from 2004 to 2012, commented, "When I was president, not a week would go by when someone from someplace else in the world would come to my office and say we would like you to help us figure out how we can built a Kendall Square where we come from."[31] Lander encapsulated the reasons behind the current standing of the district by indicating, "First of all is MIT and Harvard building great biology departments, its amazing hospitals, and its venture capitalists in this area who continue to invest larger and larger amounts in start-ups with audacious ideas but take big risk. All of these things are visionary."[32] Venture capital investment in Massachusetts biopharma increased from $0.7 billion in 2010 to $3.1 billion in 2017.[33]

The federal government also played a key role in supporting the Massachusetts technology revolution. Biomedical research would greatly benefit from the work of United States Senator Edward Kennedy (1962–2009). During his nearly 47 years of service, Kennedy was a member of many congressional committees. As chair of the Senate Labor and Human Resources Committee (1987–1995) and of the Senate Health, Education, Labor and Pensions Committee (2007–2009), Kennedy emerged as a staunch advocate for health care and biomedical science. Phillip Sharp, in an op-ed titled "In Praise of Senator Ted Kennedy for His Contributions to Biomedical Science," concluded that "few national leaders have had as significant impact on the current state of biomedical science . . . [he] quadrupled the funds supporting cancer research. New England's pre-eminence in life sciences is largely a product of his enlightened work in the Senate."[34]

The rebirth of Kendall Square was driven by the integration of cutting-edge life science research at MIT into business opportunities. Tom Leighton, a professor of applied mathematics at MIT, cofounded Akamai Technologies in 1998 during the dot-com revolution. As a delivery network responsible for the operation of the internet, the company provides content to end users. Over the years, Akamai expanded its activities to include cloud services, reaching $2.5 billion in revenues with

6,650 employees (2017).[35] Leighton was the company's chief scientist for many years before becoming its CEO in 2013. Like Biogen and Alnylam, Akamai headquartered itself at various locations in Kendall Square but, as Leighton noted, "never more than a few blocks from MIT . . . [Y]ou are at the epicenter in terms of the university . . . and that's special. So it makes perfect sense that you grow around that."[36] A key aspect of this decision relates to recruiting employees: "[you have] more of a talent pool to draw from. And we're part of a vibrant community with a lot of ideas, the desire to start something different. That's the type of culture we want to have at Akamai. You want to have people in the ecosystem and workforce like that: It keeps the company young and agile."[37] Brian Halligan, the cofounder of HubSpot, another technology company with MIT roots, echoed a similar sentiment: "It's nice being around a lot of other smart people. There's certainly an energy and a buzz that's infectious. It's very hard to quantify that stuff, but there's something to it. It's a very attractive place to work."[38] Because of these reasons, some of the most powerful technology companies in the world, including Google, Microsoft, Twitter, Apple, Facebook, IBM, and Oracle, have offices in Kendall Square.

Fueling the Kendall Square Innovation Ecosystem

Along with the academic research at MIT and the government support, there are a number of other factors that can be considered as having contributed to the ongoing growth of the Kendall Square innovation ecosystem. These include entrepreneurship competitions, the introduction of co-working spaces, and the role of real estate development, all of which should not be viewed separately but rather as interconnected elements. Like Georgia Tech, entrepreneurship competitions provided an opportunity for students and faculty at MIT to present their ideas publicly and to explore the possibility of commercializing emerging technologies. In 1989, the MIT $100K Entrepreneurship Competition was launched and, over the years, it has given birth to hundreds of companies. In the early years, the award was $10,000, but it quickly grew to $50,000 and then to the current level of $100,000. Alumni donors, along with the Sloan School and the School of Engineering at MIT, helped jump-start the initiative. Regardless, all of the participants benefit since they are able to consider how to employ technological advancements with business pursuits.

The popularity of this initiative led to the genesis of a number of other competitions that included the Pitch Contest (90 seconds to pitch start-up idea teams), the Accelerate Contest (early stage teams), and the Launch Contest (comprehensive business plan teams).[39] Akamai was part of the 1997 competition and HubSpot entered the 2005 competition. The three winning teams in 1997 (Imagen, Actuality Systems, and Virtual Ink) incorporated and remained in Kendall Square. Many of the start-ups successfully reached IPO status or were acquired by others, as did Silicon Spice, which was in the 1995 competition. Silicon Spice was sold to Broadcom for $1.2 billion in 2000.[40] The $100K Entrepreneurship Competition, the MIT Enterprise Forum Startup Competition (technology accelerator), the Harvard vs. MIT Case Competition (solving a real-life business case), and the MIT Initiative on the Digital Economy (IDE), which focuses on ways to create economic growth, are additional student opportunities. The end result of these initiatives is a heightened understanding of how technological discoveries can lead to commercialization, which in turn powers the start-up ecosystem of Kendall Square.

Growing these companies requires support. The Cambridge Innovation Center (CIC) was founded in 1999 by Tim Rowe as a shared workspace provider. One of the first of its kind, its structure helped fuel growth. Originally known as the Cambridge Incubator, the initiative started in MIT-owned space and focused on developing start-ups. But the concept failed. According to Rowe, "Some West Coast VCs gave us $17 million to give to these startups to help them. So, we gave out almost all of the $17 million, and they pretty much all failed. We figured out that we didn't really know how to do that. Giving out money wasn't going to be the solution . . . [T]his is back in 2001."[41] In response, Rowe developed a new strategy aiming to create an environment for "friends from MIT to come and do their startups again. So, we got out of the incubator business and got back to just handing out space to our friends—sharing it and making the Internet work."[42] The success was immediate. Community events followed as did other services. In 2016, CIC expanded outside Kendall Square, establishing similar operations in Miami, Florida, and Rotterdam, Netherlands. Following that, Philadelphia, Pennsylvania; Providence, Rhode Island; and St. Louis, Missouri, were added. In 2018, CIC moved to a central location in Kendall Square occupying 90,000 square feet of space. That same year, it raised $58 million to support further expansion. The company's goal is to operate in 50 cities in the next decade.[43]

An additional component, central to the continuous advancement of the Kendall Square innovation ecosystem, is the role of real estate. Dating back to the 1950s, MIT's long collaboration with the City of Cambridge expanded the institute's holdings and footprint. As the area's factories were closing and leaving for other locations in the sunbelt, MIT purchased the structures and transformed them into facilities for university use. The Heinz warehouse and the Elliott Company factory now house student affairs offices and graduate student housing. Once an ice cream factory, the Hood building became the university's High Voltage Research Lab. The MIT Museum is located at the former General Radio Company building. The Knight Science Journalism fellowship program offices, laboratories, and other administrative functions relocated to spaces formerly occupied by industry.[44]

At the same time, beyond the real estate ambitions of MIT, a number of other entities contributed to the district's ascent. Boston Properties, a major real estate investment trust, was founded in Boston in 1970. The company has a long history of subletting to government, with a major presence in Washington, DC. Beginning in 1978, the firm received approval from the Cambridge Redevelopment Authority (CRA) to be the developer of three major parcels as part of the Kendall Square Urban Renewal Plan. The long-term objective was the introduction of more than 2 million square feet of office space. In 1981, construction of the Cambridge Center complex started, eventually adding a number of multistory buildings. In 1986, Boston Properties built the Boston

Marriott Cambridge, expanding the footprint of the Cambridge Center, which was rebranded in 2015 as Kendall Center, a 24-acre campus owned and managed by Boston Properties. Since the start of the development, the CRA completed significant infrastructural projects that focused on improving transportation access and the flow of traffic. The Kendall Center has housed key tenants such as Biogen Idec, VMware, Microsoft, Google, the Whitehead Institute, Akamai Technologies, the Broad Institute, and a number of restaurants. Even The Coop, the official bookstore of MIT, is located in the area. Over the years, the scope of influence of Boston Properties grew considerably through ownership and management of office and laboratory space.

Another contributor to the real estate scene in Kendall Square is Alexandria Real Estate Equities, a Pasadena, California, firm that was founded in 1994. The company proved highly influential because it focuses on developing and leasing space to science and technology companies with emphasis on the life sciences. Biotechnology companies have unique needs, requiring an infrastructure that can accommodate laboratories, and Alexandria made that its core mission. The firm entered the Kendall Square market in 2002 and, by 2015, it had invested more than $2.3 billion in properties.[45] In 2006, Alexandria purchased the Technology Square complex from MIT for $600 million and converted portions of the development from office to laboratory space. The demand was significant since the properties leased quickly, even before the renovations were completed. By 2018, Alexandria owned 35 buildings in Cambridge, generating $318 million in rental revenues annually. Clients along Binney Street, a major district thoroughfare, included established biotechnology companies such as Sanofi, Bluebird Bio Inc., Biogen, Sarepta Therapeutics Inc., Sage Therapeutics Inc., Relay Therapeutics, Bristol Myers-Squibb Co., and Constellation Pharmaceuticals Inc., as well as start-ups like Foghorn, Sigilon, and Tango Therapeutics that have considerable capital support aiming to make a market impact. In addition, Alexandria provides space for Facebook and IBM Watson. Overall, Alexandria's work in Boston accounts for almost half of its total business, and, behind MIT, it is the largest landowner in

Cambridge.[46] Over the years, MIT has employed a strategy that retains real estate ownership through long-term leases, some of which include Boston Properties and Alexandria Real Estate Equities. Through this model, the university continues to generate revenue, which is then funneled into other office or housing projects.

The combination of staging MIT-supported entrepreneurship competitions, making quality co-working spaces available, and providing an appropriate real estate infrastructure helped create a unique culture that powered the Kendall Square innovation ecosystem. The district became closely identified with the rapidly growing biotechnology industry. However, this success created challenges. Its singular orientation as an office and research center dominated the area, making it devoid of other functions such as housing, recreation, and commercial uses. In recent years, an ambitious plan led by MIT to create a neighborhood feel has gotten underway and is expected to complement and strengthen the livability of the urban environment.

In Search of a Neighborhood

By 2010, Kendall Square was in the midst of an explosion. Adding to MIT's academic and research facilities, more than 150 biotechnology and information technology companies called the area home. Many more were in the planning stages, seeking venture capital, ready to break into the market. However, it was increasingly becoming apparent that, while very successful as an innovation ecosystem with world-class advantages that made it globally notable, Kendall Square lacked key assets that would qualitatively improve its standing to make it an even more attractive place. At a February 2010 meeting of the Kendall Square Association—a membership organization which was formed a year earlier to advocate for public policy issues that would strengthen the district—MIT President Susan Hockfield (2004–2012) commented, "Kendall Square is home to a kind of creative intensity that you don't encounter many other places on Earth: It has an entrepreneurial culture and an incredibly inspiring focus on society's important problems. If we want Kendall Square to grow and thrive over the long term, we need to make sure that the most creative entrepreneurs and most talented inventors and scientists find Kendall Square so magnetic, so appealing that they can't think seriously about 'other options.' "[47] The decades-long focus on commercializing research produced an imbalance and a lack of amenities in the form of retail, recreation, cultural attractions, and even public spaces.

Following their relocation from downtown New Haven to MIT, Hockfield and her husband Thomas Byrne were surprised at how uninhabited the area around MIT felt in the evenings and weekends. Hockfield was determined to do something: "There's no place for my husband to get a haircut. There are no amenities. You have to build something."[48] Ritch Rossi, who served as Cambridge City Manager during that time, echoed this sentiment. He admitted that it was very hard to attract restaurants to the area following the closure of Polcari's, an Italian eatery, which struggled for business in the evenings and weekends. Rossi added, "We used to go to Polcari's at lunchtime, and you would wait in line to get in. On Friday nights, you could choose any one of 250 seats."[49]

The MIT Investment Management Corporation, which oversees the university real estate activities, played an important role in reshaping Kendall Square through a project that the university dubbed the Kendall Square Initiative. A two-year process started with updated versions of planning proposals, eventually resulting in a redevelopment document centering on 26 acres of land on the eastern portion of the MIT campus. The area, known as the East Campus/Kendall Square Gateway, focused on creating a cluster of activities by transforming five MIT-owned parking lots. The final plan incorporated more residential development than initially proposed, with one-fifth of that dedicated to low- and moderate-income housing, entrepreneurial space for start-ups, commercial development, and a community benefit fund. Green space with public programming year-round, the relocation of the MIT Museum, and a new child care facility would further diversify the space. It would invite the public to engage, creating a seamless connection between MIT and Kendall Square. Underground parking and space for future academic buildings was included. Steve Marsh, managing director of MIT's Investment Management Company, noted, "We think this mixed-use opportunity is something that's really going to bring it to another level. That's our goal and we're excited about it."[50]

Three observations emerge from MIT's proposal. The first regards the effort by the institute to involve community, faculty, and staff input, all of which proved critical in the development of the plan. The second relates to a clear historical shift in the direction of MIT. In the past, the university's primary focus was the development of academic, lab, and research facilities. This mixed-use approach with dedicated land for housing, open and green corridors, retail, and innovation spaces was a clear departure aimed at invigorating the area by infusing a renewed balance of activities. Finally, the persistent need for housing, which surfaced as a theme during many conversations, proved a major

Kendall Square sign at the Marriott Pedestrian Easement (Cambridge Redevelopment Authority) next to the COOP at MIT, one of America's largest college bookstores. Courtesy of user singh lens, Shutterstock Images.

challenge. During a March 2013 review of the project by the Ordinance Committee, Fred Salvucci, a senior lecturer at MIT and former Commonwealth of Massachusetts secretary of transportation, noted that more housing was needed since the current allocation "won't solve the whole housing crisis, but those 5,000 units for graduate students competing for Cambridge housing now being used by MIT will make a much larger contribution to solving the affordable housing problem than 13 percent of a modest number of housing units. That's just tokenism. It's not going to deal with the problem." Nancy Ryan of the Cambridge Residents Alliance echoed that sentiment, indicating, "The pressure [for housing] has been incredible. Fifty or 60 affordable units is nice, but doesn't really make a dent in the problem if you've got 3,000 or so graduate students who aren't housed on the campus. And, if they're given housing subsidies by the university, it just means rents can keep going up."[51] Affordable housing has been, and remains, the most significant problem facing the area. The Committee voted favorably to move the proposal forward and in April 2013, President L. Rafael Reif and other university representatives, professors, and research directors presented the plan to the Cambridge City Council which approved the zoning by a 5–3 vote.

While MIT was advancing its own zoning proposal, the City of Cambridge, with input from neighborhood groups, participated in parallel planning efforts. In the 2000s, the city launched a coordinated initiative with a broader scope. The process included an assessment of two locations: Kendall Square (K2) and Central Square (C2). Noted as the K2C2 initiative, the areas had considerable development potential given their proximity to each other. Furthermore, identifying ways to connect the two would subsequently help improve the overall urban context. In 2013, following extensive involvement of numerous stakeholders that also included focus group findings, this community-based planning process concluded with the release of a report to guide the future of Kendall Square. The document noted the value of collaboration since a "spirit of partnership among the Massachusetts Institute of Technology (MIT), other property owners, the City, and the surrounding neighborhoods will nurture an era of shared benefit, as well as connect the community socially and physically."[52]

The K2C2 report was thorough, recommending numerous improvements on many fronts. For example, it argued for the creation of a multipurpose district. On the retail front, a single-side street orientation had dominated the area with scattered shops throughout. The creation of two-sided shopping streets would meet current demand and even attract visitors. Expanding housing and meeting the existing strong demand for research and development facilities in bio and information technology through the creation of incubators would contribute to the formation of an innovation neighborhood. Connecting these three entities (retail, housing, and office space) in upcoming renovations or new construction would help create walkable streets and continue to foster the advancement of the knowledge economy. Additional findings referenced the need to embrace sustainable design practices to nurture and strengthen the environment, as well as enhance transit flow and maintain affordable transportation options. The latter goal identified the Kendall/MIT station as a focal point. The plan also focused on the importance of urban beautification, conservation, and improvement of public open spaces. It was argued that, over time, such practices would help create a lively and inviting setting with an expanded core of recreational opportunities. Finally, the report recognized the underutilized land surrounding the Volpe National Transportation Systems Center and offered a number of options that would include a park as well as more housing.

Given the plan's scope and size, it progressed slowly in segments, project by project. The focus was first placed on the 26-acre MIT proposal as a way to jump-start redevelopment.[53] In 2016, the university received approval from the Cambridge Planning Board to erect six new buildings. Facilities will include offices and 250 new graduate student housing units, as well as the integration of plazas, retail, public spaces, and even a grocery store. Approximately 300 affordable and market rate housing units were also added. More than 100,000 square feet of storefronts will be erected to attract local businesses, improve street life, and create a sense of place.[54]

Kendall Square is currently in the midst of rapid changes as some of the planning efforts take hold. MIT is redeveloping the Volpe National Transportation Systems Center and, when completed, it is expected to add 1.8 million square feet of office space. Boston Properties is planning to develop an 18-story building with a total of 400,000 square feet that will house Google. Boeing announced the establishment of the Aerospace and Autonomy Center in an MIT anchored development. In late 2018, the French drug maker Sanofi announced a massive, 900,000-square-foot lease in the neighborhood that will house 2,700 employees. But it is not just about life science companies. Apple and banking company Capital One are looking to lease in another new building under development by MIT, joining Amazon and Facebook, which were already in the area.[55] Collectively, these forces helped shape the current standing of the district. But Kendall Square is now entering a new era, moving beyond catering only to researchers, inventors, and entrepreneurs seeking to birth successful companies or corporations wanting to locate near a nucleus of ideas and talent. The new goal is to establish an innovation hub that endeavors to cultivate an all-day atmosphere. This will be a major challenge and will require ongoing attention by its various stakeholders.

Conclusion

The transformation of the Kendall Square economy in a relatively short period of time has been impressive. This was once an area with factories that produced and distributed candy, steam boilers, paper, fire hoses, furniture, ladders, glass, coffins, bricks, and barrels. Today, it has evolved into a dense setting with offices where workers are pursuing the latest biotechnology, pharmaceutical research, medical devices, mobile apps, games, energy storage systems, and the development of high-performance database management systems. They devise and deliver social media and marketing services, internet content networks, and cloud computing. The locale has become a dynamic, rapidly evolving environment with lab incubators and start-ups trying to push the next innovation to enter the market and change the world.

But the district's continuous ascent is not guaranteed since it must address a number of unfolding threats and challenges beyond attracting and retaining the latest technology firms. These include housing affordability, a variety of services, and issues of diversity. Paramount among these is the housing question. The pressures on this area are significant as real estate interests clash with efforts to create and sustain an environment which is inclusive and responsive to multiple population segments. In recent years, redevelopment efforts alarmed neighborhood organizations, such as the Cambridge Residence Alliance and others, to the point of publicly expressing concerns about gentrification and displacement, calling for solutions to these problems. Affordability also impacts start-ups. Unless they fundraise considerable amounts quickly, they are unable to operate in the immediate ecosystem because they are priced out due to rapidly ballooning office real estate costs. It is a difficult balancing act. Leadership is essential, as is planning, collaboration, and persistence. These are the key ingredients to maintaining Kendall Square, not only as the most innovative mile on the planet, but also as a great place to live.

Leveraging for Innovation in Philadelphia

The University City Connections

J UST WEST OF DOWNTOWN Philadelphia, across the Schuylkill
River, rests University City. A dense urban area, it is considered the
academic and health care heart of the city. The University of Pennsylvania (Penn), a member of the Ivy League and a major landowner, has
been located there since 1872. To the north of Penn lies another private
university, Drexel University, which was established in 1891. Founded in
1821, the University of the Sciences in Philadelphia is south of Penn and
occupies 35 acres. Furthermore, Lincoln University—whose main campus is in outlying Chester County and is the first degree-granting, historically Black college and university (HBCU) in the nation—operates
a center on Market Street, offering select undergraduate and graduate
programs. In addition to these institutions of higher education, an impressive array of hospitals and life sciences research organizations cluster within the neighborhood boundaries. These include the Hospital
of the University of Pennsylvania, which functions under the direction
of Penn Medicine; the Children's Hospital of Pennsylvania; the University City Science Center; the Corporal Michael J. Crescenz VA Medical
Center; Wistar Institute; and the Penn Presbyterian Medical Center.

University City has a rich social history, transitioning from a white, ethnic European immigrant population in its early years to a predominantly African American neighborhood during most of the twentieth century. Following World War II, and under the auspices of urban renewal, significant redevelopment activities unfolded in the area. The 1960s brought planning initiatives which reorganized large portions of the community. Housing and business removal, new construction, and population displacement followed. Additionally, during the 1990s and early part of the 2000s, it was evident that gentrification was causing visible spatial restructuring, producing major urban change. For most observers, the higher education institutional anchors were responsible for these developments, with Penn considered as the primary driver that accelerated the massive and sustained makeover.

It is within this broader context that, in the spring of 2016, Drexel University announced a highly ambitious Schuylkill Yards project on university-owned property at an estimated cost of $3.5 billion. The emerging district will become a hub of innovation and entrepreneurship with a clustering of incubators and start-ups. Its close proximity to Center City and the nearby 30th Street Station, the third busiest intercity passenger railroad in the United States, is expected to have transformational implications. Drexel is also exploring opportunities to partner with Amtrak and other entities to introduce commercial expansion and transportation options around the station. In addition to teaching and research spaces, the project will include residential, retail, and more amenities in the form of cultural venues. Public spaces such as parks and green access connections will help fashion an interactive living and working community within a high technology ecosystem. The area is also part of the Keystone Opportunity Zone, a designation that affords considerable tax benefits to businesses as a way to induce investment in communities with underutilized land.

This chapter examines the creation of a university-anchored innovation district within a complex urban setting, subjected to a long history of mistrust and tension between the community and the adjacent institutions of higher education. Some of the questions guiding this analysis include: What are the strategic priorities and actions to overcome challenges and develop collaborative partnerships? What role does institutional leadership play in achieving the project goals? How can the local government and other city and regional entities mediate community concerns within an environment that encourages private and/or corporate sector interests? Can growth and inclusion coexist?

The Schuylkill Yards project will take more than 20 years to be fully completed. Its success will depend on larger economic forces, since launching construction of the proposed mixed-use, high-rise towers necessitates favorable conditions to ensure that presales are successful, capable of leading to building completion and eventual occupancy. Converting 14 acres of prime real estate by a university in West Philadelphia into a leading innovation hub is a very ambitious plan. However, what makes this case interesting and instructive is how Drexel's path to pursuing this development unfolds within a contested setting, since the area includes neighborhoods subjected to a history of social inequality resulting from institutionally driven gentrification and displacement.

West Philadelphia and Black Bottom

West Philadelphia is located west of the Schuylkill River, which divides this part of the city from Center City. The primary boundaries include Cobbs Creek and City Avenue to the west/northwest, Baltimore Avenue and a stretch of railroad lines to the south, and the Schuylkill River to the east and north. Its close proximity to Center City has proven crucial to the area's development. Because Center City includes Philadelphia's central business district, over the decades, the West Philadelphia neighborhoods emerged as a preferred location for many residents, providing an easy commute for those working downtown. This was also one of the early streetcar suburbs in the United States, connecting the rural setting in the outskirts to the urban core. The location of the rail lines shaped the subsequent urban expansion. During the 1890s, transportation improvements that included the electric streetcar helped further accelerate the construction of residential neighborhoods, producing increasingly dense environments that fueled rapid population growth. In 1998, in recognition of its significance, the West Philadelphia Streetcar Suburb Historic District, which is located adjacent to Woodlands Cemetery in the southwestern portion of West Philadelphia, was added to the National Register of Historic Places. Market, Chestnut, and Walnut Streets, along with Lancaster Avenue, are some of the main thoroughfares cutting through West Philadelphia.

As in many other older cities, the housing stock in West Philadelphia included primarily row homes. The use of brick made the maintenance of these dwellings economical when compared to single-family homes on larger tracts. The interior layout also maximized the available space and proved a major alternative to apartment living. Queen Anne–style housing designed and built in the latter part of the nineteenth century diversified the residential options. One of the finest examples of this can be found in the Spruce Hill neighborhood. The row homes at 4206–4218 Spruce Street were designed by George Hewitt and William Hewitt, two brothers who also introduced stately homes, as well as numerous neighborhood assets such as churches and hotels. The imposing and well-defined gables, red facades, pitched roofs, and hard lines of the Queen Anne structures proved notable. Because of their dramatic presentation, these row homes added significant architectural detail and historic value to the area. In addition to Spruce Hill, a number of other communities can be found in West Philadelphia, such as Cedar Park, Walnut Hill, Squirrel Hill, Powelton Village, and University City, among others.

During the early nineteenth century, Europeans occupied the area, primarily Irish, who were part of the large influx of immigrants to the United States in the 1820s–1840s. In the latter part of the 1800s, there was an increase in the African American population, driven by migration flows from the South. These newcomers looked for access to expanding employment opportunities and favorable social conditions.[1] After World War II, West Philadelphia was in the midst of a major demographic transition. Caucasians started to look to the growing suburban communities, which shifted the area from what was once an

economically thriving streetcar community to a collection of predominantly African American neighborhoods. Furthermore, the conversion
of grand homes into apartments contributed to diminishing housing
costs, a condition that attracted new African American residents of
limited means. While some of these changes were already in motion,
white flight and business relocations exacerbated the situation. The 1950
census revealed that 11 percent of the Italian American and 25 percent of
the Irish American population had moved out of the area. At the same
time, the African American population had increased by 72 percent.[2]

The African American population in the area was not monolithic.
Some neighborhoods, especially those in the western portion, were economically stable due to employment opportunities, primarily in public
works and other government sectors. Professional positions in teaching and mid-level management, as well as openings in sanitation and
transportation, offered those residents steady jobs. By that time, African
Americans had also benefited from making inroads into local politics,
embracing unions that they had penetrated through various leadership
positions. However, while these advancements were evident, African
Americans experienced sustained challenges. These included being subjected to redlining, racial hostility, discrimination, and social isolation. Because of this, upward mobility was limited and the opportunity
to move to suburban communities impossible.[3]

Closer to the river, and around Penn and Drexel, another neighborhood, called "Bottoms," was established. The term "Bottoms" originally
arose to geographically distinguish this location from the "Tops" found
in the western section of West Philadelphia noted above. Eventually, these
terms also informed a social separation. Black Bottom, as it became
known due to the African American population occupying the area, was a
tight-knit community but quite poor, a condition that worsened in the
1950s and early 1960s. Located northwest of Penn and west of Drexel, its
boundaries extended roughly from 32nd to 40th Streets, and from University Avenue to Lancaster Avenue. A former resident, Walter Palmer,
described Black Bottom of the mid-1950s in the following manner: "While
some German and Jewish people remained, the neighborhood was

predominantly African-American and was made up of large, extended families. Market Street was lined with run-down rowhouses, which were mostly inhabited by renting families. North of Market, large brownstones and greystones stood, while small businesses like barber shops, beauty salons, bars and pharmacies were scattered throughout the neighborhood." Another former resident, Margaret Hopkins, noted that this was a place where "everybody looked out for everybody. If you needed your rent paid, people got together to pay your rent."[4]

However, city leaders viewed Black Bottom very differently and did not focus on the social cohesion and community connectedness that existed in the neighborhood. Instead of social order, they emphasized the disorder, crime, and poor housing conditions. A report published in 1953 described the community as one in which the "occupancy of buildings changed for the worse. Decay, neglect and misuse characterized the older neighborhoods, which began to deteriorate both as to use and character. The more substantial residents moved to greener pastures and their places were filled by transient individuals and families from lower income groups. Large houses built for single families now had to make do for many households. North of Market Street, except in a few isolated spots, slum or near-slum conditions developed."[5] Additionally, "physical and social ills began to grow amid substandard housing. Crime and juvenile delinquency reared their evil heads. Hoodlum gangs roamed the Powelton-Mantua area. The efforts of the police and public agencies proved but a small deterrent."[6] According to one observer, Black Bottom was perceived to be ripe for redevelopment during the latter part of the 1940s and early part of the 1950s.[7] The slum-like conditions were so abhorrent that clearing and starting anew could prove not only beneficial but highly desirable.

The Rise of University City

The end of World War II brought about significant changes in many aspects of American life. Two federal government initiatives played a major role in the case of West Philadelphia and its higher education institutions. The first development was the Servicemen's Readjustment Act of 1944, popularly known as the GI Bill. By the mid-1950s, almost 8 million veterans had used the benefit, with a significant portion of them attending college and completing a degree.[8] Competing for the unprecedented student growth meant that colleges and universities would need to rethink their existing program offerings and plan to upgrade their facilities while exploring the addition of new buildings. The second development was the significant funds spent on research following the establishment of the National Science Foundation (NSF) in 1950. By the 1960s, federal outlays on health, science, space, natural resources, and energy were growing rapidly and so was the necessary infrastructure, as well as human and physical capital. Total research and development spending in the United States has continued to increase dramatically.[9]

In 1948, Penn announced a new campus master plan titled "The Martin Plan." Named after Sydney Martin, a highly respected Philadelphia architect, the document called for more open space, which would create opportunities for future expansion. However, the emergent federal funds allocated to research, in response to the Cold War that followed, required the creation of larger, more complex, and highly elaborate structures. Penn was challenged, given its position within a dense urban setting, a condition viewed by many as a clear liability. One analysis concluded, "From the standpoint of size, complexity, and segmentation, Penn was disadvantaged by being a landlocked urban campus standing in close proximity to the industrial city."[10] It was during the presidential tenure of Gaylord P. Harnwell, from 1953 to 1970, that Penn's fortunes changed as the university emerged as the recipient of considerable federal support for biomedical research from the National Institutes of Health and other government sources. Enrollment and the university endowment grew rapidly and new graduate programs brought prestige that transformed the institution with high-caliber faculty and unparalleled research facilities. All this improved the university's standing, helping it ascend as a leading national university and eventually one of the most prestigious institutions of higher education in the world. By the late 1960s, research and development revenues ranked Penn in the top 20 nationally. How did all this materialize?

The city had already expressed interest in addressing the struggling conditions in West Philadelphia, especially the geographical area north of Penn and west of Drexel. In 1947, Edmund Bacon, chair of the Philadelphia City Planning Commission, noted, "If present deterioration . . . is allowed to spread, the good sections to the west will be cut off from the city center by a band of blight, and their rapid decline may be expected. . . . if the area is intelligently redeveloped so as to establish a sound connection to the heart of the city, the desirable areas of West Philadelphia will tend to be stabilized." Bacon concluded by favoring redevelopment functioning within the existing university area.[11] It was clear that Harnwell had the green light. Referenced as a builder, Harnwell "disentangled the University from the creep of heavily trafficked city streets, clanging trolley lines, and tawdry commercial establishments. He built the present day West Central and West Campuses, expanded the North campus between 32nd and 38th streets, and established a sphere of influence between Chestnut Street and Lancaster Avenue . . . [all this] though not without unintended, long-term consequences for the University's community relations."[12]

Penn led by creating a coalition that included a number of actors at the city, state, and federal levels, including the Philadelphia City Planning Commission, the Redevelopment Authority of Philadelphia, and the West Philadelphia Corporation. Two developments aided the implementation process. First, through its board of trustees, Penn maintained ties to the Greater Philadelphia movement, a group of business leaders who called for an end to political corruption, which they declared a threat to economic prosperity. Second, at the same time, the public staging of the Better Philadelphia Exhibition in 1947 offered a glimpse of the future of cities by showcasing planning concepts aimed at improving urban life. A public perception favored starting anew. Clearing existing parcels and rebuilding was the proper plan of action. The Redevelopment Authority of Philadelphia, employing the provisions of the Housing Acts of 1949 and 1954, utilized government resources to support revitalization by acquiring land. In 1959, a partnership between Penn, Drexel, the College of Pharmacology and Science, and the Presbyterian and Osteopathic hospitals founded the West Philadelphia Corporation.

A nonprofit entity, the West Philadelphia Corporation focused on the redevelopment of an area from 34th and 40th Streets along Market Street. The organization's actions focused on Black Bottom and displaced more than 2,000 residents, primarily African Americans, by leveling many residential blocks after formally declaring them a slum. As the chief driver behind the execution of the plan, Penn led the swift remaking of the blighted areas. The result of these urban renewal efforts and the restructuring that followed helped form a new community which Penn branded University City. University City offered a very different image, one aimed at attracting a unique type of resident: faculty and staff employed at the nearby colleges and universities. The University City Science Center, an urban research park, and the University City High School are two examples of institutions that were added as part of this initiative.

Urban renewal dramatically altered the landscape of West Philadelphia, and Penn has since been subjected to extensive criticism regarding the handling of its surroundings. Even Edmund Bacon, who once supported the university's expansion plans, criticized how Penn handled the Hill Field, leaving it undeveloped, by noting, "I walked by it today . . . and my resentment was renewed because there it stands . . . an open parking lot and . . . a field without a single soul in it . . . It was extremely painful to take the brunt of putting people out of their houses. They lived there. They loved their houses." According to Bacon, Penn engaged in "a capricious and irresponsible utilization of a space after such destruction."[13] Hill Field stood empty for decades until Penn broke ground for a new residential building in 2014.

As the dominant player in this part of the city, the university boldly took control of what was perceived as neighborhood deterioration. Referenced as the "urban renewal university," Penn employed its power and financial strength to almost singlehandedly wipe out entire

Looking east toward the downtown Philadelphia skyline, home of the Schuylkill Yards innovation district. Cira Centre and Amtrak's 30th Street Station are in the foreground. Courtesy of user Tippman98x, Shutterstock Images.

communities.[14] In the process, it further isolated these disadvantaged areas, causing increases in crime that threatened the well-being of faculty, staff, and students. Robberies, shootings, and rapes became commonplace. On the night of October 31, 1996, the unfortunate case of 38-year-old Penn biochemist Vladimir Sled drew national attention: he was stabbed to death near campus on his way home from his office following a botched robbery attempt. The gruesome event shook the university community to its core.[15] Penn's postwar efforts to separate itself from the surrounding area by erecting physical boundaries proved misguided, as its heavy-handedness caused widespread turmoil resulting in instability, furthering neighborhood decline.

Penn attempted to reverse those conditions in the 1990s and early part of the 2000s. Under the leadership of Judith Rodin, who served as president of the university from 1994 to 2004, the institution engaged in urban redevelopment activities that focused on transforming the nearby communities, this time by aiming to strengthen their social and economic standing. Rodin identified an aggressive plan to revitalize parts of University City by pursuing five key strategies: (1) strengthen the public schools, (2) provide more housing options, (3) expand the commercial activity, (4) address safety issues, and (5) spearhead various economic development initiatives. The approach also acknowledged the presence of many stakeholders and community assets and recognized the importance of developing robust networks with local organizations. The university moved forward by managing various projects that required the collective and direct involvement of real estate developers, neighborhood groups, and other nonprofits. Dubbed the West Philadelphia Initiatives, Rodin's framework was collaborative and participatory, characterized by her desire to build trust and transparency. She also advocated for private-public partnerships, which she viewed as central to her plans. In 2007, after she had left office, Rodin reflected, "We learned that a university can play a lead role in urban transformation by changing its perspective and making a commitment to alter its ways of interacting and transacting. By reorienting itself toward fostering relationships with local businesses the University found a way for them to prosper together with us. By inviting our neighbors to join us at the table as partners in the shared work of beautifying the streets and parks, improving the public schools, reviving the commercial corridors, and reanimating the housing market, we found a way to live more productively together."[16]

However, her positive assessment has also been met with criticism. For example, it has been argued that Penn's community investment decisions following the Sled murder were not based on concerns for area residents. Rather, critics allege, these efforts were born out of necessity and self-interest since, fearing enrollment declines, Penn had no other choice but to improve the surrounding community.[17] As Maureen Rush, Penn's vice president for public safety, once noted, "We hit the wall . . . It was clearly becoming an issue for admissions."[18] The creation of the University City District followed, a partnership of area institutions and businesses focusing on community revitalization through job growth programs, public safety initiatives, and vibrant commercial corridors. The primary drivers behind the formation of University City District in 1997 were Penn and Drexel who, along with corporate sponsors, funded the initiative. "Penntrification," as it became known, fundamentally altered this historic part of Philadelphia.

The Schuylkill Yards Plan

It is against this historical backdrop that in March 2016, President John Fry of Drexel University announced the 20-year Schuylkill Yards plan. The project complements the recommendations made in a report by the Ann T. and Robert M. Bass Initiative on Innovation and Placemaking calling for a broader, coordinated strategy to pursue a series of cluster initiatives that take advantage of the city's existing research and technological assets. The report identifies the creation of a robust corridor, connecting University City and Center City and creating a massive, contiguous innovation district.[19] When completed, the Drexel project is expected to transform the immediate surroundings while serving as a catalyst for economic development. Fry brought significant expertise to this ambitious undertaking because of his prior role as an executive vice president and chief operating office at Penn under President Rodin from 1995 until 2002. While at Penn, he was instrumental in the university's outreach efforts to the community, which included University City neighborhood improvement initiatives such as strengthening the residential and commercial sectors. However, one of the major criticisms that many of the policies advanced by Penn during that period faced was that they produced considerable displacement and gentrification.

The Schuylkill Yards plan will unfold on multiple city blocks within walking distance of Amtrak's 30th Street Station, the third busiest rail station in the nation. It will include almost 7 million square feet of space dispersed as offices, laboratories, retail, residential, and a hotel. A major selling point for this massive development is its proximity via Amtrak to New York City (a little over an hour) and Washington, DC (about an hour and a half). Furthermore, easy access to City Center and the Philadelphia Airport through SEPTA, the regional public transportation authority, provides quick connections to additional locations. However, Schuylkill Yards' positioning near the universities and health science research and medical facilities in University City is its greatest strength and major attraction. Extensive public spaces and green thoroughfares are also included in the master plan.

Drexel's project partner is Brandywine Realty Trust, a Philadelphia company and one of the largest publicly traded real estate companies in the country. Brandywine brings almost 30 years of experience in constructing and managing Class A office buildings and mixed-use properties. Class A buildings are of the highest quality; they are typically newer structures with the highest rents. Brandywine has had prior engagements in the eastern part of West Philadelphia, along the shores of the river. Just north, and adjacent to Amtrak's 30th Street Station, rests the Brandywine Cira Centre, a 29-story skyscraper which was completed in 2004. Built over railyards, the Cira Centre is the result of a multidecade effort, dating back to the 1960s, to address a large section of what once was a heavily industrial area that remained underutilized along the river. Numerous initiatives to develop the site failed, including a stadium proposal for the Philadelphia Eagles. Because of its proximity to the station, the development is expected to be an asset to the Schuylkill Yards master plan, eventually helping to fuel further expansion.

In 1998, the Pennsylvania General Assembly passed the Keystone Opportunity Improvement Zone legislation, an initiative aimed at fostering economic development opportunities in areas struggling due to physical and infrastructural decay. By offering tax benefits to businesses and property owners willing to (re)locate in these areas, the goal was to reverse deterioration and induce growth. Brandywine and the Cira Centre benefited from this designation and successfully attracted tenants to occupy the $116 million office building.[20] Since that time, the tower has been viewed as an anchor development. A more recent project located just to the south of the Amtrak Station, and east of Penn along the river on former United States Postal Service land, is the Cira Centre South complex. A partnership between Penn and Brandywine on university-owned land resulted in the erection of two buildings. Following a long-term ground lease agreement that also provided the university with access to space, the FMC Tower—a 49-story sky-scraper of retail, residential, hotel rooms, and office space—opened with state-of-the-art amenities. Adjacent to the FMC Tower is the Evo Cira Centre South, a 33-story residential tower. It is evident that Brandywine has had a long and sustained presence in University City not only as a real estate developer but also as a higher education partner.[21]

Schuylkill Yards includes the construction of eight new towers and a community park, Drexel Square. Drexel Square was completed in 2019 and is part of the first phase of the project. It features an elliptical lawn that serves as a focal point, occupying six of the 14 acres reserved for public space. The greenways will connect workplace and lifestyle surroundings. Brandywine will be responsible for the design, construction, leasing, and management of the buildings in exchange for a 99-year ground lease. Drexel will maintain control of the land for which it receives rent. At the end of the lease, Drexel will gain ownership of the buildings.

In a joint opinion essay titled "Giant Step in Philly Growth" published by the *Philadelphia Inquirer*, John Fry, president of Drexel University, and Jerry Sweeney, president and CEO of Brandywine Realty Development, placed the ambitious project within a broader context. They argued that this "will be the largest in the city's history. It will include spaces designed for innovative start-up companies, research laboratories, and corporate offices, along with residential building, retail, and hotel space, and ample open green horizons . . . [T]his will be an appealing neighborhood that combines commercial buildings with some of the most welcoming public spaces in urban America, a civic commons unlike any other." Furthermore, they noted, "Its strategic location encourages easy collaborations with University City's rich mix of higher education, medical, and scientific institutions. This level of collaboration is in keeping with the concept of urban innovation districts."[22]

However, mindful of the history and tensions in the community, including the project's potential implications, the authors also focused on another aspect by articulating a social mission. They stated, "We don't want Philadelphia's success story to devolve into a tale of two cities. We can't afford to develop one small city for the educated, upwardly mobile, and mostly white, surrounded by a much larger city whose residents are under-educated, under-employed, poor, and predominantly non-white . . . Nonetheless, the impressive commercial development at the heart of our urban renaissance is not being matched by comparable progress in our high-poverty neighborhoods."[23] Given the magnitude of these claims, will Schuylkill Yards and its associated commercial and residential development have a positive impact on the community? Will this project have the capability of becoming a driver for growth that can also have long-lasting equitable results? The response by Fry and Sweeney was unequivocally affirmative, arguing that the "ambitious commercial development directly tied to a specific community agenda represents the best hope for an inclusive future for Philadelphia . . . Schuylkill Yards has been designed from day one to provide maximum opportunities for residents of adjoining neighborhoods like Mantua, West Powelton, and Belmont." They also added, "Economic opportunity for neighborhood residents is a major part of the vision . . . [W]e're not depending on a trickle-down approach."[24]

A debate about the meaning of inclusive development ensued with questions raised about access to the purported benefits. Being intentionally inclusive is obviously conceptually a well-intended objective. However, the way this plays out practically, at the neighborhood level, is more complicated. Jim Saksa, a public radio reporter, viewed the Schuylkill Yards project with skepticism, noting that gentrification would be the likely outcome as he commented, "I see this as an exciting project. I like what they are saying. I am skeptical. I think these are monumental challenges that they are facing. Market forces are going to be against them in terms of their calls for inclusion . . . Some of the things they brought up will increase the costs for tenants. To make some developments slightly less competitive for the market place will be difficult to do. That being said, if they can pull it off . . . we should start building statues to them."[25]

Lucy Kerman, vice provost of University and Community Partnerships at Drexel, focused on the benefits by differentiating between jobs

and residential opportunities. Kerman argued, "I don't think it's a con-
tradiction to say that you can invest in an area that will bring the kind
of investment that in fact Philadelphia needs, we need new jobs, we need
tax payer jobs, we need new retail . . . It does not mean that [Schuylkill
Yards] cannot be fair . . . it may not be that the tenant rates are going to
be affordable by the local community. But it does mean there will be access to the jobs . . . that education can be improved so that children can
eventually see themselves as the entrepreneurs in those businesses . . .
Job development, access to the space, beautiful public spaces that people
will feel welcome in, retail that will benefit everybody."[26] Community
members offered a different perspective to Drexel's approach to what
constitutes inclusive development. Michael Thorpe, executive director
of the Mt. Vernon Manor CDC, called instead for a collaborative, bottom-
up, not a top-down, approach—"not a lip service"—especially during the
early stages of developing the innovation district.

Community Outreach and Long-Term Implications

Since the formal announcement of Schuylkill Yards in 2016, the developers have engaged in a number of community outreach activities to
help strengthen the social and economic capacity of the surrounding
neighborhoods. Located to the north of University City, Mantua is a
working-class African American section of West Philadelphia that
struggled with violence primarily due to gang- and drug-related activities during the 1980s and 1990s. Mantua was also impacted by urban
renewal initiatives and the consequences of deindustrialization. In
2014, along with Belmont, Powelton Village, Saunders Park, and West
Powelton, Mantua was identified as a "Promise Zone." This federal designation recognizes communities that have high levels of poverty and
need revitalization. Improvements in education, health, jobs, and crime
reduction are the typical areas of focus. Encouraging investment is
another goal of Promise Zones, as is expanding affordable housing and
addressing the large number of existing vacant lots. In some cases, this
means rehabilitation or infill of existing housing stretches. In other

cases, focus is placed on targeting sites for developing rental units and improving homeownership.

In 2017, Brandywine Realty Trust pledged $5.6 million to strengthening West Philadelphia. This commitment identified a portion of the funds to assist with minority business development through low interest loans and job training in high demand sectors, including highly skilled construction jobs. The majority of the resources, however, were allocated for affordable housing, since residents expressed concerns about the impact that the Schuylkill Yards project would have on the neighborhood. The other major area of support regarded additional programming for the public schools. Mayor Jim Kenney recognized Brandywine Realty Trust by noting, "I'm particularly excited to see Brandywine's commitment to apprenticeship opportunities and career advancement . . . and just as importantly, Philadelphians who haven't yet benefitted from our city's recent development and construction boom will have the opportunity to partake."[27]

The Bulletin Building was constructed for the *Evening Bulletin* in 1954 and designed by George Howe, an influential American architect. Drexel University acquired the property in 1993 and added the ribbon windows to use as classrooms. The Bulletin Building, along with the adjacent Drexel Square and Amtrak's 30th Street Station, will serve as a focal point of the Schuylkill Yards development. Courtesy of Costas Spirou.

Drexel, on the other hand, has had a much deeper and more sustained involvement in the communities of West Philadelphia. The Dornsfire Center for Neighborhood Partnerships has historically engaged collaboratively to meet the interests and needs of various local stakeholders. Following the release of the Schuylkill Yards plan, the university announced an expansion of its current community outreach efforts to address the concerns voiced by the residents. Three specific inclusion initiatives were outlined. First, Drexel will encourage Schuylkill Yards tenants to seek and receive professional services provided by local businesses. The university will be promoting the procurement process. Second, community members will have access to construction jobs with the firms involved in the project. Third, a workforce development program will focus on preparing local residents to seek professional employment opportunities with companies occupying the development. Finally, a series of investments in neighborhood public schools will concentrate on strengthening programs to assist students and their families. Keith Orris, Drexel's senior vice president for corporate relations and economic development, noted that a comprehensive approach is essential since "we believe that if you are a child born in these neighborhoods—in Mantua, West Powelton or Powelton Village, or really throughout West Philadelphia—you should have the ability to grow up, get educated in a good public school, go to a university or college, maybe right here, and then graduate and have the ability to secure a job with a company in Schuylkill Yards."[28]

It is obviously too early to tell if these initiatives will prove successful. While some credit the Promise Zone designation as the impetus for the Brandywine and Drexel commitments, others remain cautious about the long-term implications. Samantha Porter, from the City of Philadelphia's Office of Community Empowerment and Opportunity and the City's point person on the Promise Zone, noted, "West Philadelphia is seeing a lot of growth [from Schuylkill Yards], and that gives the impression that it's equitable. There is still work to be done to ensure that growth is open to all of our neighbors."[29] John Phillips, president of the Powelton Village Civic Association, argued, "We're aware that

[Schuylkill Yards will] have significant impacts on the surrounding communities . . . a very strong community benefits agreement directly with the impacted neighborhoods [is needed]."[30] A similar skepticism was voiced by De'Wayne Drummond, president of the Mantua Civic Association, who noted, "My grandfather always used to say, 'They're coming,' Now, I know what he meant."[31] The unpredictable impact of Schuylkill Yards, combined with the increasing number of Drexel University students moving to apartments in the adjacent communities, contributes to an increased sense of uneasiness. The arrival of students generally distorts real estate values and adds pressure on housing costs. Many local organizations advocated for rezoning the area into single-family homes as a way to curb construction pressures and place controls on the overall impact deriving from conditions of residential density.

Conclusion

The Schuylkill Yards innovation district is a massive project and its implication for the Philadelphia region, the city, and West Philadelphia is substantial. For Drexel University, this ambitious, highly entrepreneurial project is part of its quest for institutional advancement, as it has the capacity to catapult the institution forward in ways that could be truly transformative. The initiative is expected to position the university for future growth in an exceedingly competitive higher education landscape. President Fry also predicted that "this 20-year, $3.5 billion project will benefit thousands of low-income families without disrupting the fabric of their neighborhoods," calling it "a major win."[32] But this effort unfolds within a historically contested urban environment. The persistent cycle of redlining, white flight, riots, and the crack epidemic made the surrounding neighborhoods ripe for redevelopment. Can rapid urban growth coincide with inclusion? The Drexel administration is clearly committed to and invested in practices that support the local community. However, while the pursuit of inclusion is welcomed, the long-term implications present considerable challenges. The corporate offices at Schuylkill Yards will attract young professionals whose need for housing will increase market rates, in the process fueling displacement and gentrification.

There are a number of key factors that made this plan possible. First, strong, visionary leadership at Drexel was exercised, by individuals with a long history of engagement as part of the Penn team involved in the community outreach efforts during the 1990s. Second, an entrepreneurial approach proved essential in utilizing the institutions' existing resources, resulting in a very strong partnership, not only with the developer but also with the public sector, to ensure continuous support. Finally, the Drexel team recognized that in order for them to achieve their objectives they must understand and attempt to address the complications resulting from operating in a complex urban environment. Beyond unfolding in a dense setting, the unique aspects of this innovation district are its massive size and enormous impact, as well as planned improvements with the addition of more public spaces. From a conceptual and a programmatic perspective, it is apparent that Drexel is committed to social inclusion by being a considerate and responsible neighbor who endeavors to support community organizations by strengthening education and housing options. Addressing existing challenges and improving the residents' well-being is of great importance to the university. However, this plan will be critically tested and, at full maturity, will probably be unable to deliver on its promises. Recreating new neighborhoods without the current residents will be the likely outcome. In that regard, Schuylkill Yards in West Philadelphia will be synonymous with Drexelfication.

Innovation in the Valley of the Sun

PHX Core and Beyond

I N THE FALL OF 2019, at a time of enrollment declines, Arizona State University (ASU) had its largest, most diverse first-year class in the history of the institution. With a 10 percent enrollment increase from the previous year, this was also the best academically prepared class ever. In addition, for the fourth straight time, US News & World Report identified ASU as the most innovative national university in the United States, noting a sustained culture of inventive thinking. Under the leadership of current ASU President Michael M. Crow, the institution has been in the midst of rapid change. Crow argued that the ascent of Arizona State was in line with a prototype that he referenced as the "New American University," which is at the forefront of higher education reinvention. The pursuit of academic excellence resides at the core of this model, which also embraces inclusiveness through innovative practices to maximize social impact. Its egalitarian orientation is always searching for innovative ideas and practices.

This chapter examines the role of ASU in the rebirth of downtown Phoenix and the planning of PHX Core, a nearby innovation district. In 2004, ASU announced a new campus in the city's center, which is located

10 miles away from the main campus in Tempe, Arizona. Today, more than 12,000 students are studying in the downtown campus, with an institutional goal of expanding that number to 20,000 over the next few years. These efforts have infused energy into the area, fermenting the renewal of a struggling city ravaged by the forces of postwar suburbanization into a robust environment that now attracts continuous commercial investment and residential growth. The PHX Core is planned to overlap parts of downtown and the adjacent Warehouse District, which is enjoying an urban renaissance. As an anchor institution, ASU is expanding its physical presence in the area and will be central to the future of PHX Core as it is transitioning into a thriving cultural and economic hub. Like other innovation districts, the goal is to attract business and technology start-ups, incubators, and accelerators. It is expected that, as the district progresses, the remaining manufacturing warehouses will undergo new adaptive uses.

In addition to the ASU Downtown campus, PHX Core will be supported by two other distinct economic entities, the Phoenix Biomedical Campus and Galvanize. Launched in 2004, the Phoenix Biomedical Campus is the result of a collaboration between the City of Phoenix, the University of Arizona College of Medicine, ASU, and the Arizona Board of Regents. The 30-acre urban medical and bioscience campus conducts biomedical research and includes clinical and academic spaces. ASU is involved by offering bioinformatic and health science education programs. The other distinct entity, Galvanize, has a total of nine campuses across the country that focus on providing co-working spaces to assist start-ups and more established companies. Workshops and other educational opportunities—such as strategies to raise venture capital, as well as skill and knowledge development—are offered to assist in fueling a culture of innovation.

The chapter concludes by discussing the Novus Innovation Corridor, a $30 billion, 330-acre, ASU-owned development in Tempe. Until recently, the land has been primarily used to generate revenue from sporting events. However, when completed, this downtown project will include more than 10 million square feet of mixed-use options for residential, business, retail, and entertainment functions. A key goal will be to take advantage of the proximity to the university and create an environment that will attract existing companies and new entrepreneurs interested in exploring pioneering industries. This will significantly boost the city, giving birth to a new economy. Finally, the chapter points to another ASU initiative within the city of Mesa, aimed at jump-starting its downtown revitalization efforts.

In the last 20 years, downtown Phoenix has undergone significant urban regeneration changes. ASU has played a critical role in this ascent, having created a downtown campus that continues to flourish. The launch of PHX Core is in part due to ASU expanding its footprint in the area. Some of the questions guiding this analysis include (1) Is the innovation district in the city's Warehouse District the outcome of the New American University's preoccupation with economic development? (2) Does ASU's intense focus on economic development shift the institution away from its primary purpose? (3) What role do public and private sector partnerships play in advancing these initiatives?

The Ascent

A public research university in the Phoenix metropolitan area, ASU has gone through significant changes as part of its efforts to serve a rapidly expanding metropolitan area. The growth has been astonishing. In just a decade, the city of Phoenix saw its population grow from 106,818 in 1950 to 439,170 in 1960. By the early 1990s, the city surpassed the million mark, and the 2010 census reported nearly 1.5 million people residing within the city borders. It is expected that the upward trend will continue, pushing the population over the 2 million mark in a few years. The growth has been equally impressive in Maricopa County, which is a major part of the Phoenix-Mesa-Glendale MSA. According to the Maricopa Association of Governments, the county's population increased from a little over 2 million in 1990 to 4 million in 2014 and is expected to surpass 5 million by 2030.[1] Recent data revealed that Maricopa County is the fastest growing county in the country.[2]

A 2007 report released by the US Conference of Mayors identified the Phoenix-Mesa-Scottsdale metropolitan area as having the fastest projected population growth in the nation, from 4.6 million (2016) to 7.8 million (2046), a 67.8 percent change.[3] More recent analyses forecast an even faster progression, indicating that, by 2040, the population will reach 10 million residents. This change will likely end up connecting Phoenix and Tucson, since the distance between the two cities is only 120 miles.[4] The rapid economic expansion is driven by three primary factors: manufacturing relocations, plentiful affordable housing, and a pleasant climate. In recent years, the regional economy has diversified considerably to include increases in bioscience and technology sectors, thus maintaining a vibrant economic outlook.

ASU has operated within this rapidly unfolding metropolitan environment, boasting five campus locations, as well as online programs. The university is part of the Arizona Board of Regents (ABOR) that also includes Northern Arizona University and the University of Arizona. Its main campus in Tempe is about a 20-minute drive from downtown Phoenix. Additionally, the Downtown Phoenix campus, the West campus, the Colleges at Lake Havasu City campus, and the Polytechnic campus offer undergraduate and graduate programs to thousands of students. In the fall of 2018, ASU was one of the largest universities in the United States, serving about 73,000 students on campus and 36,300 through ASU online for a total of more than 109,000 students.[5] ASU is also a member of the Universities Research Association (URA) and the Association of Public and Land-grant Universities (APLU).

Since the 1970s, four ASU presidents have played a crucial role in the development of the university. John Schwada served between 1971 and 1981, when the enrollment exploded from 26,000 to 40,000 students and 25 buildings were added to the campus. J. Russell Nelson followed from 1981 to 1989. During his tenure, ASU became a multicampus institution and was recognized as a research university. Lattie Coor, president from 1990 to 2002, expanded the research mission at ASU. This positioned the institution to become identified as a Research I university by the Carnegie Foundation for the Advancement of Teaching. Coor also established ASU East in 1996, which was later renamed ASU Polytechnic campus.[6]

The arrival of Michael Crow as president of ASU in 2002 signaled a major period of rapid transformation which continues today. Right from the start, Crow focused on the concept of the New American University. In fact, the title of his inaugural address was "A New American University: The New Gold Standard." He articulated his vision by outlining the importance of pursuing excellence in teaching, research, and public service. However, he also called for "providing the best possible education to the broadest possible spectrum of society. The new American university would embrace the educational needs of the entire population—not only a select group, and not only the verbally or mathematically gifted. The success of the new American university will be measured not by who the university excludes, but rather by who the university includes, and from this inclusion will come its contributions to the advancement of society."[7] This approach charted a different direction from the typical, major Research I, public universities which have made selectivity a central tenant of their reputation and distinctiveness.

At the same inauguration speech, Crow called for the university to engage in an entrepreneurial manner which he posited would be essential to ASU's continued ascent. He argued, "We must commit ourselves to exploring the entrepreneurial potential of university teaching and research . . . ASU must aggressively seek new revenue streams . . . [and] I would like to see ASU develop a reputation for its entrepreneurial boldness. The enterprise imperative must become a part of our culture."[8] This direction is pertinent to academic disciplines, which can always benefit from exploring and implementing innovative practices outside their boundaries and across interdisciplinary structures in their approaches to teaching, learning, and knowledge making. However, promoting the commercialization of technology transfer is another, central aspect of the university's entrepreneurship strategy. Beyond engaging faculty in that area, ASU focused on encouraging and supporting students to develop their own companies. An infrastructure connecting innovative thinkers, venture capitalists, and entrepreneurs created an environment conducive to furthering the entrepreneurship goal. A substantial component of meeting this objective resulted in SkySong, a project that aptly captures this orientation outside the traditional boundaries of higher education, necessitating considerable public and private sector involvement. SkySong was established in what once was a shopping center.

In 1969, Los Acros Mall opened in Scottsdale, but by the 1980s it started to experience signs of decline. These intensified in the 1990s, leading to its closure in 1999 and eventual demolition in 2001. In 2008, in collaboration with the City of Scottsdale and the ASU Foundation, ASU launched SkySong, a mixed-use, private-public partnership to be constructed on 42 acres of the former mall. It would be a technology complex with the goal of attracting innovative business. The complex, developed by Plaza Companies, is expected to reach 1.2 million square feet when fully completed. Over the years, office space sprouted up. More recently, an apartment building and amenities such as restaurants opened and, in 2019, a 157-room Element Hotel at SkySong operated by Marriott was added. ASU maintains a strong presence in SkySong by providing businesses with access to faculty, students, and programs. Additionally, incubators fuel the growth of start-up companies while the Global Growth Accelerator, a partnership between ASU and the Greater Phoenix Economic Council, aims to attract international companies to the location. Danielle Casey, director of economic development for the City of Scottsdale, recognizes the significant value of this initiative, noting that "SkySong has opened the door for the city to grow its brand as a top location of choice for tech talent as well as entrepreneurs . . . It frequently draws interest from prospective companies that are focused on attracting the best talent and identifying a location with a strong university connection." Sharon Harper, CEO of Plaza Companies, echoed a similar sentiment: "We know now one of the biggest decisions about where a company is going to locate is the existing talent base and a pipeline of talent . . . That's ASU."[9]

Initiatives like SkySong are in line with creating an entrepreneurial university and have been aggressively pursued by Crow during his tenure. Furthering access and promoting inclusion by expanding the number of minority and low-income students is another major component of the New American University model. However, in higher education circles, combining these two directions is viewed to be antithetical to what constitutes a successful public research university. The key question is: Could the achievement of academic prestige in a research-intensive institutional setting coincide with promoting diversity? According to Crow, these are not contradictory ambitions; rather, implementing this vision would help maximize the socioeconomic impact of higher education.[10]

The orientation proposed by the New American University has been perceived as visionary and lauded by many media outlets. *Newsweek* declared that Crow was "overseeing one of the most radical redesigns in higher learning since the modern research university took shape in 19th-century Germany."[11] *Time* recognized that ASU, once known as a top party school, was "clambering up another kind of list. [Crow] rode into office in 2002 vowing to build a New American University that embraced students with a wide range of backgrounds and abilities while giving élite public schools a run for their research money."[12] The *Chronicle of Higher Education* concluded that "the Arizona State University model is one to be watched. It will probably be emulated by other publicly funded research universities."[13] Crow's social transformation initiatives at ASU also received attention abroad, as the *Guardian* reported, "If Crow has designed the 'new American university', who will be game enough to attempt its British equivalent?"[14]

These accolades, however, have also been accompanied by sharp criticisms leveled against this model, charging that its approach to achieving institutional change is misguided. Primary among these concerns has been the ASU focus on generating revenue by embracing entrepreneurial practices, driven by corporate management strategies which contradict the nature and inner workings of higher education culture.[15] Reorganizing traditional academic structures into interdisciplinary units was also questioned as a radical approach that threatened the foundational contributions of basic science, theory, and data of the core disciplines. According to detractors, this could lead to supporting vocational education, provoking the eventual corporatization of the university.[16]

ASU's efforts to expand access to higher education has taken multiple forms. For example, in 2019, ASU announced InStride, a for-profit entity that connects, through a technology platform, the university with companies interested in providing higher education benefits to their employees. Rise Fund, a $2.1 billion entity managed by the real estate platform TPG, is the majority owner of this initiative. Another, more mainstream approach has been the "One University in Many Places" directive. This plan aims to shift the university from a model comprised of a main campus that has satellite campuses to one with multiple campuses that maintains and offers comprehensive academic services to students, operationally contributing to the institutional goals of excellence and access. It is this "One University in Many Places" strategy which led to the creation of the ASU Downtown campus, a move that will have significant implications for the revitalization of downtown Phoenix.

The ASU Downtown Vision: Setting the Stage for PHX Core

It is within the broader institutional context of the New American University that, in April 2004, ASU launched the creation of the Downtown campus. According to a 2004 report by the Office of the President, "There are currently weak and uneven relationships between and among the ASU campuses . . . [T]he missions of each of the anchor campuses and the extended campus must be redefined so that the sum of the parts will more effectively and efficiently serve the expanded mission of ASU conceived as a prototype New American University."[17] Additionally, the report outlined the academic programs that will comprise the new Downtown campus, which was initially referred to as the Capital Center campus due its proximity to the Arizona State Capitol.

In the spring of 2006, the City of Phoenix approved $223 million for the development of the Downtown campus. President Crow recognized that the value of this initiative goes beyond the institution, saying, "The evolution of the Downtown campus is an important statement . . . and an opportunity to leave to our children and our children's children a prosperous and vibrant urban environment in which to live."[18] Subsequently, a redesigned Public College (formerly the College of Public Programs); the College of Nursing; KAET, ASU's PBS television station; the Walter Cronkite School of Journalism and Mass Communication; the School of Health Management and Policy; and the University College were moved to the new location. Furthermore, the Herberger College of Fine Arts would begin offering programming at the Downtown campus.

The result of an extraordinary partnership between the university and the city, the campus opened in the fall of 2006 with about 3,000 taking classes. By 2009, more than 6,000 students studied at the ASU Downtown campus. Program expansion followed, fueling further growth. In 2012, the Sandra Day O'Connor College of Law announced that it would move from the Tempe campus to the downtown location with a new, $129 million Arizona Center for Law Society building.[19] ASU also acquired the Thunderbird School of Global Management, a private institution, relocating its operations to the downtown campus. A $50 million, state-of-the-art facility will serve as the school's headquarters.[20]

A major development for the downtown campus was the construction of Taylor Place, a student dormitory. The facility opened in 2008, eventually reaching full capacity. In the fall of 2018, 1,500 additional students were unable to be accommodated since they identified living downtown as their preferred choice. Some students ended up at the nearby Sheraton Grand Hotel while others lived on the Tempe campus, commuting daily to their downtown classes. Due to continued demand for student housing in 2019, ASU announced plans to develop a new, $130 million, 400-bed dorm building.[21] This dormitory was specifically designed to encourage innovation and entrepreneurship, supporting students who want to launch and grow their start-up businesses.

The Walter Cronkite School of Journalism and Mass Communication at Arizona State University in the ASU Downtown campus. The School moved to its current location in 2008, following the completion of the $71 million, state-of-the-art facility. Since then, it has had a significant impact on the campus and the city's downtown. Courtesy of user EQRoy, Shutterstock Images.

The ASU Downtown campus has proved to be a major success, reaching 12,000 students in 2019. All indications point to a continued expansion in both facilities and enrollment. Following decades of decline brought about by the postwar decentralization and the subsequent residential and commercial explosion in the suburbs, the Phoenix core and surrounding areas are now undergoing a rebirth. From 2016 to 2018, more than 6,000 new apartments or condo units have either been completed or are in development. From 2008 to 2018, more than 190 bars and restaurants opened in downtown.[22] According to former Mayor Thelda Williams, "Prior to ASU being (in) downtown, Phoenix was about as dead as a door nail . . . Streets were rolled up at 6 o'clock, there was no traffic, few places to eat and other than perhaps some sporting events, there really wasn't any reason to be downtown." Rick Naimark, who served as the deputy city manager of Phoenix when the ASU Downtown campus first launched, confirmed, "It was everything we wanted to do as the City of Phoenix to get ASU to become a major presence in the downtown community."[23] The Phoenix urban core is more vibrant now than it has been for many decades, and the population is growing at a rapid pace. In 2018, more than 18,000 people called the area home, an increase of 12 percent since 2000. It is expected that by 2023, the downtown residential population will increase by 8 percent.[24]

The energy brought by the ASU Downtown campus and the subsequent construction boom and population growth that followed was accompanied by a reorientation of the local economy. The technology and biomedical center emerged as a new economic direction, shifting away from the historical reliance on construction, real estate, and retail. In 2012, there were 67 technology companies in Phoenix with offices in the downtown area. In 2018, the number of similar companies exploded to 285.[25] In an article titled "Here Is Why Phoenix Could Be the Next Silicon Valley," Fortune magazine noted that technology jobs were up by almost 20 percent between 2010 to 2015. Additionally, between 2009 and 2011, 74 agreements by venture capital firms resulted in investments worth $332 million. In the next two years, the number of deals almost doubled with 145 agreements, worth $834 million. Along with investments in new office space and a light rail system, the article pointed to ASU as a major asset and the foremost reason for the transformation.[26]

ASU's efforts to brand itself as an innovative university have penetrated the city's identity. A recent report placed Phoenix as the 20th most innovative city in the Americas and ranked the city 58th globally. The analysis took into consideration urban centers that are talent magnets (attracting a "millennial" population with a strong live/work/play culture), innovative and transformative (maintaining a large number of start-ups and patents), learning and collaborative ecosystems (organizing clusters that generate research and development and associated with universities), and venture capital hotbeds (producing high levels of investments to give birth to businesses). The study identified the medical sector research and the presence of ASU as key contributors to the distinction.[27] WeWork, a national co-working office space company, decided to open a location in downtown because, according to a spokesperson, "It is a vibrant district for business and entertainment, and a magnet for creative industries."[28] Reflecting on the partnership between the city and ASU to create the ASU Downtown campus, former Mayor Williams noted, "We are very proud of the partnership. We are now known for innovation and for attracting the high-tech companies. It's paying off for all of us."[29]

In less than 15 years, more than $5.5 billion has been invested in the downtown area. However, this rapid growth, which has been viewed by many as a sign of progress, also brought considerable social pressures. Young professionals, enticed by urban amenities and a willingness to relocate, took advantage of inexpensive housing and services in once isolated and largely poor communities. These urban pioneers contributed greatly to creating successive waves of affluent residents moving into the neighborhoods. The subsequent rise of housing prices placed significant stress on existing residents for whom escalating rents and cost of living expenses proved detrimental to their ability to maintain their residence in the area. The outcome has been rapidly growing gentrification and displacement, quickly transitioning what were once marginalized communities into areas considered appealing to high-income professionals. A 2015 national report on gentrification that examined trends in 50 cities concluded that 20 census tracts gentrified in Phoenix since 2000. All of these geographic areas were located in or around downtown.[30] Similarly, a 2019 study of zip codes in America's 100 largest cities ranked Encanto Village as the seventh fastest-gentrifying neighborhood in the United States. The analysis considered changes in a number of areas including median household income, median home price variation, share of residents over 25 with a bachelor's degree or higher, and share of residents over 25 with a master's degree or higher.[31] Encanto Village is located just a mile and a half from the central business district.

The transformation of the Phoenix urban core has been nothing short of extraordinary. Construction is continuing at a dizzying pace with new buildings and large-scale renovations. New businesses establish themselves at record numbers, helping to formulate a new economy while attracting employees across the valley and outside the state. The residential population is exploding as more people call the area home. It is a thriving place, continuously pushing existing physical boundaries to form new neighborhoods. A new light rail system and infrastructural development such as sporting facilities and hotels have played an important role in the area's current standing. However, a vital ingredient to these changes has been the establishment of the ASU Downtown campus. It is this restructured environment which serves as the foundation for the launch of PHX Core, the city's innovation district.

The Warehouse District and PHX Core

Just a few blocks south of the downtown area, the Warehouse District has proved critical in the development of Phoenix. The district has been intimately connected to the city's commercial history. Over the years, the presence of the nearby Union Pacific Railroad helped drive the construction of warehouses in the downtown neighborhoods. By the early 1900s, a robust economy emerged, organized around the assembly and storage of various goods. These were distributed via railroads to the southwest and across the country. Rail spurs cut through the streets and many of the brick-and-concrete, low-rise buildings featured loading docks to aid the transportation process. A growing cluster of Chinese immigrants working on the railroads eventually formed a Chinatown that included a number of successful small businesses.[32]

As the adjacent downtown area diminished in importance with decentralization, an overall decline became apparent. However, in the 1990s and 2000s, artists discovered that the large empty spaces in the Warehouse District not only offered a gritty environment, which typically entices creative workers, but also proved conducive to showcasing artwork. This was especially evident in the presentation of exhibits that required ample space to display sizable pieces of paintings and sculptures. An example of this is the Bentley Gallery, which opened in 2004 in a 22,000-square-foot space, once a linen laundry facility. More recently, the local scene has flourished, with artists and young entrepreneurs moving into the area. From 2013 to 2018, the 36 area warehouses, most of which have been declared historical landmarks, have attracted 110 businesses to the district. These include art galleries, advertising and finance companies, architectural and design firms, and event planning and management services offering neighborhood venues for various-sized gatherings. Restaurants, bars, clubs, and coffee shops started to mushroom in this fourteen-by-six-block community.[33]

ASU has also contributed to the development of the Warehouse District. In 2014, ASU's School of Art started the renovation of a 40,000-square-foot facility that was once a cotton factory, transforming the space to house galleries and more than 60 studios for students pursuing the Master of Fine Arts program. The renovated ASU Grant Street Studios is a vibrant place, with artists engaging in various creative endeavors including painting, fiber art, photography, sculpture, drawing, and ceramics. The university involvement was welcomed by the city, given that the adaptive reuse approach it employed maintained the unique architectural character of the area while further aiding the revitalization of downtown, strengthening the art scene.[34] More recently, ASU's School of Art utilized its facilities at the Warehouse District to embrace community outreach. This strategy meant that the ASU galleries had to expand their operation hours while participating in the downtown Phoenix First and Third Fridays. Programming includes a wide variety of entertainment options, walking tours, art galleries, street performers, exhibits, and musical bands. The foot traffic improved the liveliness of the district, an outcome that complements the ASU vision of a uniquely different institution of higher education. The incoming director of the School of Art noted that community engagement should be pursued continuously: "Part of my job is going to be to create more impact around the concept of the 'New American University' which has to do largely with access for everybody and serving the public who are integral to Arizona."[35]

As he touted the rapid growth of downtown Phoenix and the transformation in the nearby Warehouse District, Mayor Greg Staton announced in 2016 plans for the creation of PHX Core, an innovation district that would geographically overlap portions of these two areas. The district would bring together business start-ups, incubators, accelerators, investors, university researchers, and entrepreneurs to collaborate across industries, building synergies while taking advantage of the unique pool of talents and resources. PHX Core is expected to drive the city's competitiveness, anchored by the Phoenix Biomedical Campus, ASU Downtown campus, and Galvanize. Christine Mackay, director of the Phoenix Community and Economic Development, declared, "Now, with a designated Innovation District and a solid strategic plan, the future of the PHX Core is solid, providing a place where our innovative and creative companies can form, thrive and succeed by working together."[36]

Downtown Phoenix looking south west. Chase Field and Talking Stick Resort Arena are visible to the left of the image. The Warehouse District is located to the south (left). Courtesy of user Tim Roberts Photography, Shutterstock Images.

The national media was drawn into covering the juxtaposition between old warehouses and the technology renaissance in PHX Core. As a writer for *USA Today* commented, "The rise of the warehouse district, like the mythological phoenix, began to take shape . . . Within the two square miles that house Phoenix's Warehouse District, there's ample evidence amid dozens of once-abandoned structures: 60 tech start-ups work out of a 55,000-square-foot technology-education campus run by Galvanize; a thriving electronic medical record company, WebPT, has morphed into a multimillion-dollar business employing hundreds; a reconverted warehouse, opened in 1926, is the home of advertising agency R&R Partners."[37] The WebPT facility was once a sausage factory. Galvanize operates in what once was a produce warehouse. Within months of its opening in 2017, the 55,000-square-foot facility attracted 48 companies whose employers utilize the available co-working spaces and available amenities.[38] In 2019, Silicon Valley giant Google located its cloud platform operations at Galvanize.[39]

The early success of PHX Core has caused concerns. These have primarily centered on the threat of accelerating gentrification and displacement. With many vacant lots in need of development, and existing buildings in need of updating, businesses and residents are anxious that incoming upscale housing construction will continue to push the current population out of the district. An additional source of anxiety relates to how the design of new buildings will impact the architectural character of the district.[40] Artists have been at the forefront of expressing their dissatisfaction with gentrification. Such direction will not only push them out, it will also slowly eliminate the impressive murals that many painters have painstakingly produced over the years and that currently adorn the area. In fact, Phoenix has a long tradition of muralists fabricating and showcasing various styles of street art.[41] Beyond the transformative impact that ASU has had on downtown Phoenix, the university has also aggressively pursued a massive development for downtown Tempe, as well as a new digital innovation initiative in downtown Mesa.

The Novus Innovation Corridor and the Mesa Innovation District

In early 2017, a public-private partnership between ASU, the City of Tempe, and Catellus Development Corporation, which would be the genesis of the Novus Innovation Corridor along Tempe Town Lake, was announced. Catellus is one of the largest landowners and developers in California, with a very active real estate portfolio. It focuses on transforming large plots that typically tend to be vacated manufacturing sites and closed military bases. When completed, the multiphase, multiyear project on 350 acres of university-owned land will create a mixed-use urban neighborhood that will include 10 million square feet of office, retail, and hotel space, in addition to various types of housing. Catellus estimates that it will bring 5,000 residents to the area.

Located adjacent to the university campus, Sun Devil Stadium, and the Wells Fargo Arena, the project will also benefit from nearby recreational opportunities. The local media has described its scope as "colossal." The mayor of Tempe welcomed the development by noting, "The City of Tempe is the perfect setting for the Novus Innovation Corridor and we are excited to see its potential within our borders."[42] Michael Crow described the initiative as groundbreaking regarding its long-term implications and impact, arguing that the "innovation corridor will be a constantly evolving illustration of how local and global enterprises can partner to put innovative research and technology into practice in the greater community."[43] The notion of innovation was also embraced by Catellus, recognizing the university as a leader in this area. A company executive commented that the project will bring the "type of innovation that ASU is known for."[44] The land lease agreement to private businesses will generate considerable revenue, estimated at $500 million over the next two decades for the university. These resources will be invested in ASU's athletics programs.

The Novus Innovation Corridor broke ground in the summer of 2017, and construction continues to progress as scheduled. The project has been celebrated for creating jobs and for having an economic impact that will drive future growth. However, this initiative has also added considerable luxury and market-rate housing to an already tight residential market, putting additional pressure on the availability of affordable housing options. A survey of residents by the Tempe Community Council in 2017 identified affordable housing as the greatest concern, an issue that has also been at the forefront of a recent mayoral election. For many working to strengthen the affordable housing options in Tempe, the Novus Innovation Corridor will exacerbate the existing challenges.[45]

In 2018, following an unsuccessful attempt to add an ASU campus in the downtown of nearby Mesa, the Mesa City Council approved a different plan. Specifically, to create an ASU digital technology hub which would bring academic programs in experimental design, media arts, gaming, film production, and entrepreneurial development in digital media. The facility, expected to be operational in 2021, will also house the ASU Creative Futures Laboratory. From a city council perspective, this initiative complements an ongoing effort to revitalize the downtown by forming an innovation district, connecting new and existing companies with start-ups and business incubators. City leaders argued in support of the project, since the ensuing economic growth will produce considerable local revenues that can be invested in public safety. The mayor of Mesa claimed that the university can play a significant role given that "ASU is known for innovation, and we were looking for an anchor for a new innovation district in downtown Mesa. ASU will bring a new program to Mesa, and create a lot of buzz."[46]

Conclusion

The successful ascent of Arizona State University through practices associated with the New American University concept led to the creation of ASU Downtown. The new campus at the core of the city brought energy and a sense of renewed purpose to the ailing urban center. This, in turn, helped propel the revitalization of the area. As a member of the Greater Phoenix Economic Council once asserted, "It was not until ASU came to downtown Phoenix that the place came alive. Now you see what happens as a result: You have these organic collisions between education and business, and it's all now feeding on itself."[47] The innovation district of PHX Core, while still under development, became possible in the adjacent Warehouse District. There are a number of insights that can be drawn from the case of ASU and its upward trajectory in Phoenix.

Leadership and the pursuit of a strategic institutional agenda is essential. While often criticized for embracing a business model, President Crow has managed, in a transformative manner, to position ASU as a major research, up-and-coming metropolitan university. Innovation and culture change have dominated Crow's outlook in revamping the existing, more traditional higher education orientation. This entrepreneurial outlook informed a continuous rethinking of current practices within a highly interconnected and diverse set of conditions and demands. Interestingly, the language of organizational change not only became central to the university's outlook but also penetrated the city's psyche. An Arizona mayor recently exclaimed, "Thankfully, we have the most innovative university in the world."[48]

Public-private partnerships dictated the operational orientation and strategy through which ASU has been redefined. In this regard, the university followed a path that would typically be associated with the actions of major business enterprises and real estate firms. And while the business of real estate is increasingly common in higher education, the case of ASU reveals its use and implementation at levels rarely seen as possible. ASU rationalizes these engagements as forced responses to consistent reductions, cuts, and funding limitations deriving from the Arizona state legislature. Thus, in order for ASU to meet its educational goals, it must operate differently. Growth is essential. For example, the partnership leading to the Novus Innovation Corridor in Tempe allows the university to generate revenue from the land to pay for investments in facilities for its intercollegiate athletics. Out-of-state enrollment is another revenue generating strategy which continues to flourish. Since Crow's arrival to ASU in 2002, more than 100 new buildings and other real estate projects have materialized.[49]

The combination of public-private partnerships, real estate pursuits, and innovation have shifted the university into a massive force of metropolitan change and regional economic development. ASU operates in a hyper enterprising manner, leasing land and seeking taxpayer support to fund expansions. As a major element of the city's growth machine, the institutional alignment and contributions to an emerging new economy that is oriented around technology, bioscience research, and advanced business services is truly remarkable. It is within this framework of a renewed energy that the City of Phoenix decided to launch PHX Core.

As an innovation district, with ASU playing a key role, PHX Core is expected to not only energize the city's new economy but also alter the urban environment by redeveloping the Warehouse District and its surrounding neighborhoods. However, the spatial restructuring will have a significant community impact and cause continuous gentrification, displacing existing residents while enticing new construction. Without a coordinated affordable housing strategy in place, market rates will control rental and ownership costs. For example, the area's designation as an Opportunity Zone attracted developers to the area because of the unique opportunities to generate profit. For example, ABI Multifamily, a multifamily brokerage and advisory services firm, launched the construction of ALTA Warehouse, a planned luxury development in the district. As the developer recently noted, "The Warehouse District has become a central hub for technology and innovation companies in the Phoenix area, and one of the major drivers in Downtown's emergence as a top draw . . . by bringing ALTA Warehouse into the mix . . . enhancing the depth of the region's attractiveness and contributing to its evolution toward a 24-hour area."[50]

PHX Core reveals the significant impact that higher education can have as a catalyst of urban revitalization, economic development, and as driver of technological innovation and change. It is likely that the City of Phoenix will continue to recast itself within a rapidly unfolding economic environment, and ASU will play a significant role in its future development. Charismatic leadership and a can-do attitude, even in the midst of detractors and criticism, means that the university has the capacity to chart a new direction and in the process advocate for the formulation of a new higher education model. However, its applicability may be limited. For example, ASU is located within a large urban center, and the city and state are booming given the persistent population growth. While agency has played a key role, structurally, the fortunes of the metropolitan area are a perfect match with the fortunes of ASU, as charted by Crow. These conditions are difficult to replicate elsewhere, raising fundamental questions about the potential applicability of the New American University.

But the case of ASU and PHX Core exposes some drawbacks, typically present when connecting higher education to urban economic development. Reshaping the urban environment produces winners and losers. Residents will be left behind, struggling to make ends meet since they will be unable to compete. In the process, they will be displaced and will be pushed out in search of new environments. In the end, conditions of urban inequality will be regenerated by the same institutional force, a university, that has made inclusiveness a core of its operational purpose and mantra.

Furthering the Local Innovation Ecosystem in Pensacola and Chattanooga

Pensacola, Florida, and Chattanooga, Tennessee, are midsized cities, each with a population of about half a million residents. Both are expected to grow due to their aggressive pursuits of economic opportunities around their main industries: aerospace, defense, and tourism in Pensacola, and transportation and tourism in Chattanooga. This chapter focuses on the role that the University of West Florida (UWF) and the University of Tennessee at Chattanooga (UTC) play in developing innovation ecosystems. The universities have not created innovation districts, though one exists in Chattanooga formed by the local government. However, both institutions recognize the value of engaging in this area and desire to expand their influence.

In downtown Pensacola, Co:Lab, a joint effort by the Greater Pensacola Chamber of Commerce and Pensacola State College, provides support to high-growth companies by offering entrepreneurs mentoring, as well as low-cost office and business services. Pensacola Socialdesk, an event and co-working space in the Midtown area, and Innovation Coast, a nonprofit entity, aim to cultivate the area's technology community by crafting collaborations and strengthening programming for startups. With limited local government involvement, UWF is taking the lead, coordinating existing undertakings via the newly established Division of Research and Strategic Innovation. The UWF Innovation Campus Network in downtown Pensacola draws from university partnerships with community organizations and industry. Framed around interdisciplinary knowledge clusters, it endeavors to position key academic and research initiatives, such as the Innovation Institute, the Center for Cybersecurity, and the Institute for Human and Machine Cognition, in the fabric of the city. The UWF vision is to drive entrepreneurship, expand economic opportunities, and create a tech hub to meet the needs of Northwest Florida.

In 2015, the City of Chattanooga, under the guidance of a strong mayor and city council, introduced a 140-acre downtown innovation district, retrofitting the former Tennessee Valley Authority office building following the downsizing of the utility company. Three entities are housed in the renovated 10-story Edney Innovation Center, which serves as the main entrepreneurial hub. These include Co:Lab, a highly successful business accelerator; the Enterprise Center, a nonprofit formed to support innovation and the digital economy; and Society of Work, a membership-based, shared office space group. In 2010, the installation of a fiber optic network (10 gigabit-per-second internet link to every residence and business) by EPB, the city's municipal utility company, brought instant recognition and aided the success of the Chattanooga Innovation District. In 2017, a collaborative planning process took place to transition the district to the next level. At that time, UTC, whose campus abuts the district boundaries, emerged as a significant player in its future direction. Redevelopment of existing buildings with academic, retail, and commercial purposes will formally connect the university to the district. UTC also contributes to the MetroLab Network, a city-university collaboration to solve community issues through academic research. The university plans to engage with the innovation district by promoting activities in entrepreneurship and smart city design to generate a thriving technology sector in an increasingly vibrant urban setting.

Both universities play different roles in the future advancement of the cities they call home. In fact, nurturing innovation is perceived by government groups, nonprofit organizations, and business entities to be a critical component and a prerequisite to economic growth. These two higher education institutions are very different from the others examined in this book, since they lack vast resources and are located in smaller urban settings. However, they equally endeavor to develop an environment that will enrich their core mission.

Downtown Revitalization and the University-City Connection in Pensacola, Florida

Located in the Florida Panhandle, Pensacola has an extensive history dating back to the mid-1500s. As the site of the first Spanish settlement in the United States, the city's location on Pensacola Bay offered many opportunities. The destination of multiple expeditions, the Spanish, British, and French competed to gain access and maintain control of Pensacola, since its status as a major seaport in the Gulf Coast meant profitable trade and commerce. The United States gained control of Florida in 1821, and with it, Pensacola emerged as a major political and economic center in the western portion of the state.

Near the Alabama border, Pensacola is part of Escambia County, the oldest county in Florida, with tourism and military as its main economic drivers. Since 1914, the presence of the Naval Air Station Pensacola has played a key role in the development of the city. A major training complex for those supporting the United States Navy air operations, the station also ensures extensive civilian employment opportunities. Because of its location on the Gulf of Mexico and its significant history, tourism has flourished. Annual festivals and various other recreational activities provide a significant economic boost. In 2016, visitors accounted for almost $800 million, and that figure is expected to surpass the $1 trillion mark by 2023.[1] Over the decades, the city population experienced a slight decline to about 50,000 residents. However, the Pensacola metropolitan area grew rapidly, nearing 500,000 residents.

The region is served by two institutions of higher education. In 1948, Pensacola Junior College opened, which is part of the Florida College

System. In 2010, a statewide initiative to pursue college completion elevated two-year colleges, enabling them to deliver four-year degrees. At that time, the college was renamed Pensacola State College. Currently more than 30,000 students take classes. The University of West Florida was founded by the state legislature in 1962. UWF is one of 12 State University System of Florida institutions of higher education. As a regional, comprehensive university, UWF serves a little over 13,000 students. Its main campus is located on 1,600 acres, about 10 miles from downtown. The university also operates a joint campus with Northwest Florida State College in Fort Walton Beach, about a one-hour drive to the east. This partnership campus focuses on delivering 2 + 2 programs primarily to adult learners. Finally, UWF is present in the city's historic downtown. The UWF Historic Trust manages the university's nine-acre city center campus, which includes 32 properties. Two graduate student residence halls are established downtown, along with a number of museums. Twenty-seven buildings are listed on the National Register of Historic Places.[2]

The story of Pensacola is typical to that of other cities across the United States. The rise of postwar decentralization, manufacturing decline, and the forces of globalization shifted business and residential development to the outskirts, promoting suburban development. The success of new shopping malls placed tremendous pressure on downtown stores, eventually causing closures, leaving behind abandoned buildings and empty lots. For many years, new residential construction and home renovations were nonexistent. These conditions furthered housing decay, dislocation, crime, and other social challenges. However, during the last 15 years, the downtown area has experienced a major rebirth. Much of that change is primarily contributed by prominent citizens and the business community which, along with local government, drove this revitalization.[3] In Pensacola, unlike other cities, the business community played a key role by repositioning the area as a thriving center. Some of the key projects in this makeover included the redevelopment of Palafox Street and the construction of a new waterfront stadium.

Palafox Street is a main street in downtown dating back to 1812. Once the commercial heart of the city, its function and popularity declined with the rise of suburban retailers. The availability and ease of parking access in the various malls that developed in the 1970s and 1980s significantly impacted pedestrian traffic, further diminishing its primacy. Cracked pavements and extensive vacancies were commonplace. One of the first key steps in the revitalization of Palafox Street was the establishment of the Pensacola Community Redevelopment Agency (PCRA). The agency was charged with the preservation of the historic thoroughfare that connects the Pensacola Historic District and the North Hill Historic District. Over the years, the PCRA completed a number of improvements, including converting the street from a one-way to a two-way, as well as improving the landscaping and its sidewalks. Additionally, planting trees, supporting the restoration of historic buildings, and encouraging pedestrian traffic by creating outdoor seating areas in what were once empty lots proved transformative. A number of events and celebrations are scheduled along Palafox Street and are managed by the Downtown Improvement Board. These include the New Year's Eve Pelican Drop and an Annual Mardi Gras Parade, which bring thousands in attendance every year. Business investments followed, resulting in new restaurants, coffee shops, bars, boutiques, specialty shops, and food courts. Today, Palafox Street is a lively entertainment district with adjacent residential additions facilitating its continued revival.[4]

The other major contributor to the city center was the development of a stadium, constructed along Pensacola Bay on neglected land near the downtown and the Seville Historic District. The 5,000-seat sports facility hosts the Pensacola Blue Wahoos, a minor league baseball team. Beyond baseball, the stadium also provides year-round activities to residents and visitors. These include concerts, soccer matches, theater performances, indoor and outdoor gatherings, and a plethora of community events. During the fall, it serves as home to the UWF college football games. The stadium, along with an amphitheater and a public park, comprise a complex that is collectively referenced as the Community Maritime Park project.[5] A small group of leaders spearheaded the development of the $70 million, 32-acre Community Maritime Park. The group included John Cavanaugh, president of the University of West Florida from 2002 to 2008. Cavanaugh was a proponent of the initiative, since it complemented his vision to expand the presence of UWF in downtown Pensacola. During Cavanaugh's tenure, UWF offered graduate classes in historic preservation at the Historic Pensacola Village, a cluster of homes comprising the Pensacola National Historic District. In recent years, UWF has successfully fundraised to maintain the programming of the local museums which, along with the Colonial Archeological Trail, are part of the district. He also advocated for expanding the activities of the Archeology Institute and the Maritime Museum.[6] Cavanaugh reinforced the importance of the downtown location for academic and research university units. Morris Marx, who served as UWF president from 1988 to 2002, once commented, "Given President Cavanaugh's emphasis on downtown, I am particularly pleased that we were able to locate the Institute for Human and Machine Cognition (IHMC) in the heart of Pensacola."[7]

The arrival of the next UWF president, Judy Bense (2008–2016), saw the introduction of sold-out football games played in the stadium on Pensacola Bay. Bense, too, focused her efforts on expanding the university's presence in Pensacola's urban core. New downtown locations were unveiled for the Florida Small Business Development Center at UWF, the UWF Haas Center, and the UWF Innovation Institute.[8] One area that received considerable attention during the Bense period was the historic part of the city. A new interpretive master plan by the UWF Historic Trust supported recreational and educational outreach, enhancing the visitor experience by promoting cultural heritage tourism, while also protecting and preserving the archeological zone.

In Search of a Direction: Driving Innovation in Pensacola

Given the smaller size of the metropolitan area, it is apparent that the innovation ecosystem in Pensacola is advancing at a slower pace. The State of Florida, local nonprofit organizations, the business community, and the University of West Florida have contributed in distinct ways to promoting technology and innovation. However, the arrival of Martha Saunders as president of UWF in 2017 brought considerable energy and a renewed emphasis on jump-starting existing initiatives while pursuing new pathways. From the start, Saunders articulated the need to expand and strengthen the intellectual infrastructure of the institution by focusing on the creation of knowledge clusters. It is expected that as these clusters mature, their economic outcomes will have a significant positive impact on the region and the local community. Partnerships and innovation would play a central role in this direction. Saunders articulated her ambitious outlook by stating, "I'm particularly interested in developing an intellectual infrastructure—hubs—for the support of manufacturing, innovation and commercialization . . . I expect to focus on partnerships, innovation and programming on which we can build a national and global reputation."[9]

One of the first steps to complement this vision was the launching in 2018 of the Innovation Campus Network. Part of the Division of Research and Strategic Innovation, a newly created UWF unit was charged with formulating a culture of innovation. The Innovation Campus Network is a presidential directive which attempts to connect the work of the university to regional economic development. Specifically, the goal is to address various industry challenges, a direction that is expected to improve competitiveness and subsequently fuel economic growth. Embracing an urban focus will be critical to success. According to Saunders, "The innovative knowledge clusters will have the energy of a start-up in a collegiate environment with accelerated learning and real-world challenges. Mile zero of the UWF Innovation Network will be developed in downtown Pensacola because students will be able to access many of the features in Northwest Florida that make it a place like no other. Pensacola's downtown area will serve as a living laboratory. The university and its myriad assets will be woven into the very fabric of the city."[10]

The first step in advancing the Innovation Network framework was the introduction of the Sear3D Additive Manufacturing Laboratory.

Housed in downtown Pensacola, the Lab provides 3D printing services to the community. A number of parallel initiatives followed, including the creation of the Innovation Institute. The Innovation Institute is strategically located on the west side of downtown in the historic Belmont-DeVilliers neighborhood. Operating as an educational incubator, it works closely with various entities to improve organizational performance while also facilitating strategic planning and retreats. Firmly grounded around an outcomes-based orientation, the institute staff partners with companies to advance their goals by employing innovative ideas to solve various challenges. A main activity at the Innovation Institute is offering design thinking workshops. This type of programming brings together individuals to engage in a think tank–like environment and benefit from the tools and available methods to solve challenges through collaboration. Recently, the work of the Innovation Institute helped create the University of West Florida Center for Cybersecurity.

Cybersecurity has emerged as a key UWF knowledge cluster. The university earned the National Security Agency's designation as the

Downtown Pensacola. The multi-use Blue Wahoos Stadium was designed to be used year-round for athletics and community events. The facility is home to the University of West Florida Argonauts football games, bringing thousands to downtown Pensacola. Courtesy of user Bown Media, Shutterstock Images.

National Center of Academic Excellence Regional Recourse Center for the Southeast Region. In 2019, the center moved its operations to downtown Pensacola. At the grand opening, President Saunders exclaimed, "Innovation defines how the UWF Center for Cybersecurity operates."[11] The UWF Haas Center for Business Research and Economic Development, which also relocated in downtown Pensacola, delivers data services, survey research, and industry and market analysis. In 2019, the university expanded the outreach of the Haas Center by merging it with the Office of Workforce and Industrial Innovation. This transition is expected to accelerate technology adoption and business growth. Another significant effort on the part of UWF in technology and innovation is the university's partnership with the Institute for Human and Machine Cognition, a not-for-profit research entity of the Florida University System. The scientists at the institute, along with faculty from the UWF Hal Marcus College of Science and Engineering, launched a new doctorate program in intelligent systems and robotics, the only such program in Florida. This initiative started in the fall of 2019, and closely aligns with the UWF focus on economic development and technology enterprise.[12]

All of these efforts are targeted at furthering innovation, and in the process complement projects already underway in Pensacola. For example, founded in 2017, the Invictus Knowledge Institute is a nonprofit start-up that offers information technology training to economically disadvantaged residents. The organization works with local software and cybersecurity companies to provide hands-on experiences to their clients.[13] Innovation Coast, a nonprofit consortium of area businesses, aims to encourage already well-established or rapidly growing technology companies in the northwest region of the state. A central part of its mission is the creation of an environment which helps establish and cultivate a community of technology professionals. Innovation Coast delivers support to entrepreneurial start-ups and recognizes and showcases successful technology initiatives through a popular awards program. Additionally, they oversee a well-received business plan and capital appreciation competition that affords assistance to the winning companies in the form of grants and technical services. Many other resources have been added in recent years, including making contacts with angel investors and helping to attract venture capital funds. The Innovation Coast board of directors is composed of representatives from both nonprofit and for-profit sectors. The University of West Florida has played a key role in the advancement of the organization by connecting its members to the academy. A faculty member recently served as its executive director, and the board of directors typically includes two UWF representatives.

This type of interaction between UWF and industry and community partners is evident in other areas. For example, the university's Center for Entrepreneurship supports economic innovation and brings a business leader on campus to serve as the "Entrepreneur in Residence." The Florida Small Business Development Center at UWF is an outreach effort providing business assistance to foster economic growth and stability. Furthermore, UWF supports the innovation ecosystem in Pensacola through initiatives focusing on managing start-ups. Co:Lab, a business incubator and growth accelerator also located in downtown, assists emerging entrepreneurs and their start-ups in their quest to become scalable. A university representative serves on the policy board of Co:Lab. Similarly, Pensacola Socialdesk is a co-working and event space that supports local entrepreneurs.

Pensacola's historic downtown and surrounding neighborhoods have been undergoing an urban revitalization. UWF has primarily operated in a suburban setting since its founding in the early 1960s. However, during the last few years, the institution has identified a new direction by relocating research units to downtown and by engaging in considerable activity that has influenced the redevelopment of the city's core. Targeted programming, such as the Experience UWF Downtown Lecture Series, brings scholars together to discuss the importance of the liberal arts and its meaningful and relevant contributions to social life. These efforts have intensified since the arrival of Martha Saunders, who as the sixth president of the university, injected a renewed focus and cultivated private-public partnerships, including technology, innovation, and related entrepreneurial endeavors. In the process, UWF has embraced a coordinating role, connecting and fostering various initiatives. In that regard, higher education leadership is strengthening the existing ecosystem while expanding Pensacola's economic standing.

Downtown Revival and the Urban University in Chattanooga, Tennessee

Following a population decline during the 1980s, the city of Chattanooga, located in the southeastern part of Tennessee, experienced significant growth from 152,000 residents in 1990 to surpassing 180,000 residents in 2018. The metropolitan area also grew from 476,000 in 2000 to about 530,000 in 2010.[14] The city has historically benefited from its location as a center of transportation with connecting highways to Nashville, Tennessee, in the northwest (Interstate 24); Atlanta, Georgia, in the southeast (Interstate 75); Knoxville, Tennessee, in the northeast (Interstate 75); and Birmingham, Alabama, in the southwest (Interstate 59). The rapidly evolving metro area of Huntsville, Alabama, to the southwest, is about 100 miles away, with a population nearing 450,000 residents. Additionally, an extensive network of railroads and the presence of the Tennessee River running through the city positioned Chattanooga as a major hub in the southeast region of the country.

Booming factories kept its industrial economy strong. More than 388 manufacturers operated in Chattanooga in the 1930s, focusing on the production of furniture and various equipment from aluminum to cast-iron metals. The economic activity was so robust that the city became known as the "Dynamo of Dixie."[15] A continuously expanding downtown transformed the community into an attractive place to do business and raise a family.

The manufacturing decline that followed after World War II impacted this midsized city, causing the once vibrant urban center to struggle. Like Pensacola, the residential population shift to the suburbs left behind decay, abandoned factories, and empty storefronts, with persistent disinvestment continuing into the 1970s and 1980s. In addition to these conditions resulting from deindustrialization, pollution became a major concern. Surrounded by mountains, the density of factories produced high concentrations of air contamination. In 1969, the federal government identified Chattanooga as having the dirtiest air quality in the country. Smog was considerable, causing poor visibility. In fact, residents had to drive with their car lights on during the day to be able to safely negotiate traffic conditions. In a 1971 national broadcast, Walter Cronkite referenced Chattanooga as the dirtiest city in America. Public infrastructure was crumbling and the tax base was rapidly weakening.[16] The poor environmental conditions also impacted the city's population. In 1940, Chattanooga ranked as the 66th largest city in the United States. However, by 1990, the city's ranking in the same category dropped to 117th. Successive annexation efforts did not help reverse this trend, resulting in a downtown that resembled the manufacturing cities of the upper Midwest, hit hard by economic restructuring.

Jolted by the abhorrent conditions that brought negative national attention to this once-prominent urban center, local leaders declared that something had to be done. Following discussions, the path to Chattanooga's revitalization began in the 1980s with a decision by elected officials, the business community, and local philanthropists to focus on connecting the city to its key asset, the Tennessee River. The conceptual plan included the creation of amenities which, once fully completed, would bring considerable benefits. A quality recreational infrastructure would entice to the area existing residents and could help transform the city into a regional tourist center. A booming visitor economy would help recast a new urban image, subsequently drawing business investment and even new residents. Over the last 30 years, Chattanooga experienced a robust addition of facilities, including the construction of Miller Park, Riverpark, the Tennessee Aquarium, the Creative Discovery Museum, Coolidge Park, Bellsouth Baseball Stadium, and the 21st Century Waterfront, among others. Furthermore, the once-slated-for-demolition Walnut Street Bridge was repurposed into a pedestrian connector. This asset successfully expanded the downtown's reach into new neighborhoods. More than $120 million in improvements have been invested in core infrastructure, with half of that amount deriving from philanthropic contributions. The remaining half has originated from taxes on hotels and motels as well as from the sale of publicly owned properties.[17]

All of these accomplishments helped benefit the revitalization of downtown Chattanooga. Today, thousands of visitors take advantage of new and existing attractions and enjoy a plethora of year-round activities. River City Company is charged with coordinating the city's cultural policy. With a budget of more than $3 million, this private, nonprofit organization works closely with various stakeholders such as the business community, the local government, philanthropists, and community representatives to promote the continued growth of downtown as an epicenter of culture and entertainment. An array of activities such as festivals, concerts, theater productions, symphony and opera performances, wine tastings, fireworks, art exhibits, and farmers markets create a vibrant environment. These amenities also expanded the area's residential options by fueling widespread renovations and construction of additional housing developments, primarily in the form of new apartments and condos. It is estimated that since 2015, Chattanooga's downtown has been the recipient of more than $1.2 billion in private investment.[18] The five main districts in the enlarged core of Chattanooga include Riverfront, Bluff View, City Center, MLK/University, Northshore, and Southside.

On the higher education front, the city is served by two public institutions, the University of Tennessee at Chattanooga and Chattanooga State Community College. In the latter part of the 1800s, the Methodist Episcopal Church searched for a location to establish a university in the South. Chattanooga University was created in 1886 as a private institution. A merger with Grant Memorial University in 1889, another religious-affiliated college, resulted in renaming the school in 1907 as the University of Chattanooga. In 1969, a merger with a two-year college produced the consolidated University of Chattanooga, which became part of the University of Tennessee System. In its current form, it's known as the

University of Tennessee at Chattanooga (UTC). The University of Tennessee System now includes campuses in Knoxville, Chattanooga, and Martin.[19] Enrollment at UTC steadily grew from about 2,300 students right before the transition to the UTC System in 1968 to 9,000 in 2001. During that early period, it was primarily commuters and first-generation students from the surrounding region that attended UTC. Today, with a strong focus on undergraduate teaching, it serves close to 12,000 students.

Located on 425 acres adjacent to the city's downtown, UTC endeavors to become a notable metropolitan university. Achieving that status, though, would require growing the overall enrollment, especially at the graduate level, where it has remained relatively unchanged at approximately 1,400 students. UTC is currently working on achieving an enrollment of 15,000 students in the next few years. The institution remained rather isolated and played a limited role in the resurgence of Chattanooga, except in the early 2000s, when the university and city leaders successfully attracted a center of computational engineering from Mississippi State University, which was established as the SimCenter at UTC. The purpose of the center, funded by the Tennessee Higher Education Commission, was not only to conduct high-caliber research, but also to contribute to the revitalization of the downtown. In 2017, the SimCenter was expanded to have a broader, campus-wide mission which most recently included offering a PhD and a master's degree in computational engineering.

Lately, UTC embarked on a strategy to better link with the city center and to contribute to its revival. In 2014, the university introduced an extended bus route connecting the campus to downtown. According to Michelle Morales, associate director of Auxiliary Services at the university, "We are interested in better connecting downtown to the campus community."[20] In response to a growing demand for on-campus housing in 2018, UTC completed a $70 million dormitory facility with 600 beds on Vine Street. The development included additional parking and much-needed retail student services. More importantly, though, the building is part of the West Campus Project and provides an opportunity to bring UTC closer to the urban core. In 2015, at the groundbreaking ceremony,

Aerial View of Downtown Chattanooga. New residential development and Coolidge Park are located to the left of the Market Street Bridge. The Tennessee Aquarium and the AT&T Field, home of the Chattanooga Lookouts, a minor league baseball team of the double-A Southern League, are visible to the right of the Market Street Bridge. Courtesy of user Kevin Ruck, Shutterstock Images.

Chancellor Angle noted, "[We're] looking at Vine Street as a major connection, a physical connection, that we have with our community."[21]

The university has also benefited from the nearby MLK/University District, which is undergoing a major redevelopment along the Martin Luther King Boulevard. In 1981, East Ninth Street was renamed after the civil rights leader. With a long history as the cultural center of the African American community in Chattanooga, the businesses along the thoroughfare suffered during the industrial decline and many closed. In 2012, the boulevard started to undergo a revitalization as office space, apartments, shops, a hotel, breweries, and restaurants moved to the area. Popular jazz performances in various music venues create a lively atmosphere, luring students from the UTC campus, situated just a few blocks away. However, one of the greatest opportunities for UTC to achieve its long-term goals rests with the Chattanooga Innovation District, one of the most ambitious undertakings in the history of the city.

The Chattanooga Innovation District

The Chattanooga Innovation District is the first of its kind to be established in a medium-sized American city. In 2015, Mayor Andy Berke announced the 140-acre district, anchored by the Edney Building, a 90,000-square-foot redevelopment. At its inception in the central city, the district included 12 companies within its physical boundaries. Viewed as an impetus for economic growth, it was argued that it would support the development of technology by assisting start-ups and firms at various stages pursuing innovative business solutions to advance and succeed. According to Mayor Berke, "Chattanooga's Innovation District will bring jobs, talent, and capital to our city. Coupled with the fastest Internet in the Western Hemisphere, our Innovation District will strengthen our place as leaders in the 21st century economy."[22] Berke also asserted that the district is the "healthy heart of a dynamic city . . . You will see over the next few years that the heart of our city beats stronger than ever. It's vibrant. It's energetic. It's powerful. It's propelling everything that happens in our city."[23] Bruce Katz, founding director of the Brookings Metropolitan Policy Program, recognized the initiative by noting, "Chattanooga is taking impressive steps toward catalyzing this new form of development, building on its distinctive position as America's Gig City."[24] The *New York Times*, PBS, the *Washington Post*, *Fortune*, and many other national media outlets covered Chattanooga's technological focus and transformation as a model of economic development. Even President Barack Obama referenced it as a success story in his 2015 State of the Union Address, pointing to the positive impact municipal internet can have on the local economy. At another speech in Cedar Falls, Iowa, President Obama referred to Chattanooga as "a tornado of innovation."[25] In 2018, the Chattanooga Innovation District housed 671 businesses and employed 14,000 individuals.[26]

The rise of the Chattanooga Innovation District and its subsequent success is primarily because of three major factors: (1) the Gig City initiative, (2) the redevelopment of downtown, and (3) mayoral leadership. No single factor brought about its robust ascent. Rather, an alignment of forces which have been at work for many years contributed to its current standing. UTC's role during the district's early conceptualization and execution was minimal. But the university is now poised to play a part in its future. In 2009, the Electric Power Board of Chattanooga (EPB), a government-owned electrical utility company, embarked on modernizing its electrical grid. The goal was to upgrade the meters and limit power outages by responding quickly to customers following a storm or other occurrences impacting the network. This decision was partly informed by the fact that a year earlier, Volkswagen had announced the creation of a massive assembly plant to employ, at full capacity, 2,000 workers. In order for the EPB to accomplish its goal, it necessitated the use of fiber for the system setup. The cost of developing the required infrastructure totaled almost $350 million (the federal government contributed more than $100 million to the project). Because of this investment, a citywide internet network was subsequently unveiled, capable of reaching 10-gigabit speeds. The EPB network offered incredibly fast internet service at a very low cost. Technology entrepreneurs looking to launch a business quickly discovered Chattanooga as an alternative to the high start-up costs typically found in large urban centers. Over the years this helped produce a lively, local technology ecosystem.[27] Ron Littlefield, who served as mayor at that time, noted that "Chattanooga didn't have a bad image, it just had no image. The Gig has restored our luster."[28]

Leadership at the local level proved critical. When Mayor Andy Berke entered City Hall in 2013, he advocated that the future growth of the city depended on the advancement of the downtown by powering the knowledge economy. Achieving that direction would require a collective effort. He noted, "We wanted to have a downtown where people can come and collaborate, to have open spaces that felt like they belonged to everybody. I am a believer that you don't get new ideas on your own, you get them in collaboration with other people. That's how you get your new business."[29] Berke also convinced others to support this vision. Chattanooga's infrastructural investments in downtown around culture and leisure fashioned an attractive environment with many amenities including bars, pubs, coffee shops, and restaurants. A free downtown electric shuttle, parks, rock climbing, hiking, boating, kayaking, and paddle boarding offered a plethora of outdoor recreational opportunities, and the presence of a robust music scene also tempted young residents to new housing. These developments encouraged the engagement of start-ups within a highly entrepreneurial setting. Accelerators, incubators, and co-working spaces flourished. Angel investors and venture capitalists searched for profits by responding to business opportunities and innovative technology ideas. Ken Hays, president of the Enterprise Center, a nonprofit that works to develop the city's digital economy, once commented that "cities that don't develop and promote the innovation economy are going to be left behind."[30]

Engaging UTC in the Innovation District

Even though the role of UTC in the ascent of the innovation district has been limited, a growing engagement is observed in recent years, especially in the eastern edge of the district which geographically neighbors the university. Considerable investments in upgrading adjoining facilities and building new structures contributed to expanding the area's student population. Furthermore, a renewed emphasis on improving the security in that part of campus has become a major priority, transforming the area into a lively setting. Overall, these developments have strengthened the innovation district. At the 2015 State of the City Address, Mayor Berke recognized the importance of UTC since "Chancellor Steve Angle gets the urgency and need for change. For so many reasons we are lucky to have him in our community. He has pushed through policy changes to help protect the thousands of young people who attend UTC, but there's more to do." Similarly, at the 2018 State of the City Address, the mayor commented that "under Chancellor Angle's leadership [UTC] is rising to new heights and investing in key areas like smart cities."[31]

In March of 2018, at a press conference held at the Edney Innovation Center, Berke unveiled a new framework plan for Chattanooga's

Innovation District. The plan aims to help transition the district to a more mature level by harnessing new opportunities while solidifying existing relationships and assets. Key elements of this reconstituted agenda include promoting diversity and inclusion, committing to the area's cultural history, and maintaining its authentic identity. Furthermore, arguing for a comprehensive approach, Berke called for the importance of incorporating education, addressing some longstanding social and economic challenges, and creating an urban lab to produce economic opportunities for local residents. UTC was featured prominently in this strategic orientation and is expected to play a critical role in the plan's future realization and the overall growth of the district.

The document even called for a "downtown campus" and declared that "this area on the eastern end of the Innovation District presents an exceptional opportunity to better integrate UTC into the district due to the proximity of the Mapp Block to downtown. The most successful innovation districts in the US have significant university engagement, and UTC will be such an innovation anchor for Chattanooga. The area will look less like a traditional college campus and will be more of a lively, mixed use and densely developed urban core."[32] It was argued that the rehabilitation of UTC's James A. Mapp Building would be essential to linking the university with the district. Originally a state government office, the building stood idle and later transferred to UTC after it was declared too expensive to make functional once again. The university funded a $3.3 million renovation project, providing new space to its occupational and physical therapy programs and the Executive and Continuing Education Center. The Center for Innovation and Entrepreneurship is also operating from the Mapp Building. Additionally, the plan called for new retail and commercial spaces and even a university-affiliated hotel. Other recommendations included rebuilding existing walkways, constructing a research lab on a large, underutilized university-owned lot, and making a continued commitment to upgrade the buildings along Martin Luther King Boulevard. In the end, achieving completion of the plan's various segments will seamlessly connect the UTC campus to downtown. UTC Chancellor Steve Angle commented that the presented conceptual scheme is "a great vision of a lot of pieces that can come together. What we have seen today can be [very successful]."[33]

In addition to physically uniting the university to the innovation district, new programming at UTC is expected to present greater collaboration opportunities. Some recent institutional efforts include the Center for Urban Informatics and Progress—which focuses on research related to energy, mobility, health, and public safety—and the Smart Communication and Analysis Lab—which utilizes big data to research transportation, energy, and health. UTC is also pursuing various urban systems and smart city initiatives following the university's inclusion in the MetroLab in 2017. MetroLab is a network that encourages universities and cities to engage in joint research. As a result, UTC added relevant graduate programs and pursued research with EPB. Specifically, the Martin Luther King Corridor is equipped with extensive underground telecommunications fiber. That infrastructure lends itself to serving as an outdoor laboratory in smart city research. In addition to UTC and EPB, other partners focusing on technology research contribute to the ecosystem. These include the Chattanooga Smart Community Collaborative, Erlanger Hospital, the City of Hamilton County government, as well as Co:Lab and the Enterprise Center.[34] Co:Lab, as mentioned earlier, is an accelerator that helps promote entrepreneurial growth and the Enterprise Center maintains an applied mission of employing technology to address various issues. Both entities are nonprofit with a clear emphasis on promoting innovation.

Chattanooga's growth strategies noted above are having social and economic impact. Rapid changes in the residential composition has caused increased gentrification. The introduction of new construction throughout downtown and its surrounding neighborhoods boosted housing prices which, in turn, diminished the available affordable stock. A study by the Thomas Fordham Institute concluded that the effort to attract more middle-class residents to downtown produced very high rates of gentrification in the Southside area, located around UTC. The number of African American residents declined considerably:

the analysis of one local zip code revealed that, from 2000 to 2010, the number of Caucasians increased from 7.2 percent to a staggering 45.9 percent.[35] Another analysis of 102 metropolitan areas identified Chattanooga as having one of the highest levels of economic disparities.[36] The *New York Times* reported that Chattanooga is in the midst of "a dramatic overhaul with a radical gentrification plan and an aggressive citywide push to lure artists."[37] More recently, a 2019 report stated that gentrification and displacement are the unfortunate outcomes of Chattanooga's development explosion. The report argues that the city responded to the physical decline of Chattanooga with massive investments, noting, "We call on leaders to make similar investments in the social and human capital of those who have been pushed out and largely excluded from Chattanooga's success."[38] Finally, a local observer claimed that the creation of the Chattanooga Innovation District brought considerable social unsettling, greatly contributing to decline. Specifically, there is a "deepening of income and racial inequities in the midst of metropolitan progress. That part of the Chattanooga story is not to be celebrated."[39]

In a relatively short period of time this mid-tier city experienced an impressive urban transformation. An infusion of resources along the riverfront helped create a tourist and visitor economy which, along with the arrival of major businesses and corporations, formed an environment that attracted and retained residents. A municipally led government effort, in partnership with nonprofit entities and for-profit enterprises, resulted in a physical area dedicated to innovation and collaboration. Located in the center of downtown, its activities are driving a creative and entrepreneurial economy. In order for nearby UTC to successfully develop its metropolitan mission, it will have to play a substantial role in the continued growth of the Chattanooga Innovation District. The future advancement of UTC partly hinges on those prospects, as well as its urban campus surroundings.

Conclusion

The University of West Florida and the University of Tennessee at Chattanooga are comprehensive institutions of higher education that are endeavoring to serve Pensacola and Chattanooga. After the unrest caused by postwar forces weakening both cities socially and economically, Pensacola and Chattanooga are in the process of repositioning themselves. The loss of manufacturing industry and flight to the suburbs left the once thriving downtown of Pensacola in a state of steady decline. Population loss, lack of housing, and limited retail and entertainment options resulted in a struggling commercial core. Similarly, once a burgeoning industrial town on the Tennessee River, Chattanooga has been hit hard by deindustrialization, a condition that pushed residents to the outskirts. The aftermath was devastating, creating empty factories, generating the worst air quality in the nation, and leaving behind a once vibrant downtown without businesses and a diminishing commercial sector. During the last decade, the core of both of these communities is undergoing a sustained renaissance and a rapidly improving financial climate.

Both universities recognized that economic development was a major force in their respective institutions. President Saunders at UWF recently commented, "We see ourselves as much more than an institution of higher education. We're a central hub for the Northwest Florida region, with the resources, expertise and initiative needed to drive educational, cultural and economic partnerships that make an impact far beyond our campus . . . In a university-community partnership model, everyone wins."[40] Partnerships and a sustained commitment to valuing the city has produced robust outcomes. It is also apparent that both institutions perceive the revitalization taking place in their downtowns to be beneficial. They view this as being important to their own long-term success. Even though UWF is at a disadvantage by having its main campus in a suburban location, it has maintained a continuous emphasis in the core via academic programs and other related activities. In turn, this type of engagement greatly contributes to the downtown's ongoing revival. UTC stands as a great beneficiary of the massive investments in the turnaround of Chattanooga's urban center, including the innovation district. Led by a visionary mayor and an ambitious community of businesses, investors, real estate developers, nonprofit entities, and philanthropists, UTC is collaborating to further urban revitalization.

Another commonality between these two institutions is the importance of technology, innovation, entrepreneurialism, and their desire to connect these pursuits to economic development. UTC views itself as a key supporter of the innovation district and wants to form an internal system that can support start-ups. In that regard, having a 501(c)3 in place would be essential, something that Chancellor Angle views as being a key first step to moving forward. According to Angle, "We are looking to have an entrepreneurship program [at the university] . . . [O]ne of the ideas we are looking at is having teams of students from different departments and colleges work on ideas that they want to develop, providing [them with] some startup funding from gifts that we've gotten." The university has created a unit to lead its technology commercialization efforts and to market intellectual property. This would be in line with the university's vision. Angle notes, "We would find value as a public university if we could have a program that would break even but generate economic activity or vitality for our community and region in the state of Tennessee . . . We focus on applied research not basic research."[41]

Local leadership proves crucial as both institutions look for ways to either connect to existing initiatives or contribute to the creation of new projects that have the capacity to support entrepreneurialism and technological innovation. Unlike Chattanooga, Pensacola does not possess a formal innovation district. But UWF is well poised and, if an opportunity arises, it would engage in its development. In order for Pensacola to succeed, civic leadership is essential—something that is evident in Chattanooga, where the mayor successfully managed to promote an ambitious vision, formulating an effective strategy that helped give rise to the innovation hub.

University engagement in the urban environment to support the advancement of entrepreneurialism and technology has social ramifications. Infrastructural investments in the revitalization of Chattanooga's downtown and the creation of the Chattanooga Innovation District is also remaking the social composition of adjoining neighborhoods. The construction of new housing produces rent hikes and increases property values. These changes eventually make it difficult for existing residents, predominantly minorities, to afford the reconstituted pricing structures. As a result, gentrification and displacement follow. UTC, by virtue of its location and recent efforts to geographically connect it seamlessly with the innovation district, and downtown will contribute to reshaping the socioeconomic makeup of the area. The city has already recognized these unfolding impacts. The 2018 Innovation District of Chattanooga Framework Plan attempts to address these challenges in a functionally mature downtown Chattanooga by organizing programs that focus on affordable housing. In Pensacola, the impact of UWF is more restricted due to the limited scope of its current operations in the urban core. However, UWF is increasingly contributing to the remaking of the city's center.

UWF and UTC will continue to exercise regional influence on their respective communities. Both institutions realize that technology, innovation, and partnerships are central to achieving their missions. At the same time, as public universities, they understand that economic development and community outreach are critical components of their work. Unlike the research universities discussed in the previous chapters, their scope and resources as comprehensive institutions are limited. Both of them creatively employ various networks in their quest to cluster activities and generate a geography of innovation.

Open Innovation, Higher Education, and Urban Change

A T THE 2018 World Economic Forum Annual Meeting in Davos, Switzerland, Farnam Jahanian, president of Carnegie Mellon University, reasoned that universities have a critical role to play given that a rapidly unfolding digital revolution is driving unprecedented changes. He contended that disruption should be viewed as the norm because emerging technologies will not only shape the economy but also transform social relations. Jahanian called for institutions of higher education to actively participate in the process of forming ecosystems, suggesting key areas of engagement. For example, he remarked that universities should be "embracing entrepreneurship as part of the academic experience, creating cultures where innovative thinking is inspired and nurtured . . . [S]tudents come to college seeking to make a difference in society through startups, social entrepreneurship, and other ventures of their own creation." He also posited, "In today's competitive environment, universities must also develop new partnerships with leading companies, foundations, and other research-intensive institutions . . . Corporations are recognizing the high-value, high-return offered by these collaborations." Finally, he articulated the need for "incorporating diverse perspectives into our work" while being prepared for "the next wave of disruptive innovation [to] continue to exacerbate inequality."[1]

Per Jahanian's comments, the last decade saw a significant expansion of university programming focused on a culture of creativity and business involvement. Entrepreneurial immersion is one major factor behind the recent rise of innovation districts. The economic downturn following the 2008 financial crisis also contributed to accelerating this trend. The aftermath of the Great Recession brought to the forefront many concerns about the inner workings of colleges and universities. Elected officials, the media, and even the public sharply criticized what they perceived to be an inwardly oriented enterprise with costs rising much faster than wages. In 2018, student loans made up the largest portion of the US nonhousing debt.[2] Reductions in state funding followed, forcing many higher education leaders to become externally focused and seek additional revenues. The creation of these enclaves requires real estate transactions and necessitates partnerships, typically with corporations, government entities, and other nonprofits.

There is another element which aids the establishment of innovation hubs: specifically, the connection of technological entrepreneurship to economic development and urban revitalization. This is rapidly becoming an approach that many cities are now pursuing. The activities associated with research centers, start-ups, incubators, accelerators, co-working spaces, venture capital financiers, and angel investors make it increasingly difficult to functionally differentiate between industry and academia. The mix of students and young inventors, as well as institutional services which support their goals, brings a renewed energy expected to revive ailing parts of the city. It is within this framework that universities claim the value of these unique, physically compact ecosystems as part of their advancement strategies.

The chapter begins by reiterating the importance of open innovation and clusters as the conceptual cornerstones of district development. It continues by analyzing the role and impact of university-anchored districts while comparing the six cases within a broader framework of technological and business growth. As innovative learning types, their focus is placed on recasting traditional models through the pursuit of collaborations and informing research, education, and policy. Some of the comparison categories employed in the investigation include the primary funding mechanism, the role of university leadership, and the degree to which private-public partnerships can be employed to drive development. The role of government, as well as the level of functional connectedness to campus activities, is also addressed. Finally, the identification of unique district features present in the cases, the role of the community in the decision-making process, including potential impact, and the level of university or district integration is noted. Special emphasis is placed on the economic contributions and the broader spatial and socioeconomic implications, as well as the distributional consequences. For example, these projects discourage affordable housing and encourage gentrification and displacement. The chapter concludes with a discussion about how the cases inform the future of academia in light of the recent entrepreneurial engagement direction of higher education as an agent of urban change.

Open Innovation and Clusters in District Development

For many observers and the public, corporate innovation is a contradictory term. A discussion of this reveals the motivating factors on the part of both businesses and universities for pursuing partnerships. One of the major challenges facing large business enterprises is that size, complexity, centralization, and shifts in core mission can create an organizational culture that is slow to respond. In recent years, operational challenges have derived from multiple areas. For example, advancements in technology, changes in customer service practices, and venture capital investments in competing businesses in search of swift profit opportunities present pressure points. Labor force shortages in specific areas of expertise and talent, as well as mobility of information, can generate additional unforeseen issues. Thus, it is common for many CEOs and corporate boards to look over their shoulder to fend off competition, especially when newly formed, agile start-ups threaten to take away customers and reduce market share and corresponding revenues.

There are multiple ways to respond to these difficulties. A common, and potentially the most simplistic, approach is for the corporation to amass enough capital to buy out smaller, competing enterprises. This will either remove them completely from the marketplace as direct competitors or utilize them as an additional operational asset. While these new ventures can contribute to strengthening the corporation's position in the marketplace, this tactic can be an expensive proposition that may have other unanticipated outcomes. For example, operating these acquisitions as a way to lessen competition and increase profit may contribute to creating fringe activity that, in the long term, complicates and possibly even weakens the organization's primary mission. When that occurs, it is common for a corporation to produce a new operational plan and realign itself by refocusing on its core mission. Pursuing workforce reductions, infusing financial flexibility, raising corporate capital, and identifying reinvestment strategies are some of the tactics employed to gain greater control.[3]

The corporate innovation movement is another response to these conditions. Companies have looked to strengthen their position by developing strategies which place themselves in the forefront of new technologies, products, and services. In the process, they ensure that their future market standing is solidified and protected within rapidly changing economic conditions. Managing innovation is a more nuanced, complex process when examining its structure within organizations. It is thus important to differentiate between what is termed "closed innovation" and "open innovation."[4] Closed innovation coincides with vertical integration or a more traditional approach to executing strategic innovation. Lucent Technologies and Cisco Systems offer two different perspectives. According to Henry Chesbrough,

> Consider Lucent Technologies, which inherited the lion's share of Bell Laboratories after the breakup of AT&T. In the 20th century, Bell Labs was perhaps the premier industrial research organization and

this should have been a decisive strategic weapon for Lucent in the telecommunications equipment market. However, things didn't quite work out that way. Cisco Systems, which lacks anything resembling the deep internal R&D capabilities of Bell Labs, somehow has consistently managed to stay abreast of Lucent, even occasionally beating the company to market. What happened? Although Lucent and Cisco competed directly in the same industry, the two companies were not innovating in the same manner. Lucent devoted enormous resources to exploring the world of new materials and state-of-the-art components and systems, seeking fundamental discoveries that could fuel future generations of products and services.[5]

On the one hand, closed innovation is an internally focused, large-scale orientation in search of a big discovery that could fundamentally alter existing technologies and dominate new markets. This proves restrictive, time intensive, and hard to accomplish. It also requires reliance on ideas coming from a small number of individuals. These would need to be grounded in the company's existing business models, which means that once fully developed, the innovation should complement many of the current organizational processes and practices. This connection is quite essential given the significant R&D investments that often accompany these efforts. As Chesbrough noted, "This approach calls for self-reliance: If you want something done right, you've got to do it yourself."[6] Control over this process means less flexibility, speed, and creativity than a more decentralized approach can produce.

On the other hand, open innovation has a very different orientation. It is horizontal in its alignment and accepts the value and contributions of external companies that have expertise in developing unique ideas. It relies greatly on entrepreneurs and recognizes that their specialized focus, across many areas, cannot be easily replicated by a large organization. Specifically, according to Chesbrough, "Cisco, on the other hand, deployed a very different strategy in its battle for innovation leadership. Whatever technology the company needed, it acquired from the outside, usually by partnering or investing in promising startups (some, ironically, founded by ex-Lucent veterans). In this way, Cisco kept up with the R&D output of perhaps the world's finest industrial R&D organization, all without conducting much research of its own."[7] Open innovation views this as a time of swift change. Unique markets are hence unfolding continuously and collaboration is globally essential. This then makes it much easier to embrace product acceleration without significant financial commitments.

The case of Kodak and Fuji Photo Film is an example where two entities shared a similar business core. Fuji operated at a distant second to Kodak, which dominated the market for decades. The disruptive forces ushered in by digital technology, which interestingly a Kodak engineer had created a prototype for in the 1970s, proved difficult to handle. Kodak moved slowly, did not embrace the new technology, and remained committed to past practices. It focused on integrating digital technology into existing products, thus continuing to maintain a traditional stance. Because of that orientation it lost market share and slowly faded. In contrast, Fuji took a different path by pursuing new opportunities, searching for emerging markets, and quickly shifting resources.[8] As the *Harvard Business Review* pointed out, "Companies often see the disruptive forces affecting their industry . . . Their failure is usually an inability to truly embrace the new business models the disruptive change opens up. Kodak created a digital camera, invested in the technology, and even understood that photos would be shared online. Where they failed was in realizing that online photo sharing *was* the new business, not just a way to expand the printing business."[9] After hitting a high of $30 billion in the 1990s, Kodak's market capitalization in 2016 was below $1 billion. However, Fuji's new products (Intax digital cameras and film and a smartphone printer) helped revenues increase by 15.6 percent (FY2018/Q3) when compared to the same quarter in the previous fiscal year.

Beyond engaging with external entities in industrial innovation, the open innovation model considers the important role that internal ideas can have in furthering market expansion. These ideas should not remain lost or hidden within the organization. They should become integrated in efforts that take place outside the corporate setting, since their amalgamation can strengthen the innovation process. Perspectives and technologies, that in their current form may not fit existing modes, should not be discarded due to their lack of profitability potential. Here, the creation of a broader network is key since "the user is certainly very important to open innovation, but so are universities, startups, corporate R&D and venture capital."[10] Strong partnerships become central because they have the capacity to create a highly functional and effective ecosystem. The open innovation approach recognizes the increasing complexity of the economy and supports the power and influence that division of labor can have on new discoveries. A 2006 study on the most significant sources of innovation revealed that, in order of importance, employees ranked highest followed by business partners, customers, consultants, and competitors.[11]

But this approach is not without criticism. Some dominant companies protect their position, remain closed, and still pursue an active internal innovation strategy. IBM (in hardware), Toyota, Tesla, and GE are examples of corporate giants that rely on their own research laboratories as a way to ensure control over their intellectual property rights. The difficulty of maintaining control over the technology and associated licensing is one key drawback of open innovation. A number of strategies are employed to address this challenge while fostering new ideas. These include (1) crowdsourcing, (2) user innovation, (3) spin-in, spin-out, acquisition and divestment, and (4) licensing-in, licensing out, market for technologies, cross-licensing, and patent pools. Crowdsourcing and user innovation possess a number of commonalities. The key difference between them relates to their targets. Crowdsourcing is an informal approach that relies on large and anonymous audiences to provide feedback to solve a specific problem. For example, the broader gaming community may jointly tackle a software challenge to improve a product through its next iteration. Conversely, user innovation relies on a smaller segment and focuses on a targeted audience that not only brings expertise, but interest and dedication to address pertinent issues as well. In that regard users involved in strategy gaming would be such a focused community. Another approach is for a company to identify and purchase start-ups that would operate separately but whose inventions would contribute to a broader plan. This inward-directed or inbound innovation could be the preferred method, especially in industries such as pharmaceuticals or biotechnology. Finally, instead of buying and having to manage complete businesses, licensing is a much less taxing option for a corporation to use to acquire technology and knowledge.[12]

Regardless of the issues and variety of strategies employed, open innovation has become an accepted approach to improving the position of corporations within the market. A 2013 study of large firms in the United States and Europe, with annual sales of more than $250 million, revealed strong utilization and support for the concept. Some of the key findings included that 78 percent of the firms were practicing open innovation, 71 percent indicated that the support from top management for open innovation was growing, and 82 percent noted that the firm was more engaged in open innovation practices at that time compared to three years earlier. The study participants shared that creating new partnerships, maintaining strong connections to developments in technology, and exploring and cultivating new business opportunities were key drivers behind the pursuit of open innovation. Inward or inbound innovation was the most popular strategy; more than a third of the firms reported its utilization. Conversely, crowdsourcing was the least employed strategy, since its greatest challenge was managing the transition from closed to open innovation.[13]

Higher education is increasingly playing a more important role, and universities are now major contributors to the open innovation process. For example, research grants are considered the third most popular inbound strategy employed by firms.[14] Because of their research activities and the specialization of subject inquiry, universities bring exceptional value and a wealth of possibilities. Data supports that the existence of a close relationship between the university and the firm results in an increased number of innovations.[15] Those organizations that utilize open innovation strategies and maintain an internal R&D program are even more successful in attracting university participation.[16] Finally, higher education plays a critical role in "radical innovations," which are high risk initiatives that can generate significant returns from new knowledge.[17]

Hitachi, a globally diversified Japanese conglomerate, is involved in a robust array of commercial enterprises. Its leadership has aggressively embraced and advocated for the importance of open innovation. With a strong R&D operation, Hitachi works jointly with 14 universities across the world to further research activities and maintain and develop relationships with industry, academia, and government. The Hitachi case may be the most extensive example of corporate-university partnership in the world. In the information and telecommunications arena, Hitachi collaborates with the University of Tokyo (Japan) and with Tsinghua University (China).

These collaborations focus on the development of an ultra-high-speed database engine and the employment of ICT technologies to protect the environment and strengthen sustainability. In health care, the multinational corporation is involved with Hokkaido University (Japan) and with Tokyo Women's Medical University (Japan) in creating a proton beam therapy system, as well as an automatic cell culturing system for regenerative medicine. In natural resources and energy, partnerships with Indian Institutes of Technology (India) and Universiti Teknologi Petronas (Malaysia) are aimed at the establishment of energy-saving data centers and improvements in rail systems. Formal exchanges with RWTH Aachen University (Germany), Technische Universität München (Germany), and Birmingham University (UK) focus on mapping data linkage chassis controls, engine combustion analysis and simulation, and improving fault detection using acoustics.

Hitachi also opened the Hitachi China Materials Technology Innovation Center within Shanghai Jiao Tong University (China) to advance the development of materials research, and is involved in innovation and human resource development by engaging in exploratory research with Cambridge University (UK). With the University of Campinas (Brazil), the company is evaluating the potential of creating new global markets. Finally, the corporation recently pursued a university partnership to address local economic development issues. In 2016, the Hitachi Hokkaido

University Laboratory opened on the campus of Hokkaido University (Japan) with the goal to "resolve the various societal issues being faced in Hokkaido, such as aging and declining birthrate contributing to a declining population, stagnating regional economy and global warming."[18]

Universities have also recognized their role in supporting business endeavors. The Media Lab at MIT is an example of a university project which closely interacts with corporations within the framework of open innovation. Established in 1985, the laboratory is comprised of groups that engage in cutting edge research across various disciplines. In fact, one of the fundamental strengths of the Media Lab is that it is not confined by intellectual boundaries. Rather it is driven by the desire to employ science, technology, and design principles to solve problems. Pioneering new discoveries through the use of disruptive technology is a central goal of those involved in research at the Media Lab. With an annual budget of about $75 million and over 300 patents, it is funded by 90 companies that pay a membership fee. The Media Lab involves its students and faculty in the creative process of scientific inquiry and technological advancement. The sponsoring companies have access to those discoveries, however, sometimes their expectations for ideas that can be quickly brought to market maybe too high. Joi Ito, the director of the Media Lab, recently admitted, "I've fired companies for that . . . I've told companies, you are too bottom-line oriented. Maybe we're not right for you."[19]

The notion of open innovation is widely accepted as the preferred approach for companies to think about their future and to embrace strategies and technologies in an environment that is highly competitive and unpredictable. Though there are no guarantees, it is clear that unlike Kodak, Sears, Lucent, Yahoo, Blockbuster, and BlackBerry, corporations have to move faster, adapt more quickly, and be willing to change. Altering existing business models, pursuing new ways of thinking, and interacting with individuals who can contribute diverse points of view, interests, and methods to solving problems is not a choice. A successful open model does not exist in isolation; rather, it must be cooperative, engaging, and inclusive.

Clusters are the other key concept driving the logic behind the rise of innovation districts. Michael E. Porter provides some major insights in this area, arguing for the value of these settings. According to Porter,

> Clusters are geographic concentrations of interconnected companies and institutions in a particular field. Clusters encompass an array of linked industries and other entities important to competition. They include, for example, suppliers of specialized inputs such as components, machinery, and services, and providers of specialized infrastructure. Clusters also often extend downstream to channels and customers and laterally to manufacturers of complementary products and to companies in industries related by skills, technologies, or common inputs. Finally, many clusters include governmental and other institutions—such as universities, standards-setting agencies, think tanks, vocational training providers, and trade associations— that provide specialized training, education, information, research, and technical support.[20]

Like open innovation, clusters create an environment that encourages cooperation. However, simultaneously, competition is present, which allows for a unique dynamic to unfold. Cooperation and competition are essential conditions to encourage entrepreneurship and to drive innovation.

Creating a university-anchored innovation ecosystem is a long-term proposition and its realization requires continuous commitment. Size, scope, and outcomes vary since these efforts can be extensive and multifaceted to complement the nature and aspirations of research-intensive institutions. Comprehensive and liberal arts colleges and universities may also pursue similar strategies with reduced complexity and degree of involvement, while aligning those projects to their mission. Regardless, when fully developed, innovation districts are spatially focused and always rely on an open innovation model that values and encourages a diverse exchange of ideas, perspectives, and interests. To launch these initiatives, colleges and universities must consider operating at two levels. The first is internally calibrated and serves as a prerequisite to the second, which has an external orientation. This segmentation as outlined in table 8.1 can also guide a strategic conversation among key stakeholders prior to or during the process. The level of intensity will also vary. As noted in the table, the first stage is formed around activities that help formulate a strong foundation. The next stage focuses on building capacity through internal and external undertakings. Finally, in order for the project to reach full maturity and persist in enabling growth, an external orientation of engagements is essential. This will lead to forming new connections which can result in future growth.

The rise of an innovation ecosystem is a complicated proposition, unfolding in varying stages and informed by structural factors that can advantage or disadvantage its trajectory. Additionally, planning considerations and institutional leadership can fuel or hinder the final outcome. Within this broad framework, how do the cases investigated in this book contribute to our understanding of higher education and its impact on the urban environment? The next section offers a comparative analysis, examining similarities, differences, and emerging themes.

Table 8.1. Developing a Higher Education Innovation Ecosystem

	Foundational Considerations	Capacity Building	Connect, Sustain, and Grow
Internal Orientation	Maker Spaces; Competitions; Curriculum Integration; Faculty Involvement; Undergraduate/ Graduate Research	Focused/Guided Leadership; Needs Assessment of Community Environment; Co-Working Facilities;	
External Orientation		Partnerships; Technical Assistance; Mentoring Services; Support for Start-ups; Accelerators; Incubators; University Foundation	Location; Local/State Government; Expanded Partnerships with Businesses and Corporations; Faculty Research; Research Institutes/Centers; Ongoing Community Engagement; Transportation; Amenities; Real Estate Professionals; Alumni; University Foundation

Comparative Analysis: Findings and Themes

The Tech Square and Kendall Square districts are the most mature of all the undertakings. PHX Core, Schuylkill Yards, and the Chattanooga Innovation District have reshaped the urban environment in various ways and are expected to have a significant impact as they further develop. In Pensacola, the university is increasingly involved in coordinating a number of projects. However, even though a call for a formal geographical cluster was recently advocated as a potential next step, like in Chattanooga, the government will need to play a greater role in its realization.[21] Smaller universities must rely on government action to a greater extent, since they lack the resources and capacity present at research institutions. The cases of Tech Square and Kendall Square encapsulate some of the key themes and offer comprehensive insights also evident in the other cases. Furthermore, they help identify some of the ongoing challenges facing the districts. Of the two, Kendall Square is in the most advanced state. The university has achieved a very robust ecosystem in Cambridge. Yet, at the same time, the institution is struggling to determine how to create a setting that ensures mixed-use spaces, serving multiple purposes.

Tech Square is a dynamic, continuously changing environment that has been guided and supported by Georgia Tech. The university managed to attract a number of businesses and corporations, which have aided its evolution over the years. As one of the most successful districts in the country, Tech Square is the result of a series of interconnected elements that, when put together, constitute a setting primed to fuel innovation, economic development, and urban growth. A number of initiatives proved instrumental in its location and have progressively contributed to the Tech Square ecology. Six broad elements comprise the makeup of this setting and include (1) developing the research core, (2) fueling a mindset for creativity and discovery, (3) supporting start-ups and accelerators, (4) enticing corporate innovation centers, (5) attracting corporate headquarters and similar entities in and around the area, and (6) positioning contributing retail services and pertinent university functions.

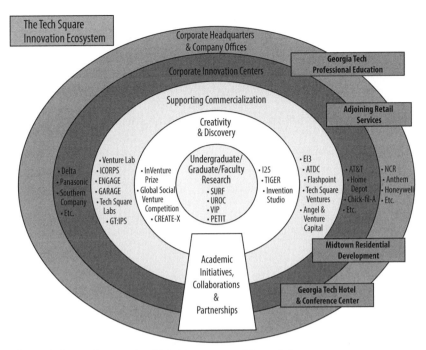

The figure contains the following labels:

The Tech Square Innovation Ecosystem

Corporate Headquarters & Company Offices

Georgia Tech Professional Education

Corporate Innovation Centers

Supporting Commercialization

Adjoining Retail Services

Creativity & Discovery

Undergraduate/ Graduate/Faculty Research

- Delta
- Panasonic
- Southern Company
- Etc.

- Venture Lab
- ICORPS
- ENGAGE
- GARAGE
- Tech Square Labs
- GT:IPS

- InVenture Prize
- Global Social Venture Competition
- CREATE-X

- SURF
- UROC
- VIP
- PETIT

- I25
- TIGER
- Invention Studio

- EI3
- ATDC
- Flashpoint
- Tech Square Ventures
- Angel & Venture Capital

- AT&T
- Home Depot
- Chick-fil-A
- Etc.

- NCR
- Anthem
- Honeywell
- Etc.

Midtown Residential Development

Academic Initiatives, Collaborations & Partnerships

Georgia Tech Hotel & Conference Center

The Tech Square Innovation District. Courtesy of Costas Spirou.

The first two elements (*developing the research core* and *fueling a mindset for creativity and discovery*) are part of Georgia Tech's efforts to distinguish itself academically and to support the intellectual experience of students. Like other universities, *developing the research core* extends beyond programs and faculty. Deliberate efforts to strengthen the academic enterprise encourage students to work in the laboratory and become intimately exposed to faculty research. This, in turn, helps undergraduates improve their success at the graduate level and beyond. Those already in graduate school can acquire a research agenda and expertise, which aids their employment options. University faculty also rely on these student engagements to further their scholarship.

The next stage *fuels a mindset for creativity and discovery*. Students have an opportunity to further their research interest and move to the next level. By using technology, they receive support to tackle unique challenges, either on their own or in teams. A number of university programs and competitions are in place to assist them in gaining a deeper understanding as they hone their research and entrepreneurial skills. Some of these activities have commercialization potential. By *supporting commercialization*, established mechanisms help propel these ideas forward and transition them into start-up status with the hopes of successfully entering the market. These include opportunities to access venture capital, and the availability of co-working spaces, legal advice, and business knowledge. *Enticing corporate innovation centers* to locate in Tech Square is another major contributor to the innovation ecosystem. A strategically unique direction and part of a broader vision, the growing presence of these centers infuses energy in the process, producing a vibrant setting. The formulation of this modern, fast-paced atmosphere has subsequently come to define the Tech Square environment and can serve as a model.

More recently, *corporate headquarters and company offices* are flocking to the area. Attracted by the growing opportunities to recruit young talent, some corporations and well-established businesses have chosen to locate in and around Tech Square. Other companies have also decided to move employees into the area. Finally, the university *positioned retail services and institutional functions* at the center of the development. A residential component gradually became evident in and around the district as Midtown ascended to become a community of choice. This added vibrancy further fueled growth as its geography underwent continuous transition, thus expanding and creating a larger and denser physical footprint.

The case of Kendall Square is one that parallels broader conditions of urban change of decay and rebirth. However, as industrial decline was in full force, MIT's ambitious agenda was rapidly and successfully unfolding, transitioning the university into a world-class institution of higher education. It is the distinctive status of MIT as an outstanding research university that gives rise to this center of innovation, first, from the 1960s to the early part of the 2000s, as an office park district, and then as a diverse business district until the early part of the 2010s.

Since around 2012, MIT's emphasis has been on sustaining and growing the district in a manner that is balanced and responsive to multiple needs. But achieving this is not an easy task given extensive pressures and demands for real estate. So, what are the key findings that emerge following a close examination of this case? What can be learned?

The MIT focus on groundbreaking research in life sciences and technology would prove critical to the ascent of the Kendall Square district. This rise is firmly grounded in the realization that cutting-edge research and discovery is purposeful and must support commercialization efforts, business creation, and advancement. Such a notion sets the stage for the development of collaborative interactions with many influential corporations that find the university's Kendall Square ecosystem inviting. Through its vast real estate ventures, the university emerged as a landlord to some of the largest companies in the world. For MIT, an open outlook and strong collaboration with industry are essential elements to improving human society and individual well-being.

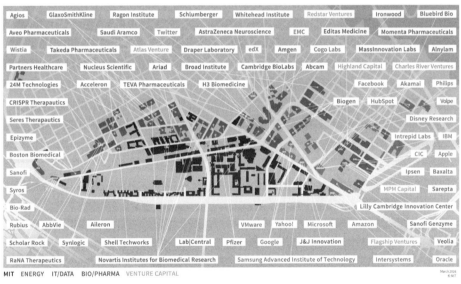

The MIT Innovation Cluster and the Kendall Square Innovation District. Photo courtesy of MIT. Used in Claudia Trillo's Smart specialisation strategies as drivers for (smart) sustainable urban development. In *Sustainable Urbanization*, ed. Mustafa Ergen, p. 187. London: IntechOpen.

MIT purposefully cultivated a culture of innovation that fuels the Kendall Square district. The university recognized the vital role of spatial and social clustering which makes new discoveries possible. Like Georgia Tech, it embraced the concept that entrepreneurs are central to innovation and staged various university competitions to support their pursuits. MIT President Susan Hockfield once noted, "Invention, innovation and entrepreneurship are the oxygen of a thriving economy."[22] Most recently, it identified the need for patent capital to further innovation. In a *Washington Post* op-ed, current MIT President Rafael Reif called for a different way to push the current limits of research from discovery to commercialization: "Today, our highly optimized, venture-capital-driven innovation system is simply not structured to support complex, slower-growing concepts that could end up being hugely significant—the kind that might lead to disruptive solutions to existential challenges in sustainable energy, water and food security, and health."[23] To address this challenge, Reif called for "innovation orchards" which would bring together "a coalition of funders from the public, for-profit and not-for-profit sectors . . . to turn new science into workable products, up to the point that they meet venture capital's five-year threshold for the journey from investment to market. This would make investing in tangible or tangible-digital hybrid innovations no riskier than investing in the purely digital."[24] Expanding the boundaries of innovation has been a defining characteristic of the MIT culture and an ongoing commitment of the university.

MIT quickly recognized that it cannot be an island since its continued success hinges on the fortunes of its immediate urban environment. This realization made the revitalization of Kendall Square a priority. Maintaining a positive relationship with the City of Cambridge, one that is engaging and collaborative, was of vital importance. Similarly, from the start, it became apparent to the city leaders that the fortunes of Cambridge and its revival path from the postindustrial urban decline that ravaged the area were connected to the ascent of the university. According to Mayor Marc McGovern, "For a couple years, we had junk bond status, we couldn't build a tree house . . . We are a small city with a tremendous amount of resources. That makes me very hopeful that we can be a city that really tackles issues of poverty and hunger and homelessness and housing because of those resources." In 2018, the high-tech tenants of Kendall Square accounted for a third of the city's tax revenues.[25] Over the years, MIT has been mindful of contributing to the city's coffers. In 2001, when MIT purchased Technology Square from Beacon Capital Partners, it kept its commercial status to ensure continuous tax payments to the city. Allan Bufferd, MIT Treasurer, noted that "this is an investment in the City of Cambridge. MIT intends to hold Technology Square in its commercial tax-paying portfolio for the foreseeable future. The Institute has allocated a significant portion of its private endowment and other funds towards investments in non-campus commercial properties in Cambridge for more than 20 years."[26] In 2004, MIT and the city signed a 40-year agreement to ensure the long-term tax protection of Cambridge. It creates a guarantee on how much property the university can maintain in commercial status. It also provides a 20 percent increase in the flat payment (PITOL) for its tax-exempt status, and a 2.5 percent annual increase thereafter. According to MIT President Charles M. Vest, "We at MIT care deeply about the health and future of this city and believe that our investment in property here is a very positive factor for the Cambridge economy."[27]

Effective ongoing planning is essential to generate and sustain this innovation district. A continuous interplay between MIT, the City of Cambridge, and the community proved critical to transitioning the area from its previous dilapidated condition to its current sought-after standing. In order for the Kendall Square innovation district to avoid becoming a victim of its own success, it must continuingly reinvent itself by responding to external and internal pressures. In 2013, when MIT received approval of its zoning petition from the city, David Maher, city councilor and ordinance committee chair, commented on the willingness of the university to adjust its proposal by being open to feedback: "MIT has done an outstanding job of listening to the Planning Board, the Council, and the community and drafting a petition that reflects that." The petition received support from the Kendall Square Association, the Central Square

Business Association, the Cambridge Chamber of Commerce, and A Better Cambridge Neighborhood Association.[28]

A combination of other key factors contributed to the development of Kendall Square. Private and public funding sources that included the university and federal, state, and local governments as well as major real estate firms and corporations would, at different junctions of its life cycle, support the district's growth efforts. MIT exemplified persistent leadership at the highest level, as successive university presidents personally engaged in crafting a vision, addressing key challenges, and pursuing the advancement of various aspects of the ecosystem. Finally, transportation was always a consideration; every plan recognized its importance, and the city council, during its review and deliberations, insisted on improvements in this area. The MIT case is unique due to the presence of extensive resources. Nevertheless, achieving and maintaining community support is complicated, and even that does not guarantee success.

Table 8.2 shows some of the common characteristics of these institutional initiatives as well as the variations between them. For example, a combination of university, foundation, city, state, and federal funds are employed in the development of these projects. However, it is important to note that the private sector plays an ever-increasing role, especially following the launch of the districts. The presence of businesses and other corporate entities is essential to furthering their desired trajectories. Strong institutional leadership is also critical in all of the cases. University presidents and other administrative and academic leaders make these efforts a priority and articulate their importance, often on the grounds of mission advancement, institutional expansion, and economic development. Private-public partnerships are another crucial component, evident in all of the cases. For example, Arizona State University maintains one of the most aggressive entrepreneurial outlooks in higher education. Without these relationships in place, universities would be unable to fully realize their goals. The government is another factor present in all of these cases. While in

Table 8.2. Comparative Analysis of Initiatives by Key Characteristics

Initiative	Institution	Primary Funding Mechanism	Institutional Leadership	Private-Public Partnerships	Role of Government	Campus Connection	Unique Features	Role of Community	Level of Integration
Tech Square	Georgia Institute of Technology	University	High	Strong	Average	Strong	Corporate Innovation Centers	Moderate	Very High Affordability Problems
Kendall Square	Massachusetts Institute of Technology	University, City, Private	High	Strong	Strong	Strong	Amenities, Major Corporations	High	Very High Affordability Problems
Schuylkill Yards	Drexel University	University, Private	High	Very Strong	Strong	Strong	Public Spaces, Housing	Moderate/High	High Gentrification Displacement
PHX Core	Arizona State University	University, City, State, Private	High	Strong	Very Strong	Above Average	Revitalization	Minimal/Moderate	Average Gentrification Displacement
Innovation Institute	University of West Florida	University, City, State	High	Average	Average	Low	Regional Development	Minimal	Low
Chattanooga Innovation District	University of Tennessee at Chattanooga	City, State, University	Low, Emerging	Strong	Very Strong	Average	Revitalization	Minimal	Low Gentrification Displacement

some cases its involvement is stronger than in others, without it, it is unlikely that these undertakings would ever materialize.

Regarding connecting the districts to the campuses, it is apparent that both Georgia Tech and MIT possess very strong levels of integration. After all, these have been in place for some time. When fully completed, Schuylkill Yards will seamlessly connect to the campus of Drexel University. While extensively involved in Tempe with the Novus Innovation Corridor, Arizona State University will continue to influence the development of the PHX Core. In fact, the university is a major driver of the technology industry. As one observer noted, "The role of Arizona State University in helping build Phoenix as a tech hub is hard to overstate."[29] Having recognized its value, the University of Tennessee at Chattanooga embarked on a concerted effort to better align with the nearby Chattanooga District, a move that is expected to strengthen its effectiveness.

The Challenges of Innovation Clusters and Other Considerations

When assessing the level of institutional integration, it is also important to consider the impact these initiatives have on the surrounding neighborhoods and the broader urban environment. The analysis reveals a strong tendency to generate significant affordability issues, displacement, and gentrification. Georgia Tech's establishment of Tech Square in Atlanta is rapidly attracting more corporate offices and new housing construction. The growth has been unprecedented in the last five years, with more changes underway. Tech Square contributes to a reconstituted socioeconomic makeup of Midtown by pricing out existing residents, making it a more expensive place to live. The robust Kendall Square ecosystem is so overwhelming that maintaining a balance of retail, residential, office, and recreational functions in the community proves a major struggle. Affordable housing is essential; as one observer once noted, "It's time we stopped sugar-coating what are basically acts of self-destructive gentrification."[30]

Similar forces are present in both Schuylkill Yards and PHX Core. The massive project in West Philadelphia will result in challenges for local residents in the surrounding neighborhoods. A community representative cautioned that attention is needed: "We've been seeing a great deal of pressure for market-rate development, not for affordability. People could be potentially pushed out if we don't create a program to offset some of that stress."[31] In Phoenix, the success of the ASU Downtown campus helped drive a revitalization of the center and the development of the PHX Core in the Warehouse District. Rental housing increases and new construction have put considerable pressure on existing residents, altering the composition of the community. The innovation district in Chattanooga is producing comparable concerns. A study of socio-spatial processes concluded that uneven development has been a key outcome of placemaking practices. Specifically, claims of the city's southern exceptionalism should be questioned, since "urban space has been, and continues to be racialized and socially stratified."[32]

So, who profits from these types of university-driven efforts? Obviously, the university is able to advance its mission and support its research and economic development objectives. Additionally, students benefit since they can take advantage of the available resources and contacts with businesses. However, a credible and comprehensive answer to this question necessitates that one recognizes the complexities embedded within these initiatives. Universities tout the commercialization contributions of their innovations, but often fail to identify the unintended distributional consequences of their actions. For example, University of Colorado Boulder Chancellor Philip DiStefano recently announced that institutional efforts from 2014 to 2018 accounted for $1.9 billion in benefits from campus entrepreneurship in the form of start-ups and industry partnerships.[33] According to DiStefano, "This supported an estimated 11,545 jobs . . . paying an estimated $732 million in wages. Much of this activity occurred in our home state, providing an impact of $1.2 billion to Colorado's economy." CU Boulder programs such as Commercialization Academy and Destination Startup were singled out for playing a key role in this success.[34] Part of the engine generating these results is downtown Boulder, an innovation hub with accelerators, incubators, and start-ups, all within a very close proximity to each other. CU Boulder operates in and contributes to that environment. Additionally, the sense of community found in a smaller town and the outdoor lifestyle for which the city is recognized are central to promoting the local technology ecosystem. However, this emerging dynamic also generates unique challenges. There is an affordable housing crisis in Boulder. Politics and zoning policies restrict opportunities for low- and middle-class residents to live in the city. Instead, baby boomer neighborhood preservationists who embrace environmentalism have been accused of advancing status quo policies that oppose approaches to increasing density. In the process, these approaches drive rental and ownership costs higher and higher, thus keeping residents from lower socioeconomic backgrounds out of city living.[35] Unfortunately, today's growing group of technology entrepreneurs supports this segregating reality. As one observer noted, "Pretty much every entrepreneur told me he or she started up in Boulder or stayed in Boulder for that same reason: It's a beautiful place to live. And it's beautiful not because the city forefathers had some nifty pro-start-up policy—but because they had the foresight to plant lots of trees, welcome a university and federal science labs, buy up lots of parkland, and then stay disciplined about preserving the beauty they had created."[36]

Even though the Boulder case involves a more nuanced interpretation of the impact, real estate firms, developers, construction firms, and corporate entities clearly stand to benefit from the rise of university-anchored innovation districts and related pursuits. In Tech Square, Portman Holdings—a fully integrated development practice firm that has erected hotels, office buildings, apartments complexes, and retail spaces internationally—recently received a 10-year property tax break worth $5 million for its third planned office tower in the district. At the nearby Coda Tower, another Portman Holdings high-rise, BlackRock is one of the world's largest investment firms. BlackRock announced that it would establish iHub, its new technology innovation center. In exchange for creating 1,000 jobs by 2024, the company expects to receive $25 million in tax breaks.[37] West Philadelphia will experience a building boom in the next couple of years valued at $2.1 billion from the Schuylkill Yards project. Construction firms will be at the forefront of monumental changes, reorganizing the geography and physical core of the area. A recent report acknowledged that the development will cause rising housing costs and fuel gentrification because it will be "pricing out residents in and around Penn and Drexel."[38] Finally, downtown Phoenix has seen an explosion of construction with developers and real estate firms emerging as the clear beneficiaries. Luxury housing and a high demand for amenities are reducing affordable options, putting pressure on current residents who see the costs of ownership and rent skyrocket.[39]

And there are other forces at play. Specifically, special attention must be paid to the implications of the recent Tax Cuts and Jobs Act of 2017. The passage of the act by Congress included the creation of 8,700 Opportunity Zones across the country, affording tax incentives to help finance initiatives in troubled communities struggling with decline and disinvestment. The goal is to encourage eligible activities leading to job creation by supporting small businesses and aiding property management. Opportunity Zones have been designated near higher education and research centers in all states. In fact, in some cases the campus rests within the Opportunity Zone. As anchors for the commercialization of knowledge, creating incubators and accelerators to support student start-ups and other entrepreneurial activities offers great potential for local growth.[40]

Some universities are already partnering with investors, and developers are exploring projects that would benefit from this legislation. Contributions to a Qualified Opportunity Fund ease that process since it allows taxpayers to financially invest while deferring capital gains. This ensures that adequate funds are gathered to move forward with a venture. Arizona State University, the University of Delaware, and the University of Illinois at Urbana-Champaign are some of the institutions that are currently pursuing prospects associated with Opportunity

Zones. Recently, Renaissance Equity Partners raised $50 million to create the Renaissance HBCU Opportunity Fund. The fund focuses on financing mixed-use developments on or near HBCU campuses.[41]

In the coming years, it is likely that more colleges and universities across the country will be involved in activities within the Opportunity Zones framework, and their actions will surely reshape the built environment. Yet the long-term effectiveness of the program is questionable. Similar to the Reagan Free Enterprise Zones in the 1980s and the Clinton Empowerment Zones during the 1990s, the goals of this comparably conceived Trump initiative will be contested. Focusing tax incentives within geographic boundaries does not automatically strengthen the socioeconomic standing of a neighborhood. Economic development does not necessarily translate to community development. These are two very different processes.

Innovation districts afford many benefits to the higher education institutions that serve as their anchors. At the same time, economic growth and job creation are by far the most apparent byproduct of their development. In their Brookings Institution report, Bruce Katz and Julie Wagner identified two additional contributions: "Innovation districts help address three of the main challenges of our time: sluggish growth, national austerity and local fiscal challenges, rising social inequality, and extensive sprawl and continued environmental degradation."[42] On the subject of social inequality, they argued, "A substantial number of emerging innovation districts across the United States are close to low- and moderate-income neighborhoods, offering the prospect of expanding employment and educational opportunities for disadvantaged populations."[43]

The inclusive nature of the purported economic outcomes noted above are debatable. The technology sector consistently relies on a highly educated, well-compensated workforce. According to census data, from 2013 to 2018, household income in the United States rose the most in technology centers.[44] These ecosystems create communities with high-income residents that push both housing costs and property taxes out of reach. This, in turn, makes it difficult for low- and middle-income families who have been unable to secure desirable housing either to buy or rent.[45] Furthermore, the speed of development to attract these employees also impinges upon any efforts aimed at affordable housing or strengthening the local social capital. The forces of change are so powerful that, in the end, social inequality remains one of the major challenges facing innovation clusters when examining their impact on the urban environment.

Conclusion

Fifty years ago, many urban universities considered leaving the city. Today, having a city presence is a major asset, and leaders of colleges and universities not only celebrate their fortunes but also work feverishly to determine how to take full advantage of their unique locations. The suburban research park venues of the 1960s and 1970s have given way to a new set of dynamics fueled by the energy and talent of young urban entrepreneurs working in a fast-paced, digital economy. A powerful cultural shift is underway, driven by a renewed urban romanticism and the benefits of walkable amenities, diversity, density, and unique housing options. These trends have helped redefine the urban core and its surrounding neighborhoods. It is within this geography of possibilities that universities anchor innovation districts, the result of both structure and agency. Postwar urban decline provided access to low-cost real estate which, alongside institutional leadership and successful partnerships, powered robust ecosystems of technological innovation.

The pursuit of innovation initiatives has intensified during the last 10 years, following the 2008 Great Recession. Two major forces contributed to these efforts. First, the declining economic conditions pressured universities to look for alternative sources of revenues. Reductions came immediately and are still in place. In 2010, public universities in Maryland saw a $48 million state budget cut.[46] In Arizona, in response to significant budget deficits emanating from the Great Recession, the state's lawmakers made some of the deepest cuts compared to other states. Even a decade later, Arizona still lagged behind the prerecession funding levels.[47] After adjusting for inflation, from 2008 to 2018, Arizona cut per-student support by 54.9 percent.[48] The Arizona case is not an outlier. According to the Center on Budget and Policy Priorities, in 2018, 41 states spent less per student than in 2008.[49] This reality forced universities to become entrepreneurially oriented and pursue profitable real estate ventures and partnerships in a more concerted manner than in the past. The second reason relates to economic development. Criticized for their unique structure and at times anachronistic, steeped-in-tradition inner workings, colleges and universities embraced an economic development agenda to showcase their worth and valuable contributions. Innovation districts came to signify and greatly complement strategies aimed at knowledge of commercialization and job creation.

At the same time, each of the cases in this book reveals a unique contribution to better understanding the relationship between higher education, technological innovation, and urban change. In establishing Tech Square, Georgia Tech provides a blueprint on how to integrate corporate innovation centers while expanding campus services, academic programming, and university activities. Even though MIT maintains a strong presence as a major real estate holder and broker in Kendall Square that benefits the university, the institution is able to successfully connect world-class research with businesses and corporations. Furthermore, MIT's attempt to coordinate and balance community functions in Kendall Square and the surrounding communities is noteworthy. Drexel University offers unique insights on creating a strategy that is attentive to and supportive of community interests. While the success of these efforts can be questioned, it is important to recognize the comprehensive nature of those initiatives. In Phoenix and Tempe, Arizona State University exemplifies an impressive entrepreneurial orientation while showcasing the potential that robust partnerships can generate. The university's New American University model, contemporary outlook, and involvement with local municipalities is truly impressive and is at the forefront of change in higher education. The University of West Florida offers insights on institutional initiatives to achieve regional progress. Finally, the University of Tennessee at Chattanooga shows that smaller, comprehensive institutions can also benefit from technological innovation by aligning closely with the local government.

It is apparent that university-anchored innovation districts can make significant contributions to economic expansion, job growth, and the institutions that guide their development. Nonetheless, there are questions about their impact on the urban environment. After World War II, many urban colleges and universities erected walls to isolate and protect themselves from the socioeconomic ills and challenges of their surroundings. This produced separation for which they were criticized. However, 50 years later, the open engagement of these technology clusters may construct similar outcomes in different ways. The creation of monolithic cultural settings of residents with high incomes fuels separation and isolation, erecting an invisible wall, thus, once again, keeping the university divorced from the realities of the city.

Chapter 1. The New Entrepreneurial University

1. Ryan Lillis. 2018. A huge UC Davis tech campus is coming to this neighborhood in Sacramento. *The Sacramento Bee.* April 13.

2. Editorial. 2018. Here's how to keep UC Davis' Aggie Square from becoming a gentrification bomb in Sacramento. *The Sacramento Bee.* April 22.

3. Felicia Alvarez. 2019. Four developers in the running to build Aggie Square. *Sacramento Business Journal.* September 16.

4. Gary May. 2019. UC Davis' Aggie Square can lead to regional prosperity. *Comstock's Magazine.* May 11.

5. Jon Marcus. 2017. Under pressure to contain tuition, colleges scramble for other revenue. *The Washington Post.* May 1.

6. Roger Showley. 2016. MetroLab: End to "ivory tower" universities? *The San Diego Union-Tribune.* May 9.

7. Nicholas Kristof. 2014. Professors, we need you! *The New York Times.* February 15.

8. Time to leave the ivory tower; university reform. 2015. *The Economist.* November 14.

9. As quoted in Steven Shapin. 2012. The ivory tower: The history of a figure of speech and its cultural uses. *The British Journal for the History of Science* 45(1): 1–27. Pp. 14, 15, 16.

10. Costs. 1927. TIME. June 27.

11. Lily Rothman. 2016. Putting the rising cost of college in perspective. TIME. August 31.

12. Peter McPherson and David Shulenburger. 2010. Understanding the cost of public higher education. *Planning for Higher Education* 38(3): 15–24.

13. Paul Campos. 2015. The real reason college tuition costs so much. *The New York Times.* April 4.

14. Jon Marcus. 2017. How university costs keep rising despite tuition freezes. *The Atlantic.* January 3.

15. Zac Anderson. 2011. Rick Scott wants to shift university funding away from some degrees. *Herald-Tribune.* October 10.

16. Jenna Goudreau. 2012. The 10 worst college majors. *Forbes.* October 11; Farran Powell. 2016. Top college majors for finding full-time work. *US News and World Report.* July 21.

17. As quoted in Clayton Christensen, Michael Horn, Louis Caldera, and Louis Soares. 2009. Disrupting college: How disruptive innovation can deliver quality and affordability to postsecondary education. Mountain View, CA: Innosight Institute.

18. Goldie Blumenstyk. 2009. In a time of crisis, colleges ought to be making history. *The Chronicle of Higher Education*. May 1.

19. Mary-Christine Phillip. 1995. Fiscal reality hits higher education's ivory tower . . . hard. *Black Issues in Higher Education* 11(26): 9.

20. Mary Sue Coleman. 2012. Mary Sue Coleman's open letter to President Obama. January 11. http://michigantoday.umich.edu/a8118/.

21. Kim Clark. 2010. The Great Recession's toll on higher education. *US News and World Report*. September 10.

22. AASCU State Relations and Policy Analysis Research Team. 2010. *Top 10 Higher Education State Policy Issues for 2010*. Washington, DC: American Association of State College and Universities. January.

23. AASCU. *Top 10 Higher Education State Policy Issues*.

24. Jon Marcus. 2017. Higher education seeks answers to leaner years. *The New York Times*. June 7.

25. Holden Thorp and Buck Goldstein. 2013. *Engines of Innovation: The Entrepreneurial University in the 21st Century*. Chapel Hill: University of North Carolina Press, p. 8.

26. Alexandra Lange. 2016. The innovation campus: Building better ideas. *The New York Times*. August 4.

27. Anna Marum. 2017. OSU to move into Meier & Frank building downtown. *The Oregonian*. November 21.

28. Joel Baird. 2016. City council oks lot sale to Champlain College. *Burlington Free Press*. November 28.

29. Jennifer Davies. 2016. UC San Diego Extension to open innovative cultural and education hub in downtown San Diego. *UC San Diego News Center*. December 12.

30. Patrick McGeehan. 2011. By deadline, 7 bids in science school contest. *The New York Times*. October 11.

31. Richard Perez-Pena. 2011. Cornell alumnus is behind $350 million gift to build science school in city. *The New York Times*. December 19.

32. C. J. Hughes. 2017. Roosevelt Island: Part of Manhattan, but apart from it. *The New York Times*. October 4.

33. Alexandra Lange. 2012. Silicon island. *The New Yorker*. October 15.

34. Madeline Stone. 2014. This is what Cornell's futuristic NYC tech campus will look like. *Business Insider*. May 8.

35. Kelsey Campbell-Dollaghan. 2013. How tech industry is quietly changing the face of American cities. *Gizmodo: Architecture*. June 18.

36. Elizabeth Harris. 2017. High tech and high design, Cornell's Roosevelt Island campus opens. *The New York Times*. September 13.

37. Bruce Katz and Julie Wagner. 2014. *The rise of innovation districts: A new geography of innovation in America*. Washington, DC: Metropolitan Policy Program at Brookings Report.

38. Luke Guillory. 2019. Board of Regents approves $4.4 million Spring Street building project for UGA. *The Red & Black*. September 11.

39. Joshua Drucker, Carla Kayanan, and Henry Renski. 2019. *Innovation Districts as a Strategy for Urban Economic Development: A Comparison of Four Cases*. Kansas City, MO: Ewing Marion Kauffman Foundation.

40. Tim Bryant. 2012. Central West End research park could double in size. *St. Louis Post-Dispatch*. October 12.

41. Tim Bryant. 2016. New $170 million Cortex development to add hotel, apartments, parking garage. *St. Louis Post-Dispatch*. October 20.

42. Victor Mulas and Mikel Gastelu-Iturri. 2016. *Transforming a City into a Tech Innovation Leader*. Washington, DC: The World Bank.

Chapter 2. The University as Innovator and Urban Leader

1. Patricia McDougall-Covin. 2011. Entrepreneurship: Myth—Mindset—Mandate. Presentation at the University of Pavia. October.

2. Christopher Jencks and David Riesman. 1968. *The Academic Revolution*. New York: Doubleday.

3. Henry Etzkowitz. 2001. The second academic revolution and the rise of entrepreneurial science. *IEEE Technology and Society Magazine* 20(2): 18–29; Henry Etzkowitz. 2004. The evolution of the entrepreneurial university. *International Journal of Technology and Globalization* 1(1): 64–77; Henry Etzkowitz and Andrew Webster. 1998. Entrepreneurial science: The second academic revolution. In *Capitalizing Knowledge. New Intersections of Industry and Academia*, ed. Henry Etzkowitz, Andrew Webster, and Peter Healey, pp. 21–46. Albany: State University of New York Press.

4. Douglas Henton, John Melville, and Kim Walesh. 1997. *Grassroots Leaders for a New Economy: How Civic Entrepreneurs Are Building Prosperous Communities*. San Francisco: Jossey Bass.

5. Joshua Kaan and Henry Etzkowitz. 2013. *The power of cultural entrepreneurship: Symbiosis of Oregon's Shakespeare Festival (OSF) and Southern Oregon University (SOU)*. European Commission: University-Business Cooperation Project.

6. Cornelius Frolik. 2017. UD, WSU, Sinclair and Clark State pledge to partner with Amazon. *Dayton Daily News*. October 23.

7. Henry Etzkowitz. 2008. *The Triple Helix: University-Industry-Government in Action*. London: Routledge; Henry Etzkowitz and Loet Leydesdorff. 1995. The triple helix—University-industry-government relations: A laboratory for knowledge-based economic development. *EASST Review* 14(1): 14–19.

8. Henry Etzkowitz, Andrew Webster, Christiane Gebhardt, and Branca Regina Cantisano Terra. 2000. The future of the university and the university of the future: Evolution of ivory tower to entrepreneurial paradigm. *Research Policy* 29(1): 313–330. P. 315.

9. Arvids Ziedonis. 2004. *Research Policy 33*. Review of *MIT and the Rise of Entrepreneurial Science*, ed. Henry Etzkowitz, pp. 177–178. London: Routledge, p. 178.

10. Jeannette Colyvas. 2007. From divergent meanings to common practices: The early institutionalization of technology transfer in the life sciences at Stanford University. *Research Policy* 36: 456–476; Jonathan Liebenau. 1987. *Medical Science and Medical Industry: The Formation of the American Pharmaceutical Industry*. Baltimore: Johns Hopkins University Press; Eliot Marshall. 1997. Need a reagent? Just sign here. *Science*. October 10; Mark Peter Jones. 2009. Entrepreneurial science: The rules of the game. *Social Studies of Science* 39(6): 821–851; Jeannette Colyvas and Walter W. Powell.

2007. From vulnerable to venerated: The institutionalization of academic entrepreneurship in the life sciences. *Research in the Sociology of Organizations* 25: 219–259; Daniel Greenberg. 2007. *Science for Sale: The Perils, Rewards, and Delusions of Campus Capitalism.* Chicago, IL: University of Chicago Press; Martin Kenney. 1986. *Biotechnology: The University-Industrial Complex.* New Haven, CT: Yale University Press; Katherine McCain. 1991. Communication, competition, and secrecy: The production and dissemination of research-related information in genetics. *Science, Technology, & Human Values* 16: 491–516.

11. Mark Peter Jones. 2009. Entrepreneurial science: The rules of the game. *Social Studies of Science* 39(6): 821–851. Pp. 840–841.

12. Henry Etzkowitz. 1998. The norms of entrepreneurial science: Cognitive effects of the new university-industry linkages. *Research Policy* (27)8: 823–833.

13. Jaroslav Pelikan. 1992. *The Idea of the University: A Re-Examination.* New Haven, CT: Yale University Press.

14. Harvey Brooks. 1993. Research universities and the social contract for science. In *Empowering Technology: Implementing a U.S. Strategy*, ed. Lewis Branscomb, pp. 202–234. Cambridge, MA: MIT Press, p. 203.

15. Henry Etzkowitz. 1998. The norms of entrepreneurial science: Cognitive effects of the new university-industry linkages. *Research Policy* (27)8: 823–833.

16. Franklin D. Roosevelt. 1944. *Letter to Vannevar Bush.* November 17.

17. Vannevar Bush. 1945. *Science—The Endless Frontier.* A Report to the President on a Program for Postwar Scientific Research. July 25. Pp. 9–23.

18. Vannevar, *Science*, 11.

19. C. Stewart Gillmor. 2004. *Fred Terman at Stanford: Building a Discipline, a University, and Silicon Valley.* Palo Alto: Stanford University Press.

20. Marvin Chodorow. 1983. Obituary: Frederick E. Terman. *Physics Today* 36(9): 90–91. P. 90.

21. Dawn Levy. 2004. Biography revisits Fred Terman's roles in engineering, Stanford, Silicon Valley. *Stanford Report.* November 3.

22. Chong-Moon Lee, William F. Miller, and Marguerite Gong Hancock. 2000. *The Silicon Valley Edge: A Habitat for Innovation and Entrepreneurship.* Palo Alto: Stanford University Press.

23. David Lempe. 1988. *The Massachusetts Miracle: High Technology and Economic Revitalization.* Cambridge, MA: MIT Press.

24. AnnaLee Saxenian. 1994. *Regional Advantage: Culture and Competition in Silicon Valley and Route 128.* Cambridge, MA: Harvard University Press.

25. Saxenian, *Regional Advantage*, 63.

26. Saxenian, *Regional Advantage*, 9.

27. Council on Governmental Relations. 1999. *The Bayh-Dole Act: A Guide to the Law and Implementing Regulations.* Washington, DC: Council on Governmental Relations. October. P. 10.

28. *The Economist.* 2002. Innovation's golden goose. December 12.

29. Cory Leahy. 2014. From idea to IPO: Entrepreneurship at UT. *UT News.* March 6.

30. Scott Maben. 2017. UW expands CoMotion collaborative innovation hub to Spokane. *The Spokesman-Review.* January 31.

31. Bob Roseth. 2013. UW launches record 17 startup companies. *UW News.* July 18.

32. John Pletz. 2017. UChicago, U of I collaboration expands in bid to foster startups. *Crain's Chicago Business.* October 19.

33. Rob Matheson. 2017. The Engine closes its first fund for over $150 million. *MIT News.* April 6. P. 19; Rob Matheson. 2017. The Engine announces investments in first group of startups. MIT News. September 19.

34. Scott Carlson. 2010. The college president as urban planner. *The Chronicle of Higher Education.* January 29.

35. Carlson, The college president.

36. Mark Funkhouser. 2015. The benefits of a town-and-gown relationship. *Governing.* February.

37. Matthew Fernandez. 2016. The question of the tax-exempt university. *Inside Higher Ed.* October 13.

38. Jim Shelton. 2013. New Haven's relationship with Yale likely issue for next mayor. *New Haven Register.* May 18.

39. Paul Huffstutter. 2004. Town wants gown to cover more expenses. *The Los Angeles Times.* January 16.

40. Sabina Deitrick and Tracy Soska. 2005. The University of Pittsburgh and the Oakland neighborhood. In *The University as Urban Developer: Case Studies and Analysis,* ed. David Perry and Wim Wiewel, pp. 25–44. Armonk, NY: M.E. Sharpe.

41. Jennifer Levitz. 2012. Ivy League school to pay city. *The Wall Street Journal.* May 1.

42. Peter Marcuse and Cuz Potter. 2005. Columbia University's Heights. In *The University as Urban Developer: Case Studies and Analysis,* ed. David Perry and Wim Wiewel, pp. 45–64. Armonk, NY: M.E. Sharpe.

43. Simon Kuznets. 1973. Modern economic growth: findings and reflections. *The American Economic Review* 63(3): 247–258. P. 252.

44. Gerald Carlino, Satyajit Chatterjee, and Robert Hunt. 2007. Urban density and the rate of invention. *Journal of Urban Economics* 61(3): 389–419.

45. Peter Hall. 1998. *Cities in Civilization: Culture, Innovation and Urban Order.* New York: Pantheon, p. 291.

46. Hall, *Cities in Civilization,* 286.

47. Hall, *Cities in Civilization,* 939.

48. Manuel Castells. 2010. *The Rise of the Network Society.* Malden, MA: John Wiley & Sons, p. 65.

49. Manuel Castells. 2001. The information city, the new economy, and the network society. In *People, Cities and the New Information Economy,* ed. Antti Kasvio, Veera Laialainen, Hikka Salonen, and Pia Mero, pp. 150–163. Helsinki: Palmenia, p. 159.

50. Castells, *Rise of the Network Society,* 506.

51. Castells, *Rise of the Network Society,* 506.

52. Castells, *Rise of the Network Society,* 436.

53. Manuel Castells and Peter Hall. 1994. *Technopoles of the World: The Making of Twenty-First Century Industrial Complexes.* New York: Routledge.

54. Richard Florida. 2003. *The Rise of the Creative Class*. New York: Basic Books; Richard Florida. 2004. *Cities and the Creative Class*. London: Routledge.

55. Richard Florida. 2002. The economic geography of talent. *Annals of the Association of American Geographers* 92(4): 743–755.

56. Costas Spirou. 2011. *Urban Tourism and Urban Change: Cities in a Global Economy*. New York: Routledge; Costas Spirou and Dennis Judd. 2016. *Building the City of Spectacle: Mayor Richard M. Daley and the Remaking of Chicago*. Ithaca, NY: Cornell University Press.

57. Scott Andes. 2017. *Hidden in plain sight: The oversized impact of downtown universities*. Washington, DC: Bass Initiative on Innovation and Placemaking at the Brookings Institution. October. P. 4.

Chapter 3. Anchoring a Redevelopment Renaissance

1. American Planning Association. 2016. Midtown Atlanta: Atlanta, Georgia. https://www.planning.org/greatplaces/neighborhoods/2016/midtownatlanta/.

2. Scott Kirsner. 2017. Top 10 cities for corporate innovation. *Innovation Leader Magazine*. May. https://www.innovationleader.com/topcities/.

3. Scott Andes and Bruce J. Katz. 2016. Why today's corporate research centers need to be in cities. *Harvard Business Review*. March 1.

4. Robert McMath, Ronald Baylor, James Brittain, Lawrence Foster, August Giebelhaus, and Germaine Reed. 1985. *Engineering the New South: Georgia Tech, 1885–1985*. Athens, GA: University of Georgia Press, p. 13.

5. McMath et al., *Engineering the New South*, 14.

6. McMath et al., *Engineering the New South*, 17–18.

7. G. P. Bud Peterson. 2013. *The First Decade of Innovation*. Speech at the 10th Anniversary of Tech Square. October 17. P. 4.

8. John Carter, interview with author, January 27, 2018.

9. Wayne Clough. 2000. *Fifth Street Project Presentation to the Georgia Tech Foundation*. June 9.

10. Wayne Clough. 1999. *The Leadership Challenge: Strategies to Seize Our Opportunities*. Georgia Tech Administrative Retreat. August 18.

11. Wayne Cough, interview with author, November 15, 2017.

12. Wayne Clough. 1999. The role of the university in revitalizing city centers. Remarks by Georgia Tech President G. Wayne Clough, Urban Land Institute. May 6.

13. Wayne Clough. 2000. *Master Plan Press Event Remarks*. June 5.

14. Wayne Clough. 2001. Remarks by Georgia Tech President. Midtown Rotary Club. February 27.

15. The Campus Master Plan (2004 Update). 2004. Georgia Institute of Technology. Version 4.4, March 23.

16. Clough, Remarks by Georgia Tech President.

17. Scott Trubey. 2015. Georgia Tech's leap over the connector paying off. *Atlanta Journal-Constitution*. September 11.

18. Blueprint Midtown: Designing our future. 1997. *Midtown Alliance*. Atlanta, Georgia.

19. Shannon Powell, interview with author, November 13, 2017.

20. Gary Goettling. 2003. A "Magnificent" gateway began with a vision. *Tech Topics*. Fall. P. 18.

21. Greg Giuffrida, Jennifer Clark, and Stephen Cross. 2015. Putting innovation in place: Georgia Tech's innovation neighborhood of "Tech Square." *Proceedings of the 10th European Conference on Innovation and Entrepreneurship*. Genoa, Italy. September. Pp. 214–222.

22. Gary Schuster. 2008. Maintaining momentum. *Speech by Interim President Schuster*. September.

23. G. P. "Bud" Peterson. 2010. Georgia Tech, a culture of innovation. *Atlanta Business Chronicle*. September 26.

24. G. P. "Bud" Peterson. 2009. Remarks by incoming President G. P. "Bud" Peterson. February 29.

25. Georgia Institute of Technology. 2010. *Designing the Future: A Strategic Vision and Plan*. Atlanta: Georgia Institute of Technology, p. 5.

26. Georgia Institute of Technology, *Designing the Future*, 11.

27. Georgia Institute of Technology, *Designing the Future*, 19.

28. Georgia Institute of Technology. Categories—CIC. Accessed May 26, 2018, http://cic.gatech.edu/participate/submission/categories.

29. Georgia Institute of Technology. Welcome to CIC! Accessed May 26, 2018, http://cic.gatech.edu/.

30. Sarah Fay Campbell. 2016. Fire HUD takes first place at Ga. Tech Inventure Prize. *The Newnan Times-Herald*. March 21.

31. Janel Davis. 2016. Georgia Tech students compete in *Shark Tank*–style invention contest. *The Atlanta Journal-Constitution*. August 16.

32. Forbes. 12 Business Incubators Changing the World. *Forbes*. Accessed June 1, 2018, https://www.forbes.com/pictures/mee45jmk/12-business-incubators-changing-the-world/#1df575e62942.

33. Tricia Whitlock. 2014. GT's VentureLab ranked 2nd best incubator in US. *Hypepotamus*. June 26.

34. Katina Stefanova. 2015. Shining the light on angel investing: Interview with Merrick Furst, CEO of Flashpoint. *Forbes*. February 15.

35. G. P. "Bud" Peterson. 2013. Changing the expectations for higher education. Speech at (co)lab Summit, The Woodruff Arts Center. September 23.

36. G. P. "Bud" Peterson, interview with author, May 14, 2018.

37. Rafael Bras, interview with author, May 14, 2018.

38. Peter High. 2017. CIO Tom Miller drives $85B Anthem's innovation studio. *Forbes*. March 20.

39. Urvaksh Karkaria and Ellie Hensley. 2017. Anthem CIO: Midtown's Tech Square is a "hotbed for innovation." *Atlanta Business Chronicle*. October 12.

40. Press Release. 2018. NCR officially opens new global headquarters in Atlanta. *NCR Corporation Media*. January 8.

41. Scott Trubey. 2019. Anthem to anchor second Midtown Atlanta tower. *The Atlanta Journal-Constitution*. May 2.

42. Midtown Alliance. 2019. *Midtown Development Activity, 2019*. April.

43. Ann Breen and Dick Rigby. 2005. *Intown Living: A Different American Dream*. Washington, DC: Island Press, p. 51.

Chapter 4. The Most Innovative Square Mile on the Planet

1. Julia Georgules. 2019. The link between innovation and real estate performance. *Boston Business Journal*. June 4.

2. Abby Goodnough. 2011. Now all these legends need is a good agent and an entourage. *The New York Times*. September 29.

3. William B. Rogers. 1846. Letter to his brother outlines a "Plan for a Polytechnic School in Boston." March 13. William Barton Rogers papers, MC 1, box 2. Cambridge: Massachusetts Institute of Technology, Institute Archives and Special Collections.

4. Rogers, Letter to his brother.

5. David Kaiser. 2012. *Becoming MIT: Moments of Decision*. Cambridge, MA: MIT Press; Julius Stratton and Loretta Mannix. 2005. *Mind and Hand: The Birth of MIT*. Cambridge, MA: MIT Press.

6. Brian Cudahy. 1972. *Change at Park Street Under: The Story of Boston's Subways*. Brattleboro, VT: Stephen Greene Press.

7. Warren K. Lewis et al. 1949. *Report of the Committee on the Educational Survey to the Faculty of the Massachusetts Institute of Technology*. Cambridge, MA: The Technology Press, MIT. P. 13.

8. Michael Kenney. 2011. Cambridgeport: Its people and their stories. *The Newetowne Chronicle*. Winter. P. 1.

9. Reena Karasin. 2018. Cambridge's candy making legacy. *Scout Cambridge*. June 14.

10. Jim Miara. 2012. The reinvention of Kendall Square. *Urban Land*. February 17.

11. Miara, The reinvention of Kendall Square.

12. John Harris. 1951. Politics and politicians: Of all of Callahan's highways, Route 128 seems to be "It." *The Boston Globe*. July 22.

13. Howard Banks. 1999. Rocket science isn't easy: Among big defense contractors, Raytheon is the best of the breed. That ain't saying much. *Forbes*. November 1; David Hughes. 1993. Raytheon targets growth within four core groups. *Aviation Week & Space Technology*. March 1; Steven Lipin and Gabriella Stern. 1997. GM unveils sale of Hughes defense arm to Raytheon Co. in $9.5 billion accord. *Wall Street Journal*. January 17; Otto Scott. 1974. *The Creative Ordeal: The Story of Raytheon*. New York: Atheneum.

14. James R. Berry. 1968. Forty years in the future. *Mechanix Illustrated*. November. Pp. 90–100, p. 93.

15. Nancy Dorfman. 1983. Route 128: The development of a regional high technology economy. *Research Policy* 12(6): 299–316.

16. Susan Rosegrant and David R. Lampe. 1992. *Route 128: Lessons from Boston's High-Tech Community*. New York: Basic Books.

17. Mark Leibovich. 1998. A tech corridor's life cycle. *The Washington Post*. March 25; David Leonhardt. 2009. The economy is bad, but 1982 was worse. *The New York Times*. January 20.

18. As quoted in Garret Fitzpatrick. 2012. Duck Pin, we have a problem. *MIT Technology Review*. August 21.

19. Robert Harvey Rollins II. 1970. *Closing of the NASA Electronics Research Center: A Study of Reallocation of Space Program Talent*. Thesis, Alfred P. Sloan School of Management, MIT.

20. Garret Fitzpatrick. 2012. Duck Pin, we have a problem. MIT *Technology Review*. August 21.

21. Nidhi Subbaraman. 2010. The evolution of Cambridge. MIT *Technology Review*. December 21.

22. Subbaraman, The evolution of Cambridge.

23. Subbaraman, The evolution of Cambridge.

24. Robert Simha. 2003. MIT *Campus Planning, 1960–2000: An Annotated Chronology*. Cambridge: MIT Press, p. 79.

25. Subbaraman, The evolution of Cambridge.

26. Sam Allis, Hiawatha Bray, Scott Helman, and Carolyn Johnson. 2011. 150 fascinating, fun, important, interesting, lifesaving, life-altering, bizarre and bold ways that MIT has made a difference. *The Boston Globe*. May 15.

27. Liz Karagianis. 2015. Discovery science is reinventing the world. MIT *Spectrum*. April 21.

28. Rae Goodell. 1979. Public involvement in the DNA controversy: The case of Cambridge, Massachusetts. *Science, Technology, & Human Values* 4(27): 36–43.

29. Michael Blanding. 2015. The man who helped launch biotech. MIT *Technology Review*. August 18.

30. Karen Weintraub. 2018. In the heart of biotech, leaders explain the Boston area's "Bioboom." WBUR. June 4.

31. Weintraub, In the heart of biotech.

32. Weintraub, In the heart of biotech.

33. Katie Lannan. 2018. Biotech, pharma, are big business for Massachusetts. *Telegram & Gazette*. August 30.

34. Phillip Sharp. 2008. In praise of Senator Ted Kennedy for his contributions to biomedical science. *Xconomy*. November 24.

35. Kelly O'Brien. 2018. Wayfair overtakes Akamai as the most valuable internet company in Mass. *Boston Business Journal*. September 12.

36. Rob Matheson. 2013. From biotech to high-tech. MIT *News*. March 20.

37. Matheson, From biotech to high-tech.

38. Matheson, From biotech to high-tech.

39. Lauren Landry. 2012. A look at 22 years of the MIT $100K Entrepreneurship Competition & 10 teams who've paved the way. BOSTINNO. March 20.

40. David Hamilton. 2000. Broadcom agrees to acquire Silicon Spice for $1.24 billion. *The Wall Street Journal*. August 8.

41. Callum Borchers. 2014. In his own words: Tim Rowe tells the Cambridge Innovation Center startup story. *The Boston Globe*. January 17.

42. Borchers, In his own words.

43. Jon Chesto. 2018. Cambridge Innovation Center raises $58m to help fund expansion. *The Boston Globe*. March 14.

44. Subbaraman, The evolution of Cambridge.

45. Carey Ross. 2015. A real estate empire grows in Kendall Square. *The Boston Globe*. April 15.

46. Rebecca Spalding. 2018. Kendall Square: How a rundown area near Boston birthed a biotech boom and real estate empire. *The Boston Globe*. October 15.

47. News Office. 2010. MIT explores plans for enlivening Kendall Square. *MIT News*. May 28.

48. Michael Blanding. 2015. The past and future of Kendall Square. *MIT Technology Review*. August 18.

49. Blanding, The past and future of Kendall Square.

50. Erin Baldassari. 2012. MIT revamps development plan for Cambridge's Kendall Square. *Cambridge Chronicle*. December 5.

51. Marc Levy. 2013. Council keeps MIT plan for Kendall Square moving; residents want 5,000 student housing units. *Cambridge Day*. March 8.

52. Cambridge Community Development Department. 2013. *Kendall Square Final Report 2013*. December. P. 7.

53. Marc Levy. 2015. What happened to K2C2? City planners decided to let developers do it bit by bit. *Cambridge Day*. November 13.

54. Tim Logan. 2016. Will Kendall Square finally feel like a real neighborhood? *The Boston Globe*. May 18.

55. Tim Logan. 2018. Apple plans to lease space in Kendall Square. *The Boston Globe*. December 19.

Chapter 5. Leveraging for Innovation in Philadelphia

1. Roger Miller and Joseph Siry. 1980. The emerging suburb: West Philadelphia, 1850–1880. *Pennsylvania History* 47(2, April): 99–146.

2. Jake Blumgart. 2017. West Philadelphia. *Encyclopedia of Greater Philadelphia*. https://philadelphiaencyclopedia.org/archive/west-philadelphia-essay/.

3. Blumgart, West Philadelphia.

4. As quoted in Jackie Rogozinski. 2002. Searching for the Black Bottom. *34th Street*. October 24.

5. Leon Rosenthal. 1963. *A History of Philadelphia's University City*. Philadelphia: University of Pennsylvania Press, p. 82.

6. Rosenthal, *A History of Philadelphia*.

7. Larry Fish. 1998. Penn, reexamining, hope it learned a lesson: Critics say a similar move 30 years ago failed to improve the area. *Philadelphia Inquirer*. May 4.

8. John Bound and Sarah Turner. 2002. Going to war and going to college: Did the World War II and the G.I. Bill increase educational attainment for returning veterans? *Journal of Labor Economics* 20(4): 784–815.

9. Neil Homer, Tobin Smith, and Jennifer McCormick. 2008. *Beyond Sputnik*. Ann Arbor: University of Michigan Press.

10. John Puckett and Mark Lloyd. 2015. *Becoming Penn: The Pragmatic American University, 1950–2000*. Philadelphia: University of Pennsylvania Press, p. 14.

11. Puckett and Lloyd, *Becoming Penn*, p. 31.

12. Puckett and Lloyd, *Becoming Penn*, pp. 26–27.

13. Puckett and Lloyd, *Becoming Penn*, p. 49.

14. Puckett and Lloyd, *Becoming Penn*.

15. Ben Hammer. 1996. Sled murder prosecutors to seek death penalty. *The Daily Pennsylvanian*. December 4.

16. Judith Rodin. 2007. *The University and Urban Revival: Out of the Ivory Tower and Into the Streets*. Philadelphia: University of Pennsylvania Press, p. 188.

17. Harley Etienne. 2012. *Pushing back the gates: Neighborhood perspectives on university-driven revitalization in West Philadelphia*. Philadelphia, PA: Temple University Press.

18. As quoted in Lois Romano. 2006. Urban colleges learn to be good neighbors. *The Washington Post*. January 9.

19. *Connect to compete: How the University City–Center City innovation district can help Philadelphia excel globally and serve locally*. 2017. The Anne T. and Robert M. Bass Initiative on Innovation and Placemaking. May.

20. Henry Holcomb. 2005. Cira Centre's glass skin is now in place. *The Philadelphia Inquirer*. July 25.

21. Sandy Smith. 2016. Drexel picks Brandywine to develop "Innovation Neighborhood." *Philadelphia Magazine*. March 2.

22. John Fry and Jerry Sweeney. 2016. Giant step in Philly growth. *Philadelphia Inquirer*. March 4.

23. Fry and Sweeney, Giant step in Philly growth.

24. Fry and Sweeney, Giant step in Philly growth.

25. Radio Times. 2016. How Schuylkill Yards could change West Philly. WHYY 91 FM. March 28.

26. Radio Times, How Schuylkill Yards.

27. Sandy Smith. 2017. Schuylkill Yards project to include major community engagement component. *Philadelphia Magazine*. June 27.

28. Sonja Sherwood. 2016. Everything you ever wanted to know about Schuylkill Yards. *Drexel Now*. March 30.

29. Jon Hurdle. 2018. Closing in on 5 years, has Mantua's Promise Zone designation laid a foundation for poverty reversal? *Philadelphia Weekly*. November 8.

30. Jim Saksa. 2017. Planning Commission hears community concerns, supports rezoning for first phase of Schuylkill Yards. *Plan Philly of WHYY*. January 18.

31. Jim Saksa. 2018. As Drexel transforms University City, communities nearby prepare for gentrification. *Plan Philly of WHYY*. July 13.

32. Jim Saksa. 2016. With new Schuylkill Yards, Drexel and Brandywine promise development without displacement. *Plan Philly of WHYY*. March 8; Jon Hurdle. 2018. Philadelphia's first step to a platform of innovation. *The New York Times*. February 20.

Chapter 6. Innovation in the Valley of the Sun

1. *Regional Fast Facts Population and Growth*. 2018. Maricopa Association of Governments. February 1.

2. Lauren Schieler. 2019. Valley transit planners battle ride-hailing growth, population explosion to keep things moving. *Phoenix Business Journal*. April 27.

3. *U.S. Metro Economies: Past and Future Employment Levels*. 2017. The United States Conference of Mayors. May.

4. Catherine Reagor. 2019. Could population growth propel Phoenix and Tucson to merge? *The Arizona Republic*. April 21.

5. Mary Beth Faller. 2018. ASU student body bigger and brighter as fall classes begin. *ASU Now*. August 15.

6. Past Presidents. n.d. Arizona State University Office of the President. Accessed May 20, 2019. https://president.asu.edu/the-office/past-presidents.

7. Michael Crow. 2002. *A New American University: The New Gold Standard.* Arizona State University Inaugural Address (November), p. 3.

8. Crow, *New American University*, 17.

9. Lorraine Longhi. 2018. Fifth and tallest building yet going up at Scottsdale's SkySong. *The Arizona Republic.* June 25.

10. Michael Crow and William Dabars. 2015. *Designing the New American University.* Baltimore: Johns Hopkins University Press.

11. Stefan Theil. 2008. Reinventing the global university. *Newsweek.* August 8.

12. Laura Fitzpatrick. 2009. Nine presidents to watch: Michael Crow. TIME. November 11.

13. Nicholas Dirks. 2015. Rebirth of the research university. *The Chronicle of Higher Education.* April 27.

14. Natalie Day. 2015. Lessons from a "New American University." *The Guardian.* October 21.

15. Bernard Wysocki Jr. 2006. Once collegial, research schools now mean business. *The Wall Street Journal.* May 4; Jack Stripling. 2010. Arizona State U. has problems, just how its president likes it. *USA Today.* July 16.

16. Stefan Theil. 2008. Reinventing the global university. *Newsweek.* August 8.

17. Office of the Arizona State University President. 2004. One university in many places: Transitional design to twenty-first century excellence. April. P. 7.

18. Debra Friedman. 2009. An extraordinary partnership between Arizona State University and the City of Phoenix. *Journal of Higher Education Outreach and Engagement* 13(3): 89–99.

19. Samantha Incorvaia. 2016. First look at the new ASU law school building in downtown Phoenix. *The Arizona Republic.* August 12.

20. Mike Sunnucks. 2018. ASU Thunderbird will move students, classes into Arizona Center offices in downtown Phoenix. *Phoenix Business Journal.* March 28.

21. Noah Huerta. 2019. ASU to build new residential hall on Downtown campus. *Downtown Devil.* April 4.

22. Jonmaesha Beltran. 2019. The rise of ASU's Downtown campus. *Downtown Devil.* February 5.

23. Mackenzie Shuman. 2018. ASU's Downtown Phoenix campus has brought innovation to the city. *The State Press.* September 9.

24. Jon Talton. 2017. In Phoenix, signs of a downtown that's ready to thrive again. *City Lab.* January 3; Harper Speagle-Price. 2017. Grappling with growth in downtown Phoenix. *Downtown Phoenix Journal.* December 1.

25. Joseph Flaherty. 2018. Sure, it's hot, schools are underfunded, but Phoenix still No. 2 in population. *Phoenix New Times.* May 29.

26. Lucinda Shen. 2016. Here's why Phoenix could be the next Silicon Valley. *Fortune.* October 14.

27. Patrick O'Grady. 2019. Phoenix snares high global innovation rank from site selection study. *Phoenix Business Journal.* April 14.

28. Ktar.com. 2019. WeWork to open coworking space in downtown Phoenix, fourth in 2019. *KTAR News.* May 2.

29. Mackenzie Shuman. 2018. ASU's Downtown Phoenix campus has brought innovation to the city. *The State Press.* September 9.

30. Mike Maciag. 2015. Gentrification in America report. *Governing*. February.

31. Jenna Martin. 2019. Why this Charlotte ZIP code ranked among fastest-gentrifying neighborhoods in America. *Charlotte Business Journal*. April 23.

32. Bradford Luckingham. 1994. *Minorities in Phoenix: A Profile of Mexican American, Chinese America, and African American Communities, 1860–1992*. Tucson: University of Arizona Press.

33. Kathy Chin Leong. 2018. A renewal for Phoenix's Warehouse District: Polished but gritty. *The New York Times*. March 13.

34. Mike Sunnucks. 2013. ASU fine arts school putting studios, programs in downtown Warehouse District. *Phoenix Business Journal*. November 17.

35. Hunter Freedman. 2017. ASU's Grant Street Studios mix art education with community. *Downtown Phoenix Journal*. August 17.

36. Business News. 2018. Phoenix launches new innovation district-PHX Core. *Arizona Business Magazine*. May 18.

37. Jon Swartz. 2017. Phoenix's tech scene is growing—in an old warehouse district. *USA TODAY*. May 20.

38. Hayley Ringle. 2017. Galvanize opens its Phoenix campus; 48 companies relocating to Warehouse District. *Phoenix Business Journal*. March 7.

39. Hayley Ringle. Tech giant to set up shop at Galvanize Phoenix. *Phoenix Business Journal*. March 14.

40. Kathy Chin Leong. 2018. A renewal for Phoenix's Warehouse District: Polished but gritty. *The New York Times*. March 13.

41. Jessica Suriano. 2018. Phoenix artists say gentrification of Roosevelt Row is pushing them out. *The Arizona Republic*. August 5.

42. Jerod MacDonald-Evoy. 2017. 1st phase of colossal ASU Tempe makeover begins; 20,000 jobs expected in all. *The Arizona Republic*. June 12.

43. MacDonald-Evoy, 1st phase of colossal ASU Tempe makeover.

44. MacDonald-Evoy, 1st phase of colossal ASU Tempe makeover.

45. Arren Kimbel-Sannit. 2019. Mayor candidate Corey Woods wants to make Tempe a cheaper place to live. Can he? *Phoenix New Times*. April 4; Paulina Pineda. 2019. Tempe is getting creative as it tackles its affordable housing problem. But is it enough? *The Arizona Republic*. May 14.

46. Lynn Trimble. 2018. Here are the latest plans to bring an ASU campus to downtown Mesa. *Phoenix New Times*. June 6.

47. Lily Altavena. 2018. Mesa exploring creating innovation district downtown, anchored by ASU. *The Arizona Republic*. January 22.

48. Altavena, Mesa exploring creating innovation.

49. Rachel Leingang. 2019. Michael Crow's imprint on ASU includes more than 100 new buildings. *The Arizona Republic*. February 28.

50. Press release. 2019. ALTA Warehouse planned for Phoenix Warehouse. *ABI Multifamily*. May 8.

Chapter 7. Furthering the Local Innovation Ecosystem in Pensacola and Chattanooga

1. Jim Little. 2018. Visit Pensacola launches new Tourism Works campaign to tout industry's impact on economy. *Pensacola News Journal*. March 21.

2. Anne Schultz. 2014. Pensacola shines day and night. *Vie Magazine*. November/December.

3. Melissa Nelson-Gabriel. 2013. Pensacola slowly luring visitors. *Temple Daily Telegram*. October 20.

4. Ennis Davis. 2019. The revitalization of Pensacola's Palafox Street. *Modern Cities*. June 24.

5. Cindy Riley. 2012. Blue Wahoos take the field in Pensacola. *Construction Equipment Guide*. July 24.

6. Charlotte Crane. 2005. Recovery effect. *Florida Trend*. June 1.

7. IHMC. 2003. John Cavanaugh inaugurated as UWF president. *Institute for Human and Machine Cognition Newsletter*. May.

8. Thomas Myer. 2016. Bense broke the mold as UWF president. *Pensacola News Journal*. December 18.

9. T. S. Strickland. 2017. Saunders takes helm at UWF. *850 Magazine*. February 27.

10. Martha Saunders. 2017. Introducing the UWF innovation campus network. *Office of the President, University of West Florida*. June 19.

11. Business News. 2019. UWF Center for Cybersecurity hosts grand opening in downtown student community institute building. *Pensacola Magazine*. May.

12. Joseph Baucum. 2017. UWF's "Innovation Campus Network" front and center at Gulf Power Symposium. *Pensacola News Journal*. October 3; Joseph Baucum. 2017. UWF expects to expand in downtown Pensacola by 2018. *Pensacola News Journal*. June 17; Martha Saunders. 2019. UWF paves the way for cyber coast. *Pensacola News Journal*. April 13; Kevin Robinson. 2019. UWF hosts best and brightest minds in cybersecurity at prestigious conference in Pensacola. *Pensacola News Journal*. April 25.

13. Carlton Proctor. 2018. Pining for change. *Florida Trend*. January 26.

14. U.S. Census Bureau. 2019. QuickFacts: Chattanooga City, Tennessee. July 1. https://www.census.gov/quickfacts/chattanoogacitytennessee.

15. David Eichenthal and Tracy Windeknecht. 2008. *Chattanooga, Tennessee*. Washington, DC: Brookings. September.

16. Mark Funkhouser. 2012. Dogtown and the dirtiest city in America. *Governing*. June 25.

17. Nancy Cook. 2013. Chattanooga's makeover secret: A river runs through it. *The Atlantic*. August 19.

18. Dave Flessner. 2019. California investment group to acquire 1400 Chestnut apartments in the Southside. *Times Free Press*. August 30.

19. Gilbert E. Govan and James W. Livingood. 1947. *The University of Chattanooga: Sixty Years*. Kingsport, TN: Kingsport Press.

20. Laura Bond. 2014. Mocs express adds downtown route. *UTC News Release*. August 8.

21. Tim Omarzu. 2015. UTC breaks ground on $70 million, 600-room dormitory. *Times Free Press*. November 18.

22. Dave Flessner. 2015. New innovation district unveiled in downtown Chattanooga. *Times Free Press*. January 13.

23. David Morton. 2015. Chattanooga looks to downtown for innovation district. *NOOGAtoday*. January 13.

24. Morton, Chattanooga looks to downtown.

25. David Flessner. 2015. Obama praises Chattanooga as "a tornado of innovation." *Times Free Press.* January 14.

26. Peter Cohan. 2018. How Chattanooga created $1.8B in startup exits in under 5 Years. *Inc. Magazine.* May 8.

27. David Martin. 2017. The real story behind Chattanooga's "Gig City" resurgence. *Washington Examiner.* August 2; Rob Martin. 2018. Gig City: How Chattanooga became a tech hub. PC *Magazine.* May 4.

28. Jason Koebler. 2016. The city that was saved by the internet. *Tech Vice.* October 27.

29. Mike Pare. 2019. Chattanooga's central district needs to "attract more major corporations," Corker says. *Times Free Press.* April 15.

30. Dave Flessner. 2017. Chattanooga's innovation district revived the city—but is it sustainable? *Times Free Press.* August 9.

31. Andy Berke. 2015. State of the City Address. *Chattanooga Office of the Mayor.* April 27; Andy Berke. 2018. State of the City Address. *Chattanooga Office of the Mayor.* April 19.

32. City of Chattanooga. 2018. *Innovation District of Chattanooga: Framework Plan.* March.

33. Mike Pare. 2018. Innovation district plan includes greater UTC presence downtown, housing, research opportunities. *Times Free Press.* March 21.

34. Shawn Ryan. 2018. UTC part of research collaborative in the city. *UTC News Release.* October 24.

35. Judy Walton. 2012. Census data noted racial shifts in Chattanooga neighborhoods. *Times Free Press.* June 23.

36. G. Scott Thomas. 2014. Income inequality is a problem everywhere, but especially in the South. *The Business Journals.* January 31.

37. The 45 places to go in 2012. 2012. *The New York Times.* January 6.

38. Joan McClane. 2019. Report: Chattanooga's development boom is pushing out its black residents. *Times Free Press.* January 16.

39. Rick Cohen. 2015. Chattanooga: A model of urban revitalization, or inequality and gentrification? *Nonprofit Quarterly.* October 9.

40. Martha Saunders. 2018. Inspiring the Gulf Coast: The UWF university-community partnership model. *Office of the President, President's Blog.* September 13. https://uwf.edu/offices/presidents-office/presidential-communication/presidents-blog/2/.

41. Monty Bruell and Susanne Burnham. 2015. *Start It Up* episode 22: UTC chancellor Steve Angle partners with startup community. WUTC88.1. May 8.

Chapter 8. Open Innovation, Higher Education, and Urban Change

1. Farnam Jahanian. 2018. 4 ways universities are driving innovation. *World Economic Forum Annual Meeting.* January 17.

2. Camilo Maldonado. 2018. Price of college increasing almost 8 times faster than wages. *Forbes.* July 24.

3. Ashish Arora, Andrea Fosfuri, and Thomas Roende. 2018. *Waiting for the payday? The market for startups and the timing of entrepreneurial exit.* Cambridge, MA: National Bureau of Economic Research. Working Paper 24350; Micah S. Officer.

2007. The price of corporate liquidity: Acquisition discounts for unlisted targets. *Journal of Financial Economics* 83(3): 571–598.

4. Henry Chesbrough. 2005. *Open Innovation: The New Imperative for Creating Profit from Technology*. Cambridge, MA: Harvard Business Review Press.

5. Henry Chesbrough. 2003. The era of open innovation. *MIT Sloan Management Review* 44(3) 35–41. P. 35.

6. Chesbrough, Era of open innovation, 36.

7. Chesbrough, Era of open innovation, 35–36.

8. Rita Gunther McGrath. 2013. *The End of Competitive Advantage: How to Keep Your Strategy Moving as Fast as Your Business*. Cambridge, MA: Harvard Business Review Press.

9. Scott Anthony. 2016. Kodak's downfall wasn't about technology. *Harvard Business Review*. July 15.

10. Henry Chesbrough. 2011. Everything you need to know about open innovation. *Forbes*. March 21.

11. *The Economist*. 2007. The love-in. October 11.

12. Julien Pénin, Caroline Hussler, and Thierry Burger-Helmchen. 2011. New shapes and new stakes: A portrait of open innovation as a promising phenomenon. *Journal of Innovation Economics & Management* 1(7): 11–29.

13. Henry Chesbrough and Sabine Brunswicker. 2013. *Managing open innovation in large firms: Survey report on open innovation*. Stuttgart: Fraunhofer Verlag. May 2013.

14. Chesbrough and Brunswicker, *Managing open innovation*, 2.

15. Jennifer Spencer. 2001. How relevant is university-based scientific research to private high-technology firms? A United States–Japan comparison. *Academy of Management Journal* 44(2): 432–440.

16. Keld Laursen and Ammon Salter. 2004. Searching high and low: what types of firms use universities as a source of innovation? *Research Policy* 33(8): 1201–1215.

17. Pedro Janeiro, Isabel Proença, and Vítor da Conceição Gonçalves. 2013. Open innovation: Factors explaining universities as service firm innovation sources. *Journal of Business Research* 66(10): 2017–2023.

18. "Hitachi Hokkaido University laboratory" to address societal issues facing Hokkaido through collaborative creation. 2016. *ENP Newswire*. June 17.

19. Making ideas into reality at MIT's "Future Factory." 2018. *60 Minutes*, CBS. Aired April 22.

20. Michael E. Porter. 1998. Clusters and the new economics of competition. *Harvard Business Review*. November/December.

21. David Musselwhite. 2017. Guest view: Innovation district good for Pensacola. *Pensacola News Journal*. April 12.

22. News Office. 2011. Martin (1958) Trust Center for MIT Entrepreneurship dedicated. *MIT News*. November 22.

23. Rafael Reif. 2015. A better way to deliver innovation to the world. *The Washington Post*. May 22.

24. Reif, Better way to deliver.

25. Rebecca Spalding. 2018. Kendall Square: How a rundown area near Boston birthed a biotech boom and real estate empire. *The Boston Globe*. October 15.

26. News Office. 2001. MIT to acquire Technology Square in Cambridge from Beacon Capital Partners. MIT News. January 12.

27. Denise Brehm. 2004. MIT enters into agreement with City of Cambridge that provides the city long-term tax protection. MIT News. December 6.

28. News Office. 2013. City of Cambridge approves MIT's zoning petition. MIT News. April 9.

29. Dees Stribling. 2018. Why Phoenix is a budding tech hub. Bisnow. March 7.

30. Paul Steven Stone. 2013. How to end our sugar-coated gentrification and save Cambridge for all of us. Cambridge Day. June 25.

31. Jon Hurdle. 2018. Philadelphia's first step to a platform of innovation. The New York Times. February 20.

32. Courtney Elizabeth Knapp. 2018. Constructing the Dynamo of Dixie: Race, Urban Planning, and Cosmopolitanism in Chattanooga, Tennessee. Chapel Hill: The University of North Carolina Press, p. 186.

33. Leeds School of Business at University of Colorado Boulder. 2019. Economic impact of tech transfer on the state and national economy. Boulder: University of Colorado Boulder Technology Transfer Office. January 8.

34. Mallory Richardson. 2019. New report pegs economic impact of CU Boulder commercialization efforts at $1.9 billion. Venture Partners at CU Boulder. March 5; Press Release. 2019. Economic impact study: CU Boulder pumped $1.9 billion into state economy between 2014 and 2018. CU Boulder Today. June 13.

35. Randy Shaw. 2018. Generation Priced Out: Who Gets to Live in the New Urban America. Berkeley: University of California Press.

36. Burt Helm. 2014. How Boulder became America's startup capital: An unlikely story of tree-huggers, commies, eggheads, and gold. Inc. Magazine. January.

37. Dawn Lim. 2018. BlackRock's next U.S. hub will be far from Wall Street. The Wall Street Journal. October 25.

38. David Murrell. 2019. Report: University City district expects $2.1 billion worth of construction to start in 2020. Philadelphia Magazine. December 2.

39. Grace Oldham. 2019. Officials: "X Phoenix" co-housing high-rise breaks barriers of geography, affordability. The Arizona Republic. May 30.

40. John Bailey. 2019. The education opportunity in opportunity zones. Education Next. July 2.

41. Dan Well. 2019. The Trump administration said these tax breaks would help distressed neighborhoods. Who's actually benefiting? The Washington Post. June 6.

42. Bruce Katz and Julie Wagner. 2014. The Rise of Innovation Districts: A New Geography of Innovation in America. Washington, DC: Metropolitan Policy Program at Brookings Report. May. P. 2.

43. Katz and Wagner, Rise of Innovation Districts, 4–5.

44. Mike Schneider. 2019. Income growth greatest in tech hubs over past 5 years. San Francisco Chronicle. December 19.

45. Jimmy Maas. 2019. How a wave of tech expansion could further strain affordability. Texas Standard. April 8.

46. Kim Clark. 2010. The Great Recession's toll on higher education. US News & World Report. September 10.

47. Jim Small. 2019. Arizona higher ed: Deepest cuts, biggest tuition increases since 2008. *AZ Mirror*. October 24.

48. Michael Mitchell, Michael Leachman, and Matt Saenz. 2019. State higher education funding cuts have pushed costs to students, worsened inequality. *Center on Budget and Policy Priorities*. October 24.

49. Mitchell, Leachman, and Saenz, State higher education funding.

Page numbers in italics signify photographs.

PHX Core, 151, 152, 199; and ASU, 27, 133–34, 198; plans for, 134, 147–48
Pincombe, Roger, 75
Poduska, William, 95
Porter, Michael E., 188
Porter, Samantha, 130
Portman Holdings, 200
Powell, Shannon, 70
Powers, Bill, 43
Prime Computer, 94
privatization, 34
professional education, 32
Project MAC, 99
Promise Zones, 128, 130

Qualified Opportunity Fund, 201

Raytheon Corporation, 93–94
real estate interests and ventures, 57, 204; and ASU, 151; in Kendall Square, 104–6, 193, 204; and Route 128, 95
Redevelopment Authority of Philadelphia, 120–21
Reed, Kasim, 81
Regional Advantage (Saxenian), 40
Reif, L. Rafael, 45, 109, 194
Renaissance Equity Partners, 202
research core, 191, 192
Riesman, David, 31
Rigby, Dick, 84–85
Rise Fund, 140
Rise of the Creative Class, The (Florida), 54
River City Company, 166
Rockefeller, John D., 7
Rodin, Judith, 48, 122–23, 124
Rogers, William Barton, 90
Roosevelt, Franklin D., 6, 35
Roosevelt Island, 20–21, 21, 22
Rossi, Ritch, 107
Route 128 (Massachusetts): corporate firms at, 93–95; development and rise of, 24, 86, 93–95; and MIT, 36, 38–40, 41, 93–94, 97; Silicon Valley difference with, 39–40
Rowe, Tim, 103–4
Rush, Maureen, 123
Ryan, Nancy, 109

S1 Corporation, 78
Sachs, Jonathan, 95
Sacramento, CA, 1–3
Saksa, Jim, 127
Salvucci, Fred, 109
Sandra Day O'Connor College of Law, 141
Sanofi, 105, 111
Saunders, Martha, 160, 163, 175
Saxenian, AnnaLee, 40
Schuster, Gary B., 71
Schuylkill Yards project: and community development, 126–28, 130, 131; and community outreach, 128; and Drexel, 27, 114, 124–28, 198; gentrification and displacement from, 127, 131–32, 199, 201; plans for, 115, 124–25, 126
Schwada, John, 136
Science, The Endless Frontier (Bush), 35–36
Scott, Rick, 10
Sear3D Additive Manufacturing Laboratory, 160–61
Seattle, WA, 55
"second academic revolution," 31–36
seed funding, 76, 81
Sharp, Phillip A., 99, 100, 101
Silicon Spice, 103
Silicon Valley, 24, 39–40, 96; and Stanford, 36, 37–38, 41, 66
Simha, Robert, 92
Sinclair College, 32
SkySong, 138
Sled, Vladimir, 122
Smart Communication and Analysis Lab, 173
Smith, Benjamin, 96
Smith, Charles G., 93
Society of Work, 155
South Boston (Seaport) Innovation District, 55–56
Southern Oregon University, 32
South Lake Union (Seattle), 55
Spruce Hill (Philadelphia), 116
Stanford University, 20; and Silicon Valley, 36, 37–38, 41, 66
start-up incubators, 42–44, 138
Staton, Greg, 147
Steinberg, Darrell, 2

Mapp Building at, 172; partnerships of, 173, 174; SimCenter at, 167
University of Texas at Austin, 43
University of the Sciences, 113
University of Utah, 16
University of Washington, 43–44
University of West Florida (UWF), 27–28, 204–5; about, 157; Center for Cybersecurity at, 161–62; and Innovation Campus Network, 154, 160–61; as innovation driver, 154–55, 159–64, 190; institutional leadership at, 159, 160, 163; partnerships of, 154–55, 160, 162–63; and Pensacola revitalization, 175, 177
University of Wisconsin–Madison, 44–45
University Research Park (URP, Madison), 44–45
UP Global, 44
urban renewal, 4, 89, 104, 121–22
user innovation, 184–85
UWF Historic Trust, 157

Varian, Russell H. and Sigurd F., 37
Varian Associates, 37
Vassar College, 7–8
VentureLab, 77, 78
Vest, Charles M., 195
Volpe, John, 96, 98
Volpe National Transportation Systems Center, 98, 111

Wagner, Julie, 202
Walter Cronkite School of Journalism and Mass Communication, 141, 142

Wang, An, 95
Wang Laboratories, 94
Warehouse District (Phoenix), 145–46, 151
Washington University in St. Louis, 25
Webb, James, 96
WebPT, 148
West Campus Project (Chattanooga), 167
West Philadelphia: African American residents in, 116–17, 128; and Black Bottom, 117–18; conditions in, 120, 121–22, 128; gentrification and displacement in, 114, 127, 131–32, 199, 201; housing in, 116, 199; location of, 115–16; Mantua section of, 128. *See also* Schuylkill Yards project; University City
West Philadelphia Corporation, 120, 121
West Philadelphia Initiative, 122–23
West Philadelphia Streetcar Suburb Historic District, 116
Williams, Sam, 66
Williams, Thelda, 142, 144
Worcester Free Institute of Industrial Sciences (Worcester Polytechnic Institute), 63
Wright State University, 32

Yale University, 49
Yamacraw Electronic Design Center, 70, 71
Young, Michael K., 44